LONDON'S GANGS AT WAR

DICK KIRBY
has also written

Rough Justice
Memoirs of a Flying Squad officer

The Real Sweeney

You're Nicked!

Villains

The Guv'nors
Ten of Scotland Yard's Greatest Detectives

The Sweeney
The First Sixty Years of Scotland Yard's Crimebusting
Flying Squad 1919–1978

Scotland Yard's Ghost Squad
The Secret Weapon Against Post-War Crime

The Brave Blue Line
100 Years of Metropolitan Police Gallantry

Death on the Beat
Police Officers killed in the Line of Duty

The Scourge of Soho
The Controversial Career of SAS Hero
Detective Sergeant Harry Challenor MM

Whitechapel's Sherlock Holmes
The Casebook of Fred Wensley OBE, KPM,
Victorian Crimebuster

The Wrong Man
The Shooting of Steven Waldorf and
the Hunt for David Martin

Laid Bare
The Nude Murders and
the Hunt for 'Jack the Stripper'

Praise for Dick Kirby's Books

Rough Justice '. . . the continuing increase in violent crime will make many readers yearn for yesteryear and officers of Dick Kirby's calibre.'
Police Magazine

The Real Sweeney 'His reflections on the political aspect of law enforcement will ring true for cops, everywhere.'
American Police Beat

Villains 'This is magic. The artfulness of these anti-heroes has you pining for the bad old days.'
Daily Sport

You're Nicked! 'A great read with fascinating stories and amusing anecdotes from a man who experienced it all.'
Suffolk Norfolk Life

The Guv'nors 'They were heroes at times when heroes were desperately needed.'
American Police Beat

The Sweeney '. . . thoroughly researched and enjoyable history, crammed with vivid descriptions of long-forgotten police operations . . . races along like an Invicta at full throttle.'
Daily Express

Scotland Yard's Ghost Squad 'Dick Kirby . . . knows how to bring his coppers to life on each page.'
Joseph Wambaugh, Author of *The Choirboys*

The Brave Blue Line '. . . simply the best book about police gallantry ever written'.
History By the Yard

Death on the Beat 'I am delighted Dick Kirby has written this book.'
Michael Winner

The Scourge of Soho 'Dick Kirby has chosen his fascinating subject well.'
Law Society Gazette

Whitechapel's Sherlock Holmes 'Dick Kirby has done an excellent job.'
The Ripperologist

The Wrong Man 'Dick Kirby gives us the gritty reality of this subject. I did not put this book down, reading it in one day, deep into the night.'
Paul Millen, Author Of Crime Scene Investigator

Laid Bare '. . . Dick lays out the evidence and challenges you to come to a conclusion regarding the culpability or otherwise of the suspects . . . he holds our hand in search of the answers to this mystery.'
London Police Pensioner

To my friend, Brigadier Henry Wilson:
I hope there's sufficient 'blood, snot and guts' in here to appease you!
And to Ann – all the way to the moon, and back.

LONDON'S GANGS AT WAR

DICK KIRBY

With a foreword by Lord (Peter) Imbert CVO, QPM, DL
Commissioner, Metropolitan Police 1987–93

PEN & SWORD
TRUE CRIME

First published in Great Britain in 2017 by
Pen & Sword True Crime
an imprint of
Pen & Sword Books Ltd
47 Church Street
Barnsley
South Yorkshire
S70 2AS

ISBN 978-1-47389-476-1

A CIP catalogue record for this book is available from the
British Library

Printed and bound in Malta by Gutenberg Press Ltd.

Pen & Sword Books Ltd incorporates the Imprints of Pen
& Sword Aviation, Pen & Sword Family History, Pen &
Sword Maritime, Pen & Sword Military, Pen & Sword
Discovery, Pen & Sword Politics, Pen & Sword Atlas,
Pen & Sword Archaeology, Wharncliffe Local History,
Wharncliffe True Crime, Wharncliffe Transport, Pen &
Sword Select, Pen & Sword Military Classics, Leo Cooper,
The Praetorian Press, Claymore Press, Remember When,
Seaforth Publishing and Frontline Publishing.

For a complete list of Pen & Sword titles please contact
PEN & SWORD BOOKS LIMITED
47 Church Street, Barnsley, South Yorkshire, S70 2AS,
England
E-mail: enquiries@pen-and-sword.co.uk
Website: www.pen-and-sword.co.uk

Contents

A quatrain from Kurt Weill, Elizabeth Hauptman & Bertolt Brecht's
Die Dreigroschenoper (The Threepenny Opera)

For in this life (I wish there was another),
Victuals are scarce and men are such brutes, you know.
We'd love to live in peace and worship one another,
But circumstances just won't have it so.

Acknowledgements

Firstly, my thanks go to Brigadier Henry Wilson for his enthusiasm and assistance; next, to Lord Imbert for his splendid foreword and George Chamier for his superb editing.

I should also like to thank the following for their administrative assistance: Bob Fenton QGM, honorary secretary to the Ex-CID Officers Association; Susi Rogol, editor of the *London Police Pensioner*; Beverley Edwards, Chairman of the Metropolitan Women Police Association; Mick Carter from The ReCIDivists' Luncheon Club; Barry Walsh from the Friends of the Metropolitan Police Historical Collection; Martin Stallion, secretary of the Police History Society; Paul Bickley, Curator of The Crime Museum, New Scotland Yard; and Alan Moss of *History by the Yard*.

I received a great deal of help from people who delved into their memories for the compilation of this book. Some wished to remain anonymous; others were not so shy and they appear here in alphabetical order: John Barnes, Richard 'Dickie' Bird, Mike Bucknole FNAVA, BA (Hons), PgC, Peter Burgess, Janet Cheal, Pat Collins, Jack Cooper, Dave Coppen, Ron Cork, Roger Crowhurst, Jeff Edwards, John Farley QPM, Dr Ken German, Martin Gosling MBE, Bob Hancock, Tom Hassell, Doug Hoadley, Graham Howard, George Howlett OBE, OStJ, QPM, Robin Jackson, John Lewis, Alick Morrison, Tony Osborn, Hugh Parker, Arthur Porter BEM, Pat Pryde, Dave Puntan, Kenneth David 'Taff' Rees, John Simmonds, Roger Stoodley, George Taylor, John Taylor, Bernard Tighe, Max Vernon, Mike Warburton, Ed Williams, Layton Williams, the late Bill Waite BEM, Keith White, Bryan Woolnough. My thanks for the use of photos go to Alick Morrison, Bernard Tighe and Ken German; others come from the author's collection. Whilst every effort has been made to trace copyright holders, Pen & Sword Books and I apologise for any inadvertent omissions.

There were some who could have provided pertinent information but for reasons best known to themselves chose not to do so. Bereft of their input, I have endeavoured to ensure that the content of this book is as accurate as possible and acknowledge that any faults or imperfections are mine alone.

By now I should have mastered the mysteries of cyberspace but due to a misspent old age I have neglected to do so. Fortunately, my daughter and son-in-law, Sue and Steve Cowper, have been on hand to rescue me, often from the most mundane of computer-generated cock-ups, and I am very grateful to them.

To them, and to the rest of my family, I pay tribute for their unfailing help, love and assistance: to my sons, Mark and Robert, my youngest daughter and her husband, Barbara and Rich Jerreat, and my grandchildren, Emma Cowper B.Mus, Jessica Cowper B.Mus, Harry Cowper, Samuel and Annie Grace Jerreat.

Most of all to my dear wife of more than fifty years, Ann, who thankfully has stuck by me, during the good and the not-so-good times.

Dick Kirby
Suffolk, 2016

Foreword

Dick Kirby, undoubtedly using the experience of his years as a working detective in the Metropolitan Police has, since his retirement from the Force, written a number of successful and popular books.

This book, *London's Gangs at War*, is an account of real-life (as they sadly were then) criminals, their exploits and their almost unbelievable violence to one another and to anyone else they considered to be standing between them and their dominant hold on the leadership of the most lucrative criminal enterprises in the West End of London and particularly in the streets and shady clubs of London's Soho district.

Some of those he writes about were what we might call 'household names', albeit for the worst of reasons. Their villainous exploits made good stories for the media, and I recall as a boy doing my daily paper round in my quiet country town and taking the opportunity to devour the reports of the activities of such well known rogues as Jack Spot, Billy Hill, Albert Dimes and, somewhat later, the infamous and equally violent Kray twins, Ronnie and Reggie. Even then I marvelled at the courage of the police officers who had to counterbalance and neutralize such violent and bloodthirsty gangland killers, who fought to control crooked clubs, fraudulent betting and gaming premises and prostitute rings.

It was only when I joined the Metropolitan Police myself and gained credibility with experience that I became aware of the courage of the officers who ran great risks to get inside information about these murderous individuals and groupings and their activities by cultivating and running informants, and the very brave undercover officers who, to gain vital information and evidence, posed as fellow villains. I never met any of the villains mentioned in this well written and very well researched book but am proud to have met and known a number of those who Dick has acknowledged as assisting with their own information about, in some cases, very risky and dangerous involvement.

This book will fill many a gap in the knowledge of serving detectives, their uniformed colleagues and all those fighting such violent miscreants now and in the future, and I congratulate and thank Dick Kirby for his patient, deep and thorough research into this subject. A book well worth reading.

Lord (Peter) Imbert CVO, QPM, DL.
Commissioner, Metropolitan Police 1987–93

Little Hubby and the Babe

With the arrival of the Second World War, the British authorities decided that the time had come to rid themselves of a gang who had been a thorn in their sides for many years – the Sabinis. These brothers from Clerkenwell had been responsible for racetrack protection and gang warfare since the 1920s, but by virtue of their Italian heritage, the leader, Charles 'Darby' Sabini, and some of his brothers and associates with Italian-sounding names were incarcerated in 1940 as 'enemy aliens'. This was a pyrrhic victory for the Home Office; it was also certainly unlawful. Firstly, the Sabinis were only half-Italian; their mother had been English and none of the brothers had even been to Italy. Next, Darby Sabini's twenty-one-year-old son, Flight Sergeant Harry Sabini, was killed whilst on active service with the Royal Air Force Volunteer Reserve. And lastly, Sabini himself was a spent force. He was a middle-aged man with no stomach for further confrontations of any kind.

During the Sabinis' internment, some of the criminal activity in London's Soho was run by racketeer 'Big Alf' White. Sentenced to five years' penal servitude in 1922 for shooting with intent (the conviction was overturned on appeal), shortly afterwards he was sentenced to eighteen months' hard labour for attempting to bribe a prison warder. A hard man in his prime, he had been beaten up by a gang of tearaways outside Haringey Greyhound Stadium in 1939 which rather knocked the stuffing out of him. Although he had formed an uneasy alliance with some Italian gangsters, he was prudent enough to keep at arm's length the gangs of Italians and Jews who ran many of the clubs. The Messina brothers, a band of violent Maltese pimps, had their girls working for them flat out (no pun intended) during wartime, but the brothers themselves kept a very low profile indeed. Prior to the outbreak of war, in order to prevent their being deported should they be convicted of a criminal offence, the Messinas had thought it prudent to take out British citizenship. This ruse now rebounded on them, since as British citizens they were subject to conscription into the armed services and warrants had been issued for their arrest; hence their self-enforced shyness. But neither the absence of the Messinas nor the nightly bombardment by the Luftwaffe meant a cessation of gang violence. Far from it.

★

Situated on the first floor of 37 Wardour Street, Soho was 'The Bridge and Billiards Club' – known to its habitués as 'The Old Cue Club' – and just before midnight on the evening of Thursday, 1 May 1941, Eddie Fleischer, aka Eddie Fletcher (who had been heavily involved with running protection rackets and who ten years previously had been arrested with Harry White, Alf's son, for maliciously wounding a Soho club owner), was attacked in the billiard hall, and not for the first time either. Ten days earlier, at three o'clock in the morning, Fletcher and an associate, Joseph Franks, had been involved in a fight with Bert Connelly, the doorman of the Palm Beach Bottle Parties Club, which was situated in the basement of the Wardour Street premises. Fletcher had taken a beating – two men were charged with causing him grievous bodily harm – and he had been barred from the club.

Now Fletcher returned to the Italian-run club and was playing pool when he was set upon by three men – Joseph Collette, Harry Capocci and Albert George Dimes (otherwise known as Alberto Dimeo or 'Italian Albert'). Dimes (with a Scottish mother and Italian father) was then twenty-five years old and at six feet two, a good-looking man and an adversary with a powerful reputation. Not only had he served short prison sentences, including one for breaking a police officer's jaw, it was also rumoured that in 1939 he had murdered a fellow gangster named Charles 'Chick' Lawrence in the East End.

At the time of the confrontation with Fletcher, Dimes was absent without leave from the RAF. But now his reputation was about to be considerably enhanced, because a pitched battle began in the billiard hall and, according to a very few of the forty customers who later made themselves available to the police as witnesses, it was Dimes who coordinated the violence. The five billiard tables were wrecked, the light shades above them were torn down and smashed, billiard balls were hurled around the room and Fletcher was attacked by the gang with coshes, cues and fists. A former club owner and a friend of Fletcher, thirty-six-year-old Harry Distleman – otherwise known as 'Scarface' and 'Little Hubby' – came to his aid. The three attackers vanished and Distleman took Fletcher, bleeding profusely from a wound on the side of his head, to Charing Cross Hospital to have the cut attended to.

And all might have been well, had Fletcher not insisted, an hour later, on returning to the billiard hall – 'In order to retrieve my coat', he said. Unfortunately for Fletcher, so did his three attackers.

★

By now, the sometime manager of the Palm Beach Bottle Parties Club had been alerted. He was thirty-nine-year-old Antonio 'Babe' Mancini and he had a hatred of Jews; whilst serving a twelve-month sentence of hard labour in 1939 for stealing a wallet, he developed the unpleasant habit of spitting in Jewish prisoners' food. This incurred the displeasure of the Jewish gang leader, Jack Spot, on remand for grievous bodily harm, who executed what was thought to be a suitably violent punishment on Mancini for his anti-social habits. Since Sabini's internment, Mancini had been partly responsible for the unity of what remained of the Italian gangs.

Mancini later said that he had gone to the billiard hall 'simply to see what all the fuss was about', although it certainly appeared that the violence which followed was orchestrated, since Thomas Mack, a former member of the Italian Mob, also arrived. He had impressive credentials: in 1922 he had been sentenced to eighteen months' hard labour for riot, and following his release, he and Mancini had both been sentenced to one month's hard labour in 1924 for assaulting a bookmaker. Twelve years later, Mack had gone on to better things when he received three years' penal servitude for his part in what became known as 'The Battle of Lewes Racetrack'.

Precisely what part Mack took in the frenzied fighting which followed it is difficult to say, since he disappeared shortly afterwards. However, it was fortunate that Albert Dimes' older brother Victor, a professional wrestler, was present, because before his sibling became deeply involved in the bloodshed he grabbed hold of him and pinned him to one of the wrecked billiard tables. It certainly saved Dimes from the gallows, because Mancini then thrust a dagger to a depth of five inches into Distleman's left armpit. As the noted pathologist Sir Bernard Spilsbury later observed, this was sufficient to sever the axillary artery and the accompanying vein. Staggering into the arms of three onlookers Distleman told them, with considerable justification, 'I am terribly hurt. He has stabbed me in the heart. Babe's done it.'

As Distleman lay dying on the pavement outside the premises, there to be found by two patrolling police officers, Mancini, by now completely out of control, chased Fletcher between the billiard tables, slashing at him with the dagger and severing the tendons in Fletcher's arm before, finally mollified, dropping the dagger and going home. Fletcher returned to Charing Cross Hospital where he was undoubtedly welcomed as a regular client.

★

Enter Divisional Detective Inspector Arthur Thorp from West End
Central police station. He was then forty years of age, a tough boxer,
much of whose service had been spent in London's West End. He
was fairly unconventional: when men complained that their wallets
had been stolen by Soho prostitutes but nobody would admit the
identities of the owners or tenants of the rooms used by the girls,
Thorp would suggest to the aggrieved party that he 'might like to
work the room over a little' – and would then avert his eyes as the
victim systematically wrecked the premises.

Mancini handed himself in the following day and told Thorp,
'As I was going upstairs, I heard somebody behind me say, "There's
Babe – let's knife him!"' He admitted slashing Fletcher but denied
murdering Distleman.

At the Old Bailey, Mancini was given the opportunity to plead
guilty to manslaughter, and this would certainly have been accepted
by the prosecution. Instead, in an act of almost unbelievable reck-
lessness, he pleaded not guilty to everything: Distleman's murder,
inflicting grievous bodily harm with intent to murder Fletcher or
with intent to cause him grievous bodily harm. This decision was
stupid for two reasons: (a) the weight of evidence was very much
against him, and (b) since Italy had declared war on Britain thirteen months previously, there were very strong anti-Italian feelings
amongst solid, middle-class British citizens, especially those who
made up a jury at the Old Bailey and who were decidedly disap-
proving of Italians wielding daggers.

In fairness, although there was little sympathy for the deceased
– he had run a team of racecourse pickpockets, had six convictions
for assault and ran a chain of brothels, together with his brother,
'Big Hubby' Distleman (otherwise known as 'Hymie the Gambler'
and thought to be a highly active police informant)[1] – the jury
nevertheless found Mancini guilty of murder, and on 4 July 1941
Mr Justice McNaughton duly donned the black cap. Mancini
appealed, first to the Court of Appeal (Criminal Division) and,
when that was rejected, to the House of Lords, all to no avail.
It was Albert Pierrepoint's first hanging as Chief Executioner at
Pentonville Prison on 17 October 1941, and as he slipped the hood
over his client's head he was rather unnerved when in a slightly
muffled voice Mancini called out, 'Cheerio!'

Following Mancini's conviction, Dimes, Capocci and Collette
appeared before the Recorder of London, Sir Gerald Dodson, on a

---

[1] And that was a correct assumption. See the author's *Scotland Yard's
Ghost Squad* (Wharncliffe Books, 2011).

charge of unlawfully wounding Fletcher. However, it appeared likely that some of the witnesses had been inappropriately 'spoken to', and on two occasions Sir Gerald plaintively asked the prosecuting counsel, 'Is it worthwhile going on with this case?' He later added to the jury, 'There is no evidence to show that they did anything more than engage in a rough-and-tumble,' and eventually Capocci was acquitted, with Sir Gerald telling the other two, 'You were probably expecting prison and no doubt you deserve it, but I am going to bind you over.'

And he did so; Dimes and Collette were bound over in the sum of £5 to be of good behaviour for a period of three years, although Dimes was later sentenced to six months' detention for his self-imposed absence from the RAF.

By the time of his death in 1942, 'Big Alf' White had shared his former associate, Sabini's, lack of success. Sabini died in 1951, penniless and forgotten, with Thomas Mack following him into oblivion two years later.

In the same way as when the Kray brothers were incarcerated, twenty-eight years after the Mancini incident, this left a void in the ranks of criminality and there were plenty of gangsters willing, indeed eager, to fill that vacuum. We'll make a start by focussing on Tommy Smithson, whose criminal career was just getting underway at the time of Babe Mancini's demise.

Chapter 1

Tommy Smithson – 'A Perfect Nuisance'

Tommy Smithson was considered to be seriously 'game' by the East Enders of the 1950s, an accolade for courage and daring normally only bestowed upon one of their own – something, in fact, he almost was. He had missed the sound of Bow Bells at birth – a necessity to claim true Cockneyship – by a distance of 178 miles, because he was born in Liverpool in 1920 (the sixth of eight children); but two years later, the Smithson family relocated to Hoxton.

He acquired a number of convictions, including a spell in Borstal, before joining the Merchant Navy as a stoker. Discharged in the 1940s, he returned to his old haunts in the East End, only to find that a large number of Maltese had set up gambling and drinking clubs as well as running strings of prostitutes, and Smithson, with his love of gambling, decided that the Maltese were ripe to be fleeced.

Smithson certainly had charisma; he was a former fairground boxer with a reputation for fighting to the point of rashness, and few of the Maltese club owners wanted a confrontation with him. He worked a crooked roulette wheel with Antonio Benedetta Mella, aka 'Big Tony', a failed (just five bouts) heavyweight boxer, and also as a croupier with George Caruana at his club in Batty Street, a side turning off the Commercial Road, Stepney. However, it was not too long before Caruana (who owned several other clubs) was transformed from employer into victim, as Smithson nipped him (as well as many other club owners) for a shilling in the pound from their dice games; and that was just the beginning.

Smithson was enhancing his reputation as well as obtaining a great deal of illicit income – much needed, because he had a fondness for silk shirts and underwear as well as being generous towards his friends. He was married but separated from his wife, and in 1948 he met twenty-year-old Zoe Progl, at that time out on licence from Borstal and later to become known as 'The Queen of the Underworld'. They had much in common: both had been Borstal inmates, both were thoroughly dishonest and, since both were highly sexed, they began a passionate affair. However, in March 1949, he left to go to Manchester on 'unspecified business' (in fact, it was an eighteen-month sentence for robbery), and by the time he returned, a year later, he discovered that he was the father of a baby boy. Annoyed that Zoe was bringing up a baby in what he accurately referred to as 'a house full of prostitutes', Smithson set up home with Progl in a flat above a café in Shrubland Road, Hackney where both mother and child were showered with gifts.

But Smithson's gaming rackets at dog tracks and clubs, crooked though they were, were losing money, and both he and Progl came to the conclusion that it might be more profitable to concentrate on more old fashioned villainy. She acquired a job as a clerk in a factory which lasted just long enough for her to discover that the weekly wages were delivered on Thursdays, for a Friday pay-out. On her final Thursday she left a window open so that later she, Smithson and two of his gang could climb in and remove the safe, containing £7,000. Within a week, their share of the loot had vanished, after Smithson's near-lunatic betting at dog tracks and 'spielers' (illegal gambling clubs), where the races, card and dice games were undoubtedly every bit as crooked as his own. A week later, silk worth £4,000 turned up in the basement of their flat, but although the police raided the premises, both Progl and Smithson managed to walk away unscathed.

Smithson also ran a billiards club in Archer Street, Soho, and his generosity extended to permitting twins who were on the run from their National Service – their names were Reggie and Ronnie Kray – to sleep there, an act of kindness never forgotten by the brothers.

However, by 4 September 1951 the romance with Progl was over. That was the date when he met twenty-seven-year-old Fay Richardson at a restaurant in Baker Street Originally a mill girl from Stockport, Richardson could not, by any stretch of the imagination be described as a raving beauty, but she was a one-time prostitute and men had found her attractive. Before they parted, Smithson presented Progl with a diamond ring worth £500 in case she fell on hard times.

Meanwhile, the romance with Fay Richardson flourished, as did Smithson's protection rackets. Unfortunately, this would bring him into contact – indirectly – with Billy Hill, the self-proclaimed 'Boss of Britain's Underworld'. Hill had left his faithful wife Aggie and had taken up with a Phyllis May Blanche Riley – known as 'Gypsy'. Allegedly a former prostitute, and the possessor of a fiery temper, in September 1953 she was annoyed by a former acquaintance, a pimp known as 'Tulip', and asked Frederick 'Slip' Sullivan to throw him out of French Henry's nightclub. Sullivan was somewhat past his sell-by date; in 1936 he had been acquitted of breaking and entering, and in 1952 it was rumoured that he was one of nine men who had participated in the £287,000 Eastcastle Street robbery, which had been masterminded by Billy Hill. Although he was rapidly approaching middle age, Sullivan did succeed in ejecting Tulip, who in fairness was much the same age – it was rumoured that the expulsion included the pimp being deprived of half an ear – but unfortunately, Tulip was protected by Smithson and therefore satisfaction was required. A savage altercation between Smithson and Sullivan ensued, the latter emerging from the confrontation with his throat cut (either as a consequence of a sharp implement being wielded or as the result of being chucked through a plate glass window). This was not the best year of Sullivan's life; later he was sentenced to twenty-one months' imprisonment for assault and following his release, in January 1955, he was stabbed to death by his girlfriend, Mary Cooper, who successfully claimed self-defence. Meanwhile, regarding the Smithson/Sullivan confrontation, Hill decided that Tommy Smithson had gone just a little too far. Smithson thought so too, because he promptly went into hiding, but within a week he was lured out on a promise from his former employer, George Caruana, that matters could be settled amicably. A meeting was arranged at the back of the Black Cat cigarette factory in Mornington Crescent, Camden Town.

That Smithson possessed limitless courage is not disputed. He was not, however, the sharpest knife in the drawer. He was accompanied to the meeting by Paddington club owner, Dave Barry, who although he had served prison sentences, including one for manslaughter, proved not to be the staunchest ally one could wish for. Smithson had brought with him a Luger, but when he was greeted by Jack Spot and told that this would be a peaceful meeting, he surprisingly handed it over – not that retention of the pistol would have benefited him, since he had forgotten to obtain any ammunition for it.

To most fighting men with a penchant for self-preservation there would surely have been the smell of danger in the air, but Smithson failed to detect it. Opinions vary as to what happened next. One version has it that a dozen thugs leapt out of a lorry and attacked Smithson; another that there were just four of them: Jack Spot, Billy Hill, Moishe Goldstein, aka Blueball, and Slip Sullivan's brother, Sonny. But whatever the case, Barry took to his heels and Smithson was subjected to a ferocious beating. He was punched, kicked, hit with an iron bar which broke his arm and, whilst Spot held him down, mercilessly slashed all over his face and body by Billy Hill – the wounds on his face alone would necessitate forty-seven stiches – then run over by the lorry (twice) and, according to various sources, either left in the street or thrown into Regent's Park. If the latter, the gang must have conveyed him there by a circuitous (and time-consuming) route – perhaps it is more likely that he was deposited in Harrington Square Gardens, which was much nearer. Hill thought, with considerable justification, that he had killed Smithson, and on Jack Spot's instructions Moishe Goldstein summoned an ambulance, prudently leaving prior to its arrival.

That Smithson did not succumb to his injuries was nothing short of miraculous; everyone – the villains out on the street, friends and acquaintances, the doctors at Charing Cross Hospital where he was found to have lost five pints of blood – expected his imminent demise. It was a view certainly shared by Divisional Detective Inspector John Gosling from Albany Street police station, who visited the hospital the following morning whilst Smithson was receiving a blood transfusion; just one eye and a corner of his mouth could be seen among the swathe of bandages covering his face.

Who was responsible for the attack was London's worst kept secret – everybody knew, including Gosling, who had spent a tremendously successful career with the Flying Squad and had been a founder member of the ultra-secret post-war Ghost Squad. He wanted nothing better than to arrest Jack Spot and Billy Hill, and if Smithson lived – he admitted that this was unlikely – he hoped to obtain a written complaint which would secure their convictions. But that time was not yet; leaving him in the care of two detectives with strict instructions not to permit any visitors, presents, letters or telephone calls, Gosling left the hospital to pursue another investigation. But when he returned, four hours later, he found Smithson sitting up in bed and lighting a cigarette, having consumed a four-course meal – and he knew immediately that someone had got to him. It was said that Spot had paid him either £500 or £1,000 (multiply by at least twenty for today's values) for his silence – and he got it. Billy Hill, in his memoir *Boss of Britain's Underworld* (Naldrett Press Ltd, 1955), in which he referred to Smithson as 'Brownson', remarked, 'But even when he was breathing what he thought was his last, he didn't sing. No, the cozzers tried everything to make him talk but that Brownson just kept his mouth shut.'

And so he did – then, at any rate. He discharged himself from hospital five days after the attack, and when his paramour, Fay, removed the bandages they revealed a total of seventy-eight stitches which had been used to sew his body back together again. Describing himself as looking like 'the tracks running into Charing Cross station', he swore revenge on his attackers. He bought a share in a nightclub in Old Compton Street which was promptly shut by the police, then swiftly purchased another which was similarly closed down.

But when he was accused of being a police informant, he was attacked again, and this necessitated another twenty-seven stitches being inserted in his well-worn face. It is highly likely that it was in a spirit of revenge that he put Gosling in the way of a stash of two million stolen cigarettes, a ton and a half of sweets (still subject to post-war rationing) and several other valuable commodities secreted in farm buildings belonging to two brothers at Pitsea, Essex. The brothers went away for three years each at Leeds Assizes, and the informant – whoever he was – received thousands of pounds worth of reward money from the loss adjusters. It was probably coincidental that, following the payout, Smithson was spotted swaggering around London's West End wearing extremely expensive suits to complement his silk shirts.

With Smithson it was a case of 'easy come, easy go'; he opened clubs and bookmaker's offices, but when the money ran out, he was raided by the police and the courts committed him to prison in lieu of paying a fine, his friends organized a whip-round to secure his release.

And so it probably would have gone on, with Smithson obtaining and losing money and delivering beatings and receiving them in return (one from former associate Tony Mella, who cut his face open), but in June 1956 Fay Richardson was arrested. She had stolen a wallet containing a chequebook and had obtained ten gramophone records from a London store by false pretences as well as a dress from a Bond Street shop; having made an appearance at the Magistrates' Court, she was remanded in custody because when arrested she declared that she was of 'no fixed abode', undoubtedly to stop the police coming round to search the premises which she shared with Smithson where they might have found goodness knows what. Her case was not improved by her stating that she was employed as a barmaid, something easily disproved, when in fact she was working as a prostitute's maid.

Now Smithson was in a quandary; all he had to his name was a 'pony' (£25); to provide an adequate defence for his girlfriend would require at least £100. He decided to obtain 'subscriptions' and his first port of call was George Caruana – after all, he and several associates armed with iron bars had frightened some cash out of Caruana a few weeks previously, on an unrelated matter. Caruana handed over £50; however, Smithson thought this was insufficient and at midnight on 13 June, he and two associates, Walter Edward Downs and Christopher John Thomas, both aged thirty, met up in Windmill Street, Piccadilly and from there went to a café in Berners Street, where they saw Caruana. Smithson demanded £100 in total and to reinforce the request head-butted Caruana in the face, knocking out a tooth. Downs produced a flick knife and lashed out at Caruana, who put up his hands to save his face; his fingers later required six stitches. It was said that Thomas held the other occupants of the premises at bay with a revolver, although this was strongly denied by him. On Smithson's instructions, Thomas took Caruana to hospital, where his wounds were treated; when they returned to the café, Caruana handed him £30 to give to Smithson.

Only when Smithson was dead would Caruana report this matter to the police; but that was in the future. Right now, with Caruana tremblingly handing over a wad of currency, a book was produced and instructions were given to start a collection for Fay's defence and to record in it the details of the benefactors and their donations. It was handed to one of the café's clientele, Philip Louis Ellul, known variously as 'The Malt', Philip Gatt or Philip Buhagian. Ellul had convictions for possessing a gun and living on immoral earnings and ran a string of what were referred to as 'second- or third-rate prostitutes'. He was a tough, stocky man, twenty-nine years of age. Presenting someone like Ellul with such a menial, book-keeping task was not just a mistake, it was nothing short of *lèse-majesté*, rather like asking the Queen to clean up after her corgis.

Ellul was well known to Smithson; the men had previously been engaged together in various kinds of dirty work. In fact, only the previous week, when the two had been the best of friends, they had taken breakfast together. However, that friendship was about to change, quite dramatically.

*

On the evening of 25 June, with Fay Richardson still lingering in her cell at Holloway Prison, Smithson arrived at 88 Carlton Vale, NW6 at 7.30 and asked to see the landlord, whose name happened to be George Caruana. When he discovered that Caruana was not there, he asked two occupants, Marlene Marian 'Blondie' Bates and Margaret Turnbull, who shared a room, if he could wait; they agreed, and he accompanied them to their room on the third floor. Within half an hour there was a knock on the front door, and a woman in the basement flat admitted Philip Ellul, together with Victor George Sebastian Alfred Spampinato, aged twenty-two, a doorkeeper of Chicksand Street, E1 and Joseph Zammit, aged twenty-six, a cook from Christian Street, Aldgate. Spampinato, like

Ellul, was a friend of Caruana, and it appeared that these two had also come to see him.

There were angry words between Ellul and Smithson, and Ellul (allegedly) said, 'You've wanted me for a long time, haven't you, Tommy?' Ellul then pulled out a .38 automatic, and as Smithson came towards him he fired; the bullet hit Smithson in the arm and as Ellul ran out of the room, Smithson shouted, 'I'll get you in the East End for this, tonight!'

He tried to open the door but was unable to do so; someone was probably hanging on to the handle outside. But then Spampinato got up, went over to the door and murmured a few words in Maltese. The door opened, and Margaret Turnbull, who had ascended the stairs, saw Spampinato holding a knife and appearing to be helping Ellul to do something with a gun. She entered the room, and as Smithson was showing his wound to her the door burst open and Ellul rushed in. Smithson pushed Miss Turnbull out of the way and she fell on to a couch; Smithson again went for Ellul, who shot him in the neck.

The three men fled in a car which had been parked thirty yards away from the house, driven by a fourth man, and Smithson staggered down the stairs and into the roadway, where he collapsed in the gutter and, according to East End folklore, said to a passing child, 'Good morning, I'm dying.' He was taken to Paddington Hospital, where he did just that.

A murder investigation commenced under the control of Detective Superintendent Albert Webb, a veteran CID officer now at the end of his service. In 1945, as a detective sergeant, he had accompanied Detective Chief Inspector Bob Fabian KPM ('Fabian of the Yard') to Warwickshire to investigate what became known as 'The Witchcraft Murder', and four years later, as a detective inspector, he had recorded the astonishing admissions from the acid bath murderer, John George Haigh, which had sent him to the gallows.

The newspapers were full of the murder – even the 27 June edition of the faraway *Sarasota Herald Tribune* excitedly (if inaccurately) informed its readers that this was 'England's first gangland killing since the 1920s' but went a little too far when they added that Smithson 'had been a friend of Jack Spot's'.

Details of the suspects were quickly circulated; at six o'clock in the morning of 27 June, Ellul and Spampinato walked into New Scotland Yard, where two hours later they were seen by Webb. Telling them he was making enquiries into the death of Smithson, Webb said, 'I believe you two men were present at the time. Would you be prepared to tell me if that is so?'

Surprisingly, senior detectives really did talk to suspects like that in those days, and just as unusually, Ellul replied, 'Sure, it was me that shot him. He was going to do me if I didn't get out of London and I don't stand for that.'

For good measure, Spampinato added, 'I was with him when he shot him. He's my friend and what he says is OK by me.'

Ellul then said, 'I'll tell you the whole set-up, if you like', and proceeded to do so in a written statement, which in part read:

> I backed into a corner by the door and pulled out a gun which I was carrying inside the top of my trousers. I pulled the trigger and it clicked. Then he came towards me with the scissors and I hit him with my hand. He fell on the bed, then he flew back at me. I pulled the trigger again, and I shot him. He was still standing up and I walked out of the door . . . I didn't intend to kill him. I didn't even know I was going to see him that day.

The same evening, a Flying Squad team pulled up outside an address in Berners Street, W1, and collected Zammit, who was taken to Harrow Road police station. At 7.30 pm, he was seen by Webb, who told him that he believed that he was present during the shooting of Smithson, and Zammit replied, 'Yes, I was with Philip and Victor.'

The driver of the getaway car, Louis Magri, was traced and questioned. He was not charged, but Ellul, Spampinato and Zammit were – with the capital murder of Tommy Smithson.

An inquest at St Pancras Coroner's Court was opened and adjourned on 28 June; three weeks went by, and then at Willesden Magistrates' Court Mr E.C. Jones outlined the case for the prosecution to the magistrate, saying that Ellul had told the police that after the shooting, he had thrown the gun over a fence in Camden Town. He had also stated, said Mr Jones, that he and Spampinato had gone by train to Manchester and thence by taxi to Salford. Seeing in the newspapers that Smithson was dead, they had decided to return to London and go to Scotland Yard.

Marlene Bates gave evidence, telling the magistrate, 'Philip pulled out a gun and as he pulled it out, Tommy went towards him. There was a shot. After he fired, Philip ran straight out of the room.' After relating how Smithson had tried unsuccessfully to open the door and Margaret Turnbull came in, Miss Bates described how when the door burst open again Smithson pushed Miss Turnbull out of the way:

> As he did so, Ellul came bursting into the room. Smithson put his arms out in front of him and made to go at Philip.

> Then Philip shot him. I saw nothing in Smithson's hands.
> I covered my face with my hand. It was terrifying. The
> next thing I saw was Philip going out of the room.

She was then shown a pair of scissors but stated she was not sure if they were in the room at the time.

Margaret Turnbull – she had now changed her address to Queen's Gardens, Bayswater – told the court that she had seen Ellul shoot Smithson.

Wishing to paint a complete picture of the murder victim, James Burge for the defence asked Superintendent Webb, 'Is it right that Smithson was a bully with a reputation for ruthless violence?'

Webb replied that he had looked through Smithson's record and could see no evidence that he had ever used a weapon: 'When he committed violence, when he was convicted, he did the damage with his hands and feet.'

This provided an opening which all defence lawyers love, because it enabled Burge to sneer, 'I'm sure he would be grateful for that tribute.'

A submission that Zammit had no case to answer was rejected by the magistrate, the three men pleaded not guilty to the charge of murdering Smithson, reserved their defence and were committed for trial at the Old Bailey.

★

With the three prisoners remanded in custody, Billy Hill and the Kray twins attended the showbiz-style funeral of Tommy Smithson on 4 July 1956. Hundreds of spectators – not all of them necessarily mourners – assembled outside the house of Smithson's mother, in London Fields, Hackney an hour before the procession set out for St Patrick's Roman Catholic Cemetery, Langthorne Road, Leytonstone. Women carrying babies, schoolchildren carrying their satchels, old men in macintoshes and cloth caps and young men with hard faces watched as the funeral cortège passed by. Unfortunately, the hearse suffered a flat rear offside tyre, which had to be hastily changed, but then the procession recommenced with six more Rolls-Royces containing family and friends following the hearse; behind the cortège were fifty more private cars and tradesmen's vans. There were over a hundred bouquets, wreaths and tributes: 'Tommy from neighbours', one read; another simply 'From a friend'; a third one said enigmatically: 'Memories from Porkie'. This was a prescient memento from one Arthur 'Porkie' Bennett, recently released from eight years' preventative detention for razor-slashing. There were two floral dice composed of white daisies and cornflowers, one showing four spots, the other three – a gambler's lucky seven. Not so lucky was Fay Richardson; her application for bail was refused, so she remained in Holloway prison. Instead, she sent a wreath with the words, 'Till we meet again. Love, Fay'. In contrast to Fay Richardson's desire to be present, a firm decision not to attend was made by Tommy Smithson's pretty blonde widow, Jessie. They had parted in 1945, and both she and their daughter were conspicuous by their absence.

There were huge crowds around the graveside, and workers from the nearby Central Line railway tracks looked on as the priest intoned the words, 'Is this a lesson to us? No matter how we spend our lives, whether for good or evil, death always awaits us . . . '

East End sentimentality went beyond mawkishness when the bookmaker Sammy Samuels, who had clashed with members of 'The Brummagem Hammers' racetrack gang in 1922, offered the opinion that Smithson 'was as harmless as a day-old chick'. Smithson's mother had the words 'No one so true and kind' engraved on her son's memorial. However, seeing as how they were referring to the man whose watchword was 'pay up, or get cut' it is fairly certain that there were some – George Caruana amongst them – who might have disagreed with those sentiments.

*

One month later, on 3 August, Fay Richardson appeared before Mr A.W. Cockburn QC, the Chairman of the London Sessions, and pleaded guilty to the three charges of theft and false pretences; in fact, she cleared out the entire chequebook because she asked the Chairman to take a further nineteen offences into consideration when he placed her on probation for three years. However, a condition was imposed on the probation order: that she return to live with her mother in Stockport and not return to London during the next three years.

And so Fay Richardson left, saying farewell to her prostitute employer and pausing at the graveside of her former lover to silently bid him adieu – 'Till we meet again'. Then she was gone. When she next reappeared in London, there would be a short-lived marriage to Alec Sadler, another to Stan Davies, a receiver and Kray associate, a slightly longer liaison with a man who, like Smithson, had been a boxer and whose murder she would witness – he, too, was shot. She also took up with Ray Rosa, a South London hardman of Turkish extraction who had been flogged in prison; he died in a car crash. It appeared that Mrs Davies, formerly Sadler, née Richardson, was accompanied by the angel of death.

*

The trial of the Ellul and Spampinato – no evidence was offered against Zammit and he was discharged – commenced at the Old Bailey on 18 September 1956 before Mr Justice Ashworth, who eight years later would be the last judge in England to send two murderers to the gallows. The Crown's case was conducted by Mr R.E. Seaton QC. 'Reggie' Seaton was a tremendously keen prosecutor and was much admired – by the police, that is.

Another competent barrister (who would go on to become a judge) was Edward Clarke QC, who appeared as defence counsel for Ellul and who told the jury that during the attack upon Caruana by Smithson and his two associates, Caruana had told Smithson, 'I haven't any money coming in. You've had £1,500 from the club since coming out of prison'.

According to Ellul, Smithson had replied, 'I could get money from Billy Hill but I don't want anything to do with him. The only difference between me and him is that he takes ten shillings in the pound and I only take five shillings. I don't ask you people for money, I demand it.'

In addition, Ellul told the court that a day or two before the killing, Smithson had told him, 'If you don't get out of London, I'll do you', and consequently, Ellul moved his address. On the day of the killing he had bought an automatic pistol and nine rounds of ammunition from 'a coloured man in Poplar'.

'I thought I'd be safer with a gun,' Ellul told the court. 'Smithson and his gang had threatened me with a gun.' Describing how he went to 88 Carlton Terrace on the evening of 25 June to wait to see Caruana, Ellul told the court that he had entered 'Blondie' Bates' room to find Smithson there:

> While talking to Miss Bates, I saw her looking at some-thing and turning round, I saw Smithson with a pair of scissors in his hand. He said, 'I'm going to have you now.' He made a swing at me and I pulled out the gun. I ducked and hit him on the chin with my fist and he fell on the bed. He jumped up in no time and was after me. I thought he was going to hit me and I shot him. I walked out of the room but I returned after Spampinato had told me that Smithson had been hit. I said I would try and reason with him and help him. Smithson jumped at me with the scissors. I raised my right hand and a shot was fired by me. I rushed out. The last I saw of Smithson was him following me down the stairs. I had no idea he was injured. Spampinato had nothing to do with the firing of the shots.

The following day, Spampinato gave evidence and told the court that he had no quarrel with Smithson ('a rough fellow, who had beaten up people in a club') whom he had known for four years, and 'had never got in his way'.

Referring to the time of the shooting, Spampinato's barrister, Mr E. St George, asked him, 'Did you interfere in any way with what was going on between Ellul and Smithson?'

'I tried to help Smithson when he was hurt', replied his client.

In cross-examination and referring to when Ellul returned to Miss Bates' room and fired the second and fatal shot, Reggie Seaton (who a few years later would become the Chairman of the Inner London Sessions) tore into Spampinato: 'That was a visit to finish off Smithson, who was being a perfect nuisance to you, was it not?'

'No, sir', replied the prisoner.

'And when the first shot was fired, you urged your friend to go back and do it again', insisted Seaton.

'That is what you are saying', replied Spampinato sulkily.

'And in case it misfired, you had got a knife?'

'No, sir. I never had a knife in my life', replied Spampinato.

Louis Magri had been called as a prosecution witness, to prove that he had conveyed the three men to the flat prior to the shooting and had driven them away afterwards. However, he was a better witness for the defence, because he told the jury that Smithson had visited several clubs and was an expert in obtaining money by threats: 'Smithson was proud of his reputation of being violent and boasted of the beatings-up he had given.'

The next day, 21 September, Mr Justice Ashworth summed up the evidence and told the jury:

> Before you can convict Spampinato, you have to be satis-fied that he was a party to the firing of the shot by Ellul. You might think that Spampinato was there just trying to help but not wanting to injure anybody. Unless you can find in him any intention to be a party to the killing of Smithson, he is entitled to be acquitted.

And he was; he walked off into the sunset with his girlfriend, 'Blondie' Bates. It was a different verdict for Ellul, for whom the judge donned the black cap and issued the death sentence. However, the jury had added a recommendation for mercy and this was heeded by the Home Secretary, Major Gwilym Lloyd-George TD, PC (later 1st Viscount Tenby), who just over a fortnight later, on 8 October, recommended a reprieve. He had refused to commute the death penalty for Ruth Ellis in 1955 (the last woman to be hanged in England), but the Labour politician Samuel Sidney Silverman, who was a passionate opponent of the death penalty, had introduced a private member's bill to abolish it which was passed by 200 votes to 98 on a free vote in the House of Commons on 28 June 1956. Although the bill would be later defeated in the House of Lords, it was probably sufficient to influence the Home Secretary's decision.

Ellul had escaped the hangman's noose by just forty-eight hours; but he would spend the next eleven years in prison.

★

On the day that Ellul was sentenced to death, another trial got underway at the Old Bailey. Almost as soon as removing the black cap, Mr Justice Ashworth commenced presiding over the trial of Walter Edward Downs and Christopher John Thomas, who were charged with inflicting grievous bodily harm on George Caruana and with possessing a firearm with intent to endanger life. Thomas pleaded not guilty to both charges; Downs pleaded guilty to the first charge but not the second, a plea which was immediately accepted by the utterly incompetent Christmas Humphreys QC, so the case was considerably weakened from the start.

Downs therefore left the dock and the trial commenced against Thomas, who told the jury that when he entered the room at the café in Berners Street, Caruana, whose hands, he noticed, were bleeding, was sitting in a corner. He also noticed that Downs had a knife in his hands. 'I took the knife from him and put it in my pocket', he virtuously told the jury. 'I accompanied Caruana to hospital and later returned with him to the café. I never possessed a gun in my life. Caruana seemed frightened of Smithson and he gave me £30 to give to Smithson.'

Without Downs in the dock, with Smithson unavoidably absent, Ellul having other things on his mind and Christmas Humphreys conducting the prosecution, it took no time at all for the jury to acquit Thomas of both charges.

Downs, on the other hand – a three-time loser – was brought up from the cells for sentence. Mr Justice Ashworth said:

> I have got to deal with you on the footing that you took part in the most brutal assault on Caruana. I have seen the weapon and the thought of you and Smithson setting about that man and reducing him to a pitiful state of ter-ror compels me to impose a quite severe sentence.

He then sentenced Downs to three years' imprisonment.

There was just one more matter to consider. Remember the diamond ring which Smithson had given to his previous paramour, Zoe Progl, in the event that she fell upon hard times?

Well, it appears that she did. Detective Sergeant Terry O'Connell of the Flying Squad (later Commander O'Connell QPM) spotted her in two clubs, The Rehearsal and The Plonker, endeavouring to sell the ring; when he saw her at an address at Chelsham Road, Clapham on 19 February 1960 he not unnaturally wished to know if it was stolen. She told him that she had had the ring for years, that Smithson had given it to her and that she had pawned it 'dozens of times at Attenborough's in the West End'. By the time she made an application for the ring to be returned under the Police Property Act at Marylebone Magistrates' Court on 2 January 1962, she did so under escort from Holloway Prison, where she was serving a four-year sentence of corrective training for six cases of receiving and false pretences, imposed the previous year at Southampton Quarter Sessions. After she told the magistrate, Mr Geoffrey Raphael, that she 'didn't know where Smithson got the ring and didn't ask him', the ring worth, in her estimation, 'a few hundred, I should say', was restored to her.

And that appeared to be the end of a sordid series of events which culminated in the death of Tommy 'Scarface' Smithson, except for one matter: just about everything said by the defendants during his murder trial was a lie. George Caruana would experience several more brushes with mortality, and seventeen years would pass before anything like the truth would unfold.

CHAPTER 2

Tommy Smithson – the Maltese Syndicate

Following the demise of the Kray brothers – you'll have to be patient, we'll come to them in due course – a gap appeared which the East End's underworld was keen to fill. Leonard 'Nipper' Read was aware that this would happen and he entreated the Home Office to establish a permanent squad instead of his ad hoc one, and eventually they did.

The Serious Crime Squad was thus formed, and on 29 March 1971 it was headed by Detective Chief Superintendent Albert Samuel Wickstead, then approaching his forty-eighth birthday. Short and stocky, a career detective with twenty-three years' service, he tore through the underworld like an avenging angel wielding a flaming sword. Utterly unscrupulous in his treatment of criminals, he was known as 'The Old Grey Fox', and the East End villains were terrified of him. Two of the most violent characters were once hauled into his office and, after Wickstead had finished 'telling them their fortune', he flung his door open and astonished members of his team were amazed to see the two thugs on their knees with tears streaming down their faces.

'Look at 'em!' roared Wickstead. 'The terrors of the East End! They don't look so fucking terrifying now, do they?'

This was not an isolated incident; Wickstead had that effect on criminals.

The first on Wickstead's list were contemporaries of the Krays, the Dixon brothers. Taking a leaf out of Nipper Read's book, Wickstead's evidence came from other criminals who received his ultimatum: 'Come over to my side or end up in the dock!' Many of them did and provided the evidence for the extortion rackets, the woundings and the beatings which resulted in sentences of twelve years for George Dixon and nine years for his younger brother, Alan.

Next on the agenda were the Tibbs family from East Ham; Wickstead exposed a shocking catalogue of shootings, stabbings and bombings against rival factions which led to seven members of the gang being sentenced to a total of fifty-eight years' imprisonment.

That was the East End tidied up, so where next? The West End of London beckoned; a group known as 'The Maltese Syndicate' were running vice – and just about everything else – in Soho. The profits from prostitution and pornography were enormous, and there was more than enough left over to bribe some very stupid, very crooked police officers – as unscrupulous in their way as Wickstead was in his.

The head of the Maltese Syndicate was not Maltese at all – his name was Bernard Silver and he was an East End Jew, born in 1922. Shortly after taking command of the Serious Crime Squad, Wickstead had heard his name and in accordance with the maxim 'know thine enemy' started asking questions about him. Silver had heard of Wickstead's enquiries and wanted a meet with him – not to confess to any of his misdeeds but to see if a deal could be brokered. Ed Williams, then a detective sergeant, who met Silver in the foyer of Tintagel House (then Wickstead's headquarters), told me:

> He didn't look well. He wasn't a tall man; I'd say five foot six to seven. I do recall he was wearing an ill-fitting grey/ green suit. His whole appearance was 'crumpled'. His face was pale and pasty. He looked more like a man awaiting execution than a person in control of the situation. When Silver extended his hand to me, I shook it and was conscious that he held on to my hand for far too long, for the specific purpose of making it very clear that he was a freemason, as I was at that time.
>
> Bert remained seated when I walked Silver into his office. Silver extended his hand, which Bert took. As they released hands, Bert's face was furious. He said, 'I saw what you did then, and that's going to get you nowhere.' I assumed that Silver had also given Bert a sign that he was 'on the square'. I knew that Bert was also a freemason.
>
> Silver said, 'I hear that you want to see me over something in the past, some old problems. Is that true? Are you bringing me in?'
>
> Bert smiled the Wickstead smile and said, 'Where did you hear that?' Silver said, 'Is it true?'
>
> Bert said, 'When I decide to bring you in, if I decide to bring you in, you'll be the first to know about it . . .'
>
> Silver was patently afraid and Bert's strategy may have been to let that Fear fester. Bert seemed pleased with the encounter, knowing full well that he had said a temporary farewell to his criminal prey. I sensed that 'The Old Grey Fox' was preening his whiskers.

News of Wickstead's new enterprise in Soho – and his interest in Silver – naturally filtered out, and it reached the fox-like ears of Commander Wallace Virgo, the head of C1 Department at the Yard, the department of which Wickstead's Serious Crime Squad was just one section.

Virgo was extremely well informed; it was said that sparrows were unable to fart without his being aware of it. It was also rumoured that Virgo could hear the rustling sound of a £5 note falling on to a mattress from a distance of five miles; what was more, he was as straight as a corkscrew.

Virgo therefore decided to pay a courtesy call to Wickstead's headquarters, which had now moved to the old married quarters at Limehouse police station. Placing an envelope containing £500 on Wickstead's desk, Virgo blandly informed him that a similar sum would be made available to him, every week – with the proviso that he stay out of the West End.

This, I assure you, was symptomatic of the bare-faced arrogance of those crooked detectives; Virgo must have been mightily surprised when with a roar of rage Wickstead threw him and his bribe out of his office. But Wickstead went further than that. Previously, all of his reports had been submitted to the commander of C1, for onward transmission through the chain of command; it was necessary, a courtesy and common sense for the commander to see what Wickstead was doing at Limehouse, and Virgo was the head of Wickstead's department.

Overnight, that changed. Wickstead's reports now went nowhere near Virgo's office; instead, they went right over his head to the desk of Deputy Assistant Commissioner Ernie Bond OBE, QPM, who was in charge of 'C' Department's operations. Bond was a very tough character who had been David Stirling's sergeant in the wartime Special Air Service; he was worshipped by the rank and file CID officers and, in turn, he admired the Serious Crime Squad.

'Every time you come to my office', he would good naturedly grumble, 'you leave my fucking drinks cabinet bare!'

Although Wickstead was a heavy smoker, he seldom drank; but he ensured that his staff kept Ernie Bond's drinks cabinet fully stocked.

Now Wickstead and his men were meeting their informants, getting a breakdown on who did what in Soho – and there was an additional bonus. Quite apart from vice and prostitution, the word on the street was that Silver had been responsible for the murder of Tommy Smithson.

★

Silver and his lieutenant – 'Big Frank' Saviour Mifsud, an eigh-teen-stone former Maltese police officer – had been running brothels and gaming clubs in the East End during the 1950s. The Messina gang who had run prostitution in Soho had been bro-ken up, its members imprisoned, deported or deceased. Just four months prior to Smithson's murder, Silver was one of eight men and one woman who had been acquitted on charges of living on immoral earnings, and the way was becoming clear for Silver to gain a substantial toehold in the West End. However, any sign of weakness would be catastrophic; and Tommy Smithson had been making himself very busy in threatening Silver and other ponces in the East End for protection payments – as his assassins were told, 'This punk has got to be exterminated.'

After Ellul and Spampinato had initially fled to Manchester following the murder of Smithson, they were contacted by the Syndicate and ordered to return to London and surrender them-selves to the police. They were told that they would be convicted of manslaughter but would be rewarded to such an extent that they would never need to work again. Eleven years after Ellul's close brush with the hangman's noose he was released and went to col-lect his impressive reward. Instead, sixpence was contemptuously tossed on the floor and he was told to get out and never return. Spampinato received the same peremptory dismissal, without even the benefit of sixpence.

Ellul had gone to the United States, Spampinato to his native Malta. Unsurprisingly, both were bitter, disgruntled – and pen-niless. Could they be found? And if they could, might they be induced to return to the United Kingdom to give evidence against the Syndicate?

Enquiries therefore needed to be made in Malta, and this pre-sented a problem. Originally a British possession, the island had been awarded the George Cross for displaying courage during the Second World War. However, following its independence in 1971, Dominic 'Dom' Mintoff had become Prime Minister. Although his wife was English, he dismissed the British Governor General, annulled the British defence agreement and expelled the Commander-in-Chief of the NATO naval forces. Consequently, Malta was a political hot potato.

Normally, for British police officers to make enquiries in a for-eign country, a *Commission Rogatoire* (Letter of Request) had to be prepared and signed by the Director of Public Prosecutions, politely requesting the competent judicial authority of that coun-try to assist the officers in their investigations. However, that was precisely what could not be done in this case. But since Malta was a popular holiday destination, Wickstead was able to demonstrate his fox's wiliness. His officers untruthfully recorded in the duty book that they had taken annual leave, became 'tourists' and spoke to quite a number of the island's residents during their stay; they also received immense help from a local police officer, Inspector Fred Calleja.

Victor Spampinato, now in a fairly impoverished state, was traced with the assistance of a Maltese informant by Detective Sergeants Bernie Tighe and John Lewis to a casino in the early hours of the morning. After several clandestine meets he made a written statement implicating Silver, Mifsud and Anthony Mangion in the murder of Smithson and eventually he agreed to return to the UK. George Caruana was also seen by the officers; he gave a statement but refused to come back. He had been the subject of planned assassinations, it was said, by the Kray twins at the behest of Bernie Silver – first by dynamiting his car, then by means of a crossbow.

There was another important witness to trace who was believed to be in West Germany; this task was given to the late Detective Sergeant Terry Brown GM and Bernie Tighe. The latter told me:

> Terry Brown and myself spent a week or so, initially in the Reeperbahn district of Hamburg, as we were told that Frank 'The Snake' Dyer, a ponce, had fled there with his wife. We visited many, many sex clubs and saw things that would make you blush. [You, a hardened Squad officer, blush?!] Even saw a couple having sex on a trapeze whilst swinging over the audience. However, having exhausted our enquiries, we received further information that Dyer and his wife were in Frankfurt.
>
> There was an immediacy in tracing him, as two contract killers had left the UK to silence Dyer and his wife. Much time was spent in the vice area of Frankfurt and eventually we found the wife in a sex club – also Dyer. They were taken into protective custody by police, and Terry and I persuaded them to return to the UK.
>
> It was imperative to keep Dyer's and his wife's location secret and as she was Welsh, a safe house was found in Wales, where they were debriefed. They gave important background to the running of the Syndicate.

Now that Spampinato's testimony had been secured, it was essential to find Ellul. Wickstead flew to the States and liaised with the Federal Bureau of Investigation and the New York Police

Department. He then discovered that he was probably on the wrong side of that massive continent – because Ellul was believed to be on America's west coast, in or around the San Francisco area. The editor of *Inside Detective* magazine provided help, circulating Ellul's photograph and details with the request that Ellul, or anybody knowing his whereabouts, should contact Wickstead immediately.

Philip Ellul was eventually spotted on a park bench by two San Francisco Police Department inspectors, Nate Padrini and Bob Martin. He agreed to return to England, and Detective Chief Inspector Ken Tolbart and Detective Sergeant John Farley (later Detective Superintendent Farley QPM) flew out to meet him and escort him back.

Farley told me, 'I spent a whole day debriefing Ellul. I took a thirty-page statement from him; he had no compassion, gave cold-blooded details, showed no remorse, never laughed.'

Both Ellul and Spampinato gave graphic details of the killing: Ellul had been armed with the gun, which had jammed after the first shot, while Spampinato, despite his previous denials, had been in possession of a knife. After the gun's mechanism had been cleared, Ellul's second, fatal, shot had hit Smithson in the neck.

Despite the panicky excuses which both men had used in court, Ellul had in fact told his companion, 'Leave him to me'. And Spampinato's previous assertion that he had tried to help Smithson now had a hollow ring to it when he admitted, 'Blood started coming out. Thick blood like liver, from his mouth ... I was really enjoying myself.'

So who had supplied the gun? Not 'a coloured man in Poplar' as Ellul had previously stated. The person responsible was said to be a certain Joe Farrugia, who had disappeared. Bernie Tighe discovered from an informant that he was in the Canary Islands, where he held an interest in a drinking/sex club. Now Mr Farrugia's hedonistic lifestyle at Gran Canaria was suddenly interrupted. Moored off the coast of the south-western resort of Puerto Rico in his boat and enjoying the attention of two West End prostitutes, his day was spoilt by the arrival of Bernie Tighe; but he was allowed to resume his intemperate behaviour after Tighe departed, taking with him a written statement in which Farrugia implicated Silver in the murder.

★

Wickstead's officers had been working non-stop; apart from the Smithson investigation, they had amassed sufficient evidence to be able to charge the Syndicate with offences of kidnapping and conspiracy to live off immoral earnings. The raid to scoop everybody into the net was scheduled for 4 October 1973, but on the previous day it was discovered that every one of the suspects had vanished. To Wickstead's fury, there proved to be a traitor in the ranks of the Serious Crime Squad, but with insufficient evidence to prosecute him, the officer in question was merely transferred. Wickstead now set about establishing a disinformation exercise: search warrants were supposedly withdrawn, newspaper stories were published which suggested that he had no further interest in the Syndicate and he carried out a raid on a pornographic bookshop with a view to hammering home the point that his interest in the West End was porn, not vice.

It worked. As the weeks went by, one by one the members of the Syndicate returned to their old haunts in the capital. And then on 30 December 1973, John Lewis received a tip from an informant that Bernie Silver was back in London.

'I phoned Bernie Tighe at home', Lewis told me, 'and we kept observation on Silver's flat at Wilton House, Knightsbridge. We saw the light go out in his flat and moments later he left, together with his girlfriend, Kathleen Ferguson, and they were arrested.'

With Silver saying, 'Mr Wickstead, what can I say? You obviously done your job. I can't say we weren't expecting it, can I?', now the other members of the Syndicate were pulled in. On New Year's Eve 1973, at Marlborough Street Magistrates' Court, Silver and Anthony Mangion were charged with two incitements to murder and they and four other defendants were charged with conspiracy to live on immoral earnings. The magistrate, Neil McElligott, remanded them in custody.

Frank Mifsud had initially vanished with the others in October, but information was received that he was in Southern Ireland. Ed Williams and Detective Inspector Brendan Byrne flew to Dublin, where they liaised with officers from *An Garda Siochána.*

'Dublin CID officers took us to Mifsud's bolt-hole, which turned out to be a very ordinary house on a bleak Dublin estate', Williams told me. 'They agreed to keep covert surveillance on the property and we flew back to London.'

But when Silver was arrested, the squad were shocked to discover that Mifsud had slipped away just prior to the arrival of the arrest team. He would not resurface for some considerable time.

However, both Ellul and Spampinato gave impressive evidence at the Magistrates' Court, sufficient to commit Silver and Mangion to the Old Bailey on a charge of murdering Smithson. Afterwards, they returned to their respective homelands, promising to return to give evidence at the trial.

The murder trial was listed for 16 September 1974; it was post-poned indefinitely after the Crown made an application for Mifsud to join the other two accused in the dock. But on 19 September, the trial of Silver and ten other men – mainly Maltese – commenced. They faced charges of living off immoral earnings, assaulting and attempting to imprison a witness and perverting the course of justice.

The trial lasted exactly three months; on 19 December, seven men were jailed, with Silver receiving the heaviest sentence for conspiracy to live off immoral earnings: six years' imprisonment and a fine of £30,000. Mangion was sentenced to five years, with a fine of £10,000.

And now Ellul and Spampinato reneged on their respective deals. According to rumour, Ellul's non-cooperation had been purchased by the Syndicate for £60,000. Roger Stoodley was one of the officers who flew to San Francisco and discovered that significant and substantial improvements had been made to Ellul's flat; the occupier refused to see them. Spampinato had allegedly received £30,000 – half Ellul's payment, but then the cost of living was cheaper in Malta than in the United States. He was now living in a villa with a five-car integral garage which overlooked B'kara, and driving a very smart car. He, too, was disinclined to speak to the police.

Nevertheless, there was sufficient evidence for the murder trial to go ahead; and on 8 July 1975, whilst Mangion was acquitted, Silver was found guilty both of murdering Smithson and of plotting to murder him. He was sentenced to life imprisonment on the first charge and ten years' imprisonment, concurrent, on the second.

Early the following year, John Lewis traced Frank Mifsud to Switzerland, from where he was extradited; he stood trial for Smithson's murder at the Old Bailey in March 1976. Denying that he had told a detective that 'Smithson was a blackmailer and he got what he deserved . . . he was always trying to make me look small', Mifsud told the court that not only did he know nothing about Smithson's murder, but that 'I liked him very much. We were friends.' He also stretched veracity to near breaking point when he described Billy Hill as 'a kind gentleman who lent money', but by now Billy Hill's star had waned and perhaps some of the Old Bailey's jurors were unaware of his fearsome reputation.

Mifsud was acquitted of Smithson's murder; he was found guilty on a separate charge of perjury, sentenced to five years' imprisonment and fined £50,000.

On 18 October 1976 Silver successfully appealed against his murder conviction, after Lord Justice Lawton said that the prosecution had built its case on the evidence of disreputable witnesses: 'A conviction based solely on such slender foundations cannot be regarded as safe or satisfactory.' Thirteen months later, Mifsud, too, successfully appealed against his conviction, sentence and fine.

And to put the tin hat on matters, in January 1977 Thames TV broadcast a programme called 'An Exercise at Law'. In it, both Ellul and Spampinato claimed they had never met Bernie Silver and that he had nothing to do with Smithson's murder.

So in that case, why say that he did? Did they commit perjury the first time they appeared in court – or the second? It must have been one or the other. And were their statements to the police the truth – or an attempt to pervert the course of justice? It was a case involving conspiracies and incitements to murder, as well as murder itself, and also perjury, assault, kidnapping and attempts to pervert the course of justice. A line from Shakespeare's *Hamlet* suggests, 'Something is rotten in the state of Denmark' – or was it closer to home, such as at the Old Bailey?

CHAPTER 3

Jack Spot & Billy Hill

A great deal – and a great deal of nonsense – has been written about the gang leaders Jack Spot and Billy Hill, especially in their vainglorious autobiographies. However, because both played such a decisive part in bloody gang warfare in London, especially in the 1950s, their backgrounds merit a mention.

William Charles Hill was born on 13 December 1911, in Cleveland Street, St Pancras, London, one of twenty-one children of a mostly villainous family. Unable to remember all of his siblings' names, it was inevitable that young Billy would become a thief, and so he did. Aged fourteen, he broke into a tobacconist's kiosk and was sent to an approved school for five years. A petition was hastily collected by the neighbours, and on appeal his punishment was reduced to one of two years' probation. It was an ill-deserved act of clemency, because with a father who was a fighting drunk, a mother who was a receiver of stolen goods and an older sister who was one of the notorious 'Forty Elephants' gang of shoplifters, there was nothing in Billy Hill's family background that could even remotely be described as stable.

By 1928 Hill had been responsible for a series of burglaries and in January 1929 he was sentenced at the Inner London Quarter Sessions to three years' Borstal Training. It was his first taste of custody and Hill didn't like it, not one little bit. He whined, believing that the harsh regime he was experiencing was somebody else's fault. Eight months later he escaped, broke into a house, was disturbed by a maid and savagely attacked her; he was sentenced to nine months' hard labour, plus twelve strokes of the birch, which he liked even less than Borstal. Following his release, Hill carried out a couple of burglaries, then was arrested for being a suspected person and received twenty-one days' imprisonment, after which he was sent back to Borstal.

Early in 1932, he was arrested once more for being a suspected person and collected 'a carpet' – for the uninitiated, three months' imprisonment, the time it took to weave a carpet on a prison loom.

Incidentally, Spot and Hill were not the only ones to embellish their legends; Billy Hill was still a well-known name in 1959 when Fred Narborough published his memoirs and he jumped on the bandwagon when he stated that as a Flying Squad officer he had provided Hill with 'his first gaol sentence', claiming responsibility for Hill's second arrest for 'sus'. However, not only had Hill served two prison sentences and a Borstal prior to that arrest but Narborough's tenure on the Flying Squad did not commence until ten months later.

More burglaries followed, for one of which, in January 1934, Hill was sentenced to three years' penal servitude. He met up with Charles 'Ruby' Sparks on his release and between them they carried out a series of smash-and-grabs as well as safe-blowings; Hill also found time to meet Agnes Kirkwood, and she became his loyal and long-suffering wife.

However, Hill had little time to get used to domesticity; he was arrested for shopbreaking, perhaps unwisely given bail and then again arrested, once more for shopbreaking. At the County of London Sessions in October 1936, he received twenty-one months' imprisonment for the first offence and six weeks later, at the Middlesex Quarter Sessions, four years' imprisonment, concurrent, for the second.

So to summarize Hill's achievements during the first thirty years of his life: he had learnt a great deal about criminality and stolen a goodly amount of valuables, but since he had been sentenced to over eleven years' in the penal system, including hard labour, penal servitude and a birching, he had had little time to savour the fruits of his labours. In addition, he let no insult go by unpunished; he carried a razor or a knife, which he would use to great effect when slashing or 'chivving' an opponent on the face, leaving a V-shaped scar. Now let's leave Hill for the moment and concentrate on his contemporary, Jack Spot.

★

A couple of years younger than Hill, Spot was born Jacob Comacho on 12 April 1913, the youngest of four children and the son of Jewish parents originally from Poland. He was also known as John or Jack Comer but was eventually referred to as Jack Spot, either because of the large mole on his cheek or because, as he was prone to say, 'I was always on the spot.' He was brought up in Myrdle Street, Whitechapel, an area of grinding poverty. The houses were overcrowded, dilapidated and so damp that their rear walls bulged outwards.

The borough surveyor was asked if he considered this dangerous but laconically replied, 'Not that they'll fall over; they prop each other up.'

The young Spot had a series of employments and indulged in a little petty larceny; by the time he was sixteen he was running protection rackets in the Petticoat Lane area, taking a 'pension' from the stallholders. He was now over six feet tall, a good boxer and a better fighter.

Aged twenty, he was arrested for being a suspected person and was simply bound over to be of good behaviour in the sum of forty shillings. His next brush with the law came two years later, when for housebreaking he appeared at the Middlesex Quarter Sessions and was placed on probation for two years; once again, he was bound over to keep the peace in the sum of £10 for a period of two years.

That was the extent of the punishment for his thieving criminality, and he was lucky – his next conviction for dishonesty would come many years later, and as with his two previous convictions, he would be humanely dealt with.

But Spot's claim to fame came on 4 October 1936 at 'The Battle of Cable Street', an all-out clash between Sir Oswald Mosley's fascist blackshirts, Jews, communists and the police. Some 6,000 police officers were on duty and in the civil disorder which followed 150 arrests were made and 175 people were injured, including women, children and 73 police officers.

Charging the black-shirted hordes who menaced the Jews whom he had sworn to protect, lashing out left and right with a chair-leg which he had lined with lead, flattening Mosley's bodyguards before he was knocked unconscious and later sentenced to six months' imprisonment, Spot was battered but unbowed and became the hero of the Jews of Whitechapel.

Unfortunately, none of this was true: no squashed bodyguards, no chair-leg and no prison sentence. But it was a convincingly told tale and many people believed it. Billy Hill might have been a prolific and much admired thief, who paid the families of his gang a pension when they were in prison, but he had not yet become a legend in his own lifetime. Spot had, and all without the encumbrance of a prison sentence. However, matters were about to change.

★

Two of Spot's staunchest friends since boyhood were Morris Goldstein (aka Moisha Blueball) and Bernard Schack (also known as Schechter, Shackter and 'Sonny the Yank'). They had been running a series of lucrative protection rackets when Nat Simmons decided on a similar enterprise which spilled over into Spot's territory. Simmons had previously been an ally; in fact, Spot had given evidence against Jimmy Wooder, one of four men sentenced to hard labour for slashing Simmons at Fox's Club, Dean Street in 1937. But now there was bad feeling between the two factions and blood spilled on both sides, which culminated in an attack at the Somerset Social Club in Little Somerset Street, Whitechapel. Simmons was slashed with a razor and Hymie Jacobs was hit with a milk bottle; the police were called and Spot, Goldstein and Schack were arrested for inflicting grievous bodily harm. When their case was heard on 31 March 1939 at the Mansion House Justice Room, Goldstein's case was dismissed but not so Spot's and Schack's; both were sentenced to six months' hard labour.

Upon his release from prison, Spot's marriage in 1936 (it may have been what used to be described as a 'common law' marriage) to Mollie Simpson, who had born him a son, collapsed. However, on the credit side, he had made friendships in prison, including an alliance with the greatly feared Upton Park Gypsies.

Shortly after Spot's release, Hill was about to re-enter the penal system. He was arrested on 26 June 1940 for a smash and grab; he was in company with Harry Bryan and George Ball, but not Charles 'Ruby' Sparks. Although Hill and Sparks often worked together, Sparks was on the run from Dartmoor, having granted himself a little unofficial parole during a sentence of five years' penal servitude. Hill received a visit from the head of the Flying Squad, Detective Chief Inspector Peter Beveridge, and a conversation between the two men took place. Was a little horse-trading carried out? Well, look at it this way. The very next day, Sparks, who had been at liberty for five months and sixteen days, was arrested in a Flying Squad ambush – they knew exactly where to find him. And although Hill was the undisputed leader of the smash and grab offence (and had the convictions to prove it), whilst Bryan and Ball went off to prison for three years apiece, Hill pleaded guilty to an offence of conspiracy which carried a maximum of two years' imprisonment – which is what he received. Blimey.

*

In 1940 Spot joined the Army and served in the Royal Artillery for three years; he was not posted overseas and his service was not particularly distinguished, since it was interrupted by incidents of fighting and disruption in barracks. He was discharged on medical grounds in 1943 and moved north, to Leeds, Manchester and Birmingham, where he ran protection rackets, before returning to the club scene in London's West End.

As previously mentioned, the head of the White family, Alf, had been a hard man in his time; in 1935 he and two of his sons had been jailed for twelve months, with hard labour, for assault, but now his power had waned and he died in 1942. Nevertheless, in 1946 the remainder of the White family tried their luck on Jewish bookmaker Moses Levy, who was also past his sell-by date, attempting to force him off his pitch at Yarmouth racecourse. Levy appealed to Spot to help him, and Spot did just that. The White faction backed down, and it would have been better if the gang had dispersed immediately – but they did not. Perhaps both sides were at fault; Spot, referring to the White family, would later say, 'I made a mistake. I let the fucking King's Cross mob come back. I should have wiped them out.'

Meanwhile, no sooner had Billy Hill been released from prison than he was scooped up once more for being a suspected person and sentenced to one month's imprisonment. It was not very much longer before he was again arrested, this time for robbery with violence, and given his previous record he was fortunate to be weighed-off with just four years' imprisonment.

It was following his release that Hill and Spot got together to force a confrontation with the White family and their gang. This was supposed to take place on the night of the Joe Baksi/Bruce Woodcock final eliminator at Haringey for the world heavyweight title, but the head of the Metropolitan Police's No. 2 District, the newly promoted Detective Superintendent Peter Beveridge, heard of it and waved a big stick in the combatants' direction. It worked on that occasion, but within a few weeks a confrontation did take place between the two factions and the Whites retired defeated. They probably fared better than Bruce Woodcock – knocked down three times in the first round (when his jaw was broken) and twice more in the second, he gamely struggled on until the referee stopped the fight in the seventh. Woodcock suffered a detached retina and was nearly blinded by the bone splinters from his smashed jaw; he was out of the ring for eighteen months.

However, the Hill/Spot merger was short-lived because Hill was arrested for a warehousebreaking, of which he always claimed he was innocent. Once again unwisely granted bail, Hill took the opportunity to flee to South Africa, but not for long; upon his return he was sentenced to three years' imprisonment.

Whilst Hill was incarcerated, Spot financed (but did not participate in) what, on the face of it, was a rather spectacular coup: a raid on the newly built Heathrow Airport. Goods worth £224,000 were stored in a warehouse, together with a safe containing jewellery valued at £13,900; gold bullion valued at £250,000 was also

due to arrive. With the help of an inside man it was decided to
drug the guards' coffee with phenobarbitone and gain possession
of the safe keys. Fine in concept but doomed to failure, as the
eleven men of Spot's and Hill's gangs discovered. The plan had
been infiltrated from the start; the three 'drugged guards' were
members of the Flying Squad and a great many of their colleagues
were secreted behind packing cases in the warehouse. During the
battle royal that ensued, shocking injuries were inflicted on both
sides, and whilst three of the gang escaped, at the end of the confrontation eight of the remaining robbers lay unconscious on the
ground. Heavy sentences were imposed: gang members received a
total of seventy-one years' penal servitude.[2] Spot was not arrested
and consoled himself with Margaret 'Rita' Molloy, a beautiful Irish
girl whom he had met at Haydock Park races prior to the abortive
raid. They moved into Flat 12F, Hyde Park Mansions, Cabbell
Street, just off the Edgware Road, a four-bedroom, three-bath-
room apartment with two reception rooms, at today's prices worth
£1,700,000. So besotted was Spot with Rita that he neglected to
pay pensions to the families of his incarcerated gang; that was a
big mistake.

According to whom you believe, upon Hill's release from prison
he was met either by Spot in a Rolls-Royce or by Aggie in a more
mundane vehicle. Hill now leased the New Cabinet Club; he and
Spot also ran a club at Southend. These were good years for the
two, but less so for Hill's marriage. In 1951 he met Phyllis 'Gypsy'
Riley and following an unkind remark about her made by 'Belgian
Johnny' aka Jean Baptiste Hubert, a convicted ponce, Hill striped
him with a razor so badly that he was obliged to get Spot to visit
Hubert in hospital to placate him – and ensure his silence – with
a sizeable wad of cash. Getting Spot to clear up after his excesses
would become a habit. It happened with Tommy Smithson a couple
of years later, and in 1954 Hill was acquitted of slashing Freddie
Andrews after the victim conveniently lost his memory.

In between times, Hill masterminded the Eastcastle Street robbery, where £287,000 was stolen, and two years later, a robbery of
£46,000 in bullion. No one was convicted of these offences; not
Hill and certainly not Spot, who was left out in the cold on both
enterprises.

---

[2] For a full account of this exciting encounter, see *The Sweeney – The
First Sixty Years of Scotland Yard's Crimebusting Flying Squad 1919-
1978* (Wharncliffe Books, 2011).

There were cracks in the Spot/Hill partnership and they were beginning to show. Spot had married Rita in 1954 and with his new-found domesticity, and the birth of two daughters, it was widely thought that he was 'going soft'. The word was put about – possibly by Hill – that he was a grass, and when the colourful newspaper reporter Duncan Webb, who ghosted Hill's autobiography, wrote a series of newspaper articles which tended to ridicule Spot, this led to a serious blunder – on Spot's behalf. He arranged a meeting with Webb and knocked him down; the fall broke Webb's wrist. Spot was arrested and Webb could not be straightened – obviously, Hill would not even try. Spot was fined £50 with 20 guineas costs, and worse, Webb sued him and received £732 in damages. Never underestimate the power of the press; Spot was now on a slippery slope.

Spot ran point-to-point racecourse pitches, and these should be explained so that the reader is fully aware of what it entailed. Jockey Club officials allocated most pitches and these were bound by the Club's strict rules, which prohibited welshing or any other disreputable behaviour. However, on some courses there was ground available outside the Club's jurisdiction, known as 'the free side'. Spot had bought up some of these latter pitches and leased them out for £25 per day to his favoured associates; it meant that unprincipled bookmakers could erect a stand and make a book without any interference from the Jockey Club. This naturally attracted the most unscrupulous individuals, and competition was keen to acquire such pitches; deep resentment was also caused amongst those who were excluded.

The Italian Mob, under Pasquale Papa, wanted control of Spot's point-to-point pitches. Born in 1894 in Islington, Papa, taking the ring name of Bert Marsh, boxed as a flyweight and a bantamweight between 1917 and 1925, winning thirty-nine of his fifty-nine bouts, although he was fortunate to have kept his licence, since in 1922 he was sentenced to six months' hard labour for unlawful wounding. Marsh was thought to be the brains behind the theft of gold bullion at Croydon Airport in 1936, and the same year, after being acquitted of murder, he was sentenced to twelve months' imprisonment for the manslaughter of a gang member. Interned as an enemy alien with his allies, the Sabini brothers, during the early part of the Second World War, Marsh was a well-respected member of the Soho underworld and employed Albert Dimes as a strong-arm man. Now, at the Epsom August Meeting in 1955, Marsh demanded that Spot hand over control of his pitches; this might well have caused an ugly scene, except that the police intervened.

Spot decided to enlist the assistance of Reggie and Ronnie Kray, but they were not really interested. Like most feral animals, the brothers could smell fear; and with his power on the wane, although Spot may not have been shaking in his boots he was certainly apprehensive.

It was on 11 August 1955, when Spot was in his club, The Galahad, in Charlotte Street, right on the borders of Soho, that he received a summons – Albert Dimes wanted to see him. It was high time for the powder keg to explode, and it did.

CHAPTER 4

Strange Happenings in Frith Street

It was probably no more than a quarter of a mile from Spot's club to Frith Street, and it was there at about 11.30 am that Spot – who was in a steaming temper – saw Albert Dimes talking to Sebastian Buonacore (or possibly Boonacore or Boonacote), a street commission agent.

'Albert, I want to talk to you', snapped Spot and the two men walked off together.

Buonacore would later say he saw 'an instrument' in Spot's hand and then saw Dimes run off towards the junction with Frith Street and Old Compton Street Spot pursued Dimes and chased him into a continental fruit shop, where Spot repeatedly stabbed him with a knife in his face and body shouting, 'You want to be a fucking tearaway, how do you like that?'

According to some newspaper reports, the shopkeeper's wife, forty-five-year-old Sophie Hyams, hit Spot on the head with some very heavy scales – this was later denied by her – and her husband Hyman said there was so much blood flowing it was difficult to see what was going on and that Dimes seemed to be 'all-in' but then 'he suddenly regained his strength and managed to get the knife from Comer. For a moment, Dimes hesitated and then he turned and attacked Comer, striking him in the side and neck.'

Dimes started to lean against a girder and Hyman Hyams thought he was going to pass out, whilst Spot slowly slumped to the floor. Bert Marsh rushed into the shop and took Dimes away in a taxi, while Spot staggered into a nearby barber's, groaned, 'Fix me up' and fainted. The two men were taken to different hospitals, Spot to the Middlesex, where he was found to have a number of facial wounds, one over his left eye and others to his left cheek, his ear and his neck, as well as four cuts to his arm and two more to the side of his chest, one of which had penetrated his lung.

At Charing Cross Hospital Dimes was described as being 'severely shocked'. He had a six-inch wound to the left side of his forehead which had penetrated to the bone and required twenty stitches, and two stab wounds, one in the stomach (which just failed to penetrate the abdominal cavity), the other in the left thigh, close to the knee, as well as minor lacerations to his chin and left thumb.

Now just for a moment, let's leave the two battered warriors leaking blood over the pristine floors of two hospitals and consider this. There are various accounts of what happened in Frith Street – one is that Spot punched Dimes on the chin and another is that Spot stabbed Dimes – but whatever the circumstances, the undeniable fact is that Dimes ran away. This was witnessed by dozens of people (few of whom came forward to deliver their testimony to the police), but that does not really matter. The point is this: if, following the initial assault on Dimes, Spot had stood his ground and left Dimes fleeing down the street for dear life, it would have reflected very well indeed on him. Dimes, a reputed hard man, working for the very well respected Bert Marsh, himself a tough nut, would have been scorned by the underworld; and whilst it is by no means certain, it is likely that Spot's reputation would have risen considerably from the depths to which it had sunk. There certainly would not have been a prosecution. But of course that didn't happen, because Spot permitted his lunatic temper to get the better of him. Consequently, we now return to the afternoon of the affray, when Dimes was seen by Detective Inspector Eric Shepherd from West End Central police station who asked him who was responsible for his injuries.

'You know as well as I do, it was Jackie Spot', Dimes replied, adding, 'but I'm not prossing [prosecuting].' Later, he made a statement in which he said:

> I was standing in Frith Street, reading a paper. I had a friend with me. A tall man came along. I don't know his name . . . Without more to do, he pulled a knife from his pocket and attacked me. He cut me about the head and face and I was covered with blood.

That statement, prosecuting counsel at the Old Bailey would later tell the jury, with masterly understatement 'was not quite true'.

The same officer interviewed Jack Spot, who told him, 'It's between me and Albert Dimes and nothing to do with you.' Asked if he would make a statement, he replied, 'It's our business. Leave us alone to settle it.'

Dimes was kept in hospital for four more days, and on 20 August Spot was told he would be taken to 'C' Division's West End Central police station for a chat with his nemesis, Detective Superintendent Bert Sparks.

At that time Sparks was forty-eight years of age and in his twenty-eighth year of service. He knew 'C' Division, inside out – this was his fourth posting, and he would spend a total of over thirteen years there. At six feet, one and a half inches tall, Sparks was hard as nails; his nickname was 'The Iron Man' and this was underlined by an incident six years earlier when, whilst off-duty, he helped arrest three men, one of whom was armed with a loaded revolver. It brought him commendations from Tottenham Magistrates' Court, the Chairman of the Middlesex Sessions and the Commissioner of the Metropolitan Police, to add to his growing total of twenty-four commendations.

Ever since Sparks had broken up a gang fight in the 1930s – he carried a scar which had required seven stitches on his forehead as a memento – he had had a definite down on gangsters; and Spot was one of those at the top of his list. Just as the Prevention of Crime Act 1953 was placed on the statute books, so Spot was arrested for possessing an offensive weapon. Although he pleaded guilty and was fined just £20, Spot later claimed that he had been fitted up and morosely blamed 'that cunt Sparks', who had arrived at West End Central just a week before. In fact, Sparks had told Spot to 'stay out of Soho', wise counsel which Spot failed to heed.

The day following the talk with Spot, Sparks interviewed Albert Dimes, and this time Dimes declared that he wanted to tell the whole truth about the feud between Jack Spot and himself:

> I saw he was holding a fairly long-bladed implement. I could not see whether it was a dagger or a knife. It cut me on the side of the hand. I turned and ran down Frith Street I realized that Spot was out to do me some terrible injury and I had nothing to help myself with. I went into the fruit shop and . . . I think I said, 'Someone is trying to kill me.' Almost instantly, Spot was on top of me again and I felt a jab in the stomach. I was beginning to feel very weak. I remember grabbing the hand and my left thumb was cut on the weapon . . . I don't want to kid you, but in the struggle between us, I must have cut him with the knife. If I did use it, I was struggling for my life.

Both men were charged with inflicting grievous bodily harm with intent to do so, possessing an offensive weapon and causing an affray.

Spot's response was, 'Why me? Albert did me and I get knocked off.'

Dimes reply was along the same lines: 'Spotty does me up and I get pinched. That don't seem fair.'

They appeared at Marlborough Street Magistrates' Court and having been remanded in custody for a week, on 29 August were committed to the Old Bailey for trial.

Dimes was represented by Billy Hill's pet barrister, Patrick Marrinan (of whom we shall hear a lot more later), who told the court that his client had acted in self-defence, having been attacked by 'this other murderous, treacherous rascal'. Dimes was allowed bail in the sum of £250 with two sureties in similar amounts.

Not so Spot; he was committed in custody after Sparks told the court that he had intimated that if released on bail he would abscond to Ireland. The following night, Spot was placed in a special cell at Brixton prison after he had been found with injured wrists.

The trial commenced on 19 September before Mr Justice Glyn-Jones. Reggie Seaton appeared for the Crown, Miss Rose Heilbron QC appeared for Spot and G.D. 'Khaki' Roberts QC for Dimes, but it was a short-lived affair. The judge decided upon separate trials for the two men and directed the jury to find both not guilty of causing an affray.

After 'Khaki' Roberts successfully argued, 'Were the prosecution really saying he was in unlawful possession of the knife? It is grotesque in its absurdity. The man was defending himself for his life', Dimes was found not guilty of possessing an offensive weapon. With Dimes free on bail, the trial against Spot – remanded in custody – recommenced the following day before the Recorder of London, Sir Gerald Dodson.

During the case for the Crown, Buonacore and, perhaps surprisingly, Bert Marsh gave evidence, as well as the Hyams family, the latter being undoubtedly amongst the few truthful witnesses, either for the prosecution or the defence. Despite Spot's barrister, Rose Heilbron, suggesting that Dimes was the aggressor and that Spot had gamely hung on to his wrist in an attempt to make him drop the knife, fifty-year-old Hyman Hyams stuck to his guns.

'No, ma'am', he replied. 'I was there. I saw enough, ma'am.'

Bert Sparks told the court that following an anonymous tip-off he had found a bloodstained knife in a paper bag in Soho Square. It certainly did not point to the guilt of Spot; he had collapsed 100 metres away before being taken to hospital. Frankie Fraser (of whom we shall be hearing a great deal more) subsequently claimed that the knife planting had been carried out by him and Bert Marsh.

Now Miss Heilbron outlined the case for the defence. She told the jury that Spot was a bookmaker who occupied a betting pitch at racecourses; in order to occupy a good pitch he found it necessary to book several, choose a good one and let out the others. However, a few days before the fight in Frith Street, Spot had received a note telling him that he had to keep away from all racecourses and point-to-point meetings and that Dimes would take care of him if he did not.

Giving evidence, Spot told the court that he had been going to racecourses for twenty years and that he would pay £300 for ground and let it out to other bookmakers, keeping a pitch for himself.

Asked by Miss Heilbron if anyone was jealous of him, Spot replied, 'Yes. Bert Marsh, Basta[3] and Italian Albert.' Dimes, he said, 'was a bit of a strong-arm man hired by Marsh. In August, Dimes said, "You have all the best pitches; I think it's time you were finished".'

Spot said he took no notice of that remark but later received a telephone message from Dimes which led to the confrontation in Frith Street According to Spot, 'Dimes said, "This is your final warning. I don't want you to go away racing any more . . . It's about time somebody else had your pitches".'

Spot claimed the two men started pushing each other until Dimes suddenly produced a knife and started stabbing at him. 'I put my hand up and the knife went through my arm', he said and went on to describe how Dimes stabbed him in the face with the knife. 'I was trying to defend myself because he was definitely trying to kill me.'

And then it was the turn of a defence witness, Christopher Glinski, an interpreter who entered the witness box and corroborated Spot's account, practically word for word. He had read about the case when it was reported at the Magistrates' Court and, he told the jury, 'It did not correspond with what I had seen, so I telephoned the defence solicitor.'

The following day, there was another surprise witness in the form of the Revd Basil Claude Hudson Andrews, an eighty-eight-year-old retired Church of England clergyman of 44 Inverness Terrace, Bayswater; he, too, had felt impelled to contact Spot's solicitor after reading a newspaper account which failed to accord with his recollection of the incident. 'I had read an account of the fight in a newspaper and was surprised to see the fairer man (Spot) described as the aggressor. It astonished me, I thought "Dear me!" because the dark man (Dimes) was the aggressor.' He had not contacted the solicitor immediately, he admitted, but did so after the matter began to prey on his mind.

So what had the venerable gentleman seen? This is what he told the court:

> Two men were pushing one another and the darker of
> the two had a steel instrument in his hand and he struck
> at the head of his opponent, a fair-haired man. The man

---

[3] 'Basta' is Italian for 'Enough!' Spot was undoubtedly referring to Sebastian Buonacore, whose nickname was 'Vesta'.

who was much fairer held up his arm to shield himself
and in so doing, I imagine he got a pretty serious wound
in the arm; I don't know. What I do know is that I saw
the dark-haired man strike the other man in the face and
blood issued pretty freely from the wound. I felt pretty
disgusted with the whole thing. I didn't want to get
mixed up in it so I cleared out and left Soho and went
into Oxford Street

The jury took little time to acquit Spot of both charges – just sixty-four minutes, in fact – and with a complete lack of dignity he
danced up and down in the dock, his hands above his head, celebrating his victory like the boxer he had once been, until he was
rebuked by the judge: 'Behave yourself, Comer!'

As Spot left the dock, so Albert Dimes stepped into it to face
the same judge and prosecutor, who told the jury that they would
have to ask themselves, having due regard for the injuries which
Spot had received, whether Dimes was acting in self-defence or
if one man had started the attack and the other had 'taken it up'.

The weekend now intervened and on Monday, 26 September
Reggie Seaton threw in the towel, telling the Recorder:

> The prosecution has now had an opportunity of consider-
> ing the position in the light of what happened in the other
> case. The conclusion we have arrived at, subject to your
> approval, is that it would be quite wrong, in the circum-
> stances, to convict Dimes.

The Recorder agreed, saying:

> From the moment that the verdict was returned on
> Friday, this position began to develop. Having regard to
> what happened on Friday, it would be manifestly unjust
> that this man should be put on his trial. It would be quite
> improper for the jury to be asked to find him guilty, espe-
> cially when witnesses in the case said that the other man
> was the assailant.

The jury were brought in to be told by the Recorder of London:

> It is better that I should say no more at the moment . . . so
> I won't. There is much that could be said but it is enough
> that now, on my direction, you should return a verdict of
> not guilty.

The jury did so, and Dimes, too, left the court a free man.

The case became known as 'the fight that never was', but there was a lot more to it than that. With the ensuing, predictably mocking publicity – the *Sunday Chronicle* had already published Spot's memoirs and he was also being championed by the *Daily Sketch*, whilst the *People* ran a story in which Spot was allegedly quoted by Dimes as whining, 'Don't cut me, Albert – please don't cut me!' – the Home Secretary was furious. Public confidence in both the police and the judicial system had taken a very hard knock indeed, and when Peter Kirk, the Conservative MP for Gravesend, asked, 'If, in view of the evidence submitted at the trial, he would take powers to close temporarily any racecourse habitually frequented by known criminals', the Home Secretary, realizing that this would mean the closure of every racetrack in England, plus a considerable loss of revenue to the exchequer, demanded that Scotland Yard conduct an enquiry into the whole affair. The Yard was ready for that one. No sooner had the commissioner put the telephone down on the seething Home Secretary than he appointed Ted Greeno to the task.

CHAPTER 5

A Very Dodgy Clergyman

The Revd Basil Andrews, described variously as 'a clerk in holy orders', 'an unlicensed parson' and 'a sponger', was the despair of several bookmakers. It was not only Andrews' history of debts and borrowings which had never been repaid; it was also said that for the sum of £300 he had introduced a seventy-two-year-old man to a girl of sixteen, who Andrews claimed was his niece and who, at the age of twenty-one, stood to inherit £100,000. It was further suggested that he had carried out a bogus marriage, again for £300 (although when this was later put to him in court, he cried, 'Good gracious! Whoever heard of such a thing?'); and when the scrounging from his fellow clergymen began to spiral out of control, his bishop had admonished him regarding his behaviour. He had fiercely repudiated these and other unkind accusations, and his declaration of innocence, published in the *Daily Sketch*, read as follows:

> I am fully aware that cowardly people who dare not come forward into the light of day are suggesting that I am a fraudulent witness and that I hoodwinked Mr Comer's legal advisors.
>
> I would recall to you that when I gave my evidence last week, I gave it on my solemn oath, and I need not remind you that I am a Clerk in Holy Orders, also.
>
> I therefore wish to affirm in the most solemn terms that what I said in the witness box was the whole truth and nothing but the truth. I wish to deny that I have committed perjury.
>
> I wish to deny that I have any hope of material gain from having come forward as a witness. I did so only in the interests of truth, and I am willing to tell the police that, if they come to me.
>
> Any financial difficulties due to my change of address and my harmless flutters in the sporting world are only temporary, due to my age and inexperience.
>
> Those who are dunning me will soon be repaid if they have patience – some debts have been repaid, already.
>
> My innocent walk in Frith Street that day has made me finish up in a nest of trouble, with enemies in an underworld I never dreamed existed.

I am a man of peace, as well, I hope, as one of God's humblest servants and workers.

I would like to bring about a reconciliation between the parties in strife who seem to have forgotten that, by what they have done, they are debasing the sacred Brotherhood of Man.

Andrews was now summoned to No. 1 District Headquarters for a distinctly uncomfortable interview.

★

Even though he had just celebrated his fifty-fifth birthday and was now in his thirty-fourth year of service, Detective Chief Superintendent Ted Greeno was still one of the Yard's most successful detectives. He had served for eleven years on the Flying Squad, was an astute murder investigator and knew the underworld inside out. Any criminal who challenged his authority would be taken on, whether in a pub, a racetrack or the street, and knocked flying. Greeno's informants were numerous and his success was not only measured by the fact that he had been commended by the commissioner on no less than eighty-six occasions and appointed MBE; it was also endorsed by Billy Hill, who acknowledged that Greeno was 'one of the Yard's best thief catchers'.

Greeno had been appointed as one of 'The Big Five' at No. 1 District Headquarters on 3 January 1955. No chair-bound warrior he; within one month of his appointment, as soon as he heard that the safe at Martin's Bank in St James had been blown and £20,621 stolen, he knew immediately who was responsible. Greeno was out from behind his desk, grabbed hold of Bert Sparks and went to work. It resulted in the conviction, three months later, of twenty-nine-year-old Howard Henry Lewis, who was sentenced to seven years' imprisonment; and since forty-three-year-old Alfie Fraser was the proud possessor of seventeen previous convictions, it meant that he was more than eligible for his sentence of ten years' preventative detention.

Now Greeno conferred with the Deputy Commissioner, Sir Ronald Howe KBE, CVO, MC and the Assistant Commissioner (Crime), Sir Richard Jackson CBE, who handed him a number of anonymous notes, one of which had been sent to 'Khaki' Roberts, Dimes' counsel, who passed it on to the Yard.

It led to some rather pertinent questions being directed at the Revd Andrews, who now told Greeno that on 13 September – midway between Spot's and Dimes' committal and the commencement of their trials – he was approached by a Peter Macdonough at the Cumberland Hotel. He was asked if he wished to earn £25; in order to do so, said Macdonough, he would have to say untruthfully that he was in Frith Street at the time of the fight and give an equally dishonest account of what he had seen. This Andrews readily agreed to do, and the two men went into a lounge in the hotel, where four persons were seated; two of them were Spot's two close associates, Morris Goldstein and Bernard Schack. Macdonough, Andrews told Greeno, introduced him to the gathering as 'the clergyman who's willing to give evidence on Spot's behalf', and not only was great enthusiasm displayed by those present but Schack kept repeating, 'We're saved, we're saved!' The following day, Andrews was picked up from his address and driven to Hyde Park Mansions, where he met Rita Comer and told her he would do whatever he could to set her husband free. Of course, Andrews had never met Jack Spot, who was then in custody, so when Goldstein, Macdonough and Schack briefed him on what he had to say, Dimes, allegedly the aggressor, was described as 'the dark man' holding the knife. Goldstein emphasized that Andrews must familiarize himself with the surroundings of Frith Street, and Rita Comer promised him £25 before he gave evidence and £25 afterwards. The next day, 15 September, Andrews was again driven to Spot's flat; the same people from the previous day were present, plus the car driver, there was another rehearsal, in great detail, of the fictitious story Andrews was to tell and Spot's appearance was described to him.

Andrews and Macdonough went to the offices of Spot's legal representatives, Peters & Peters in Wimpole Street, where they saw solicitor Bernard Abraham Perkoff; in the waiting room were three men, including Goldstein and Schack. When Andrews told his story to Perkoff, Goldstein was present, constantly interrupting and assisting with the story, and the next day Andrews signed his statement.

On Sunday, 18 September, Andrews visited the area of the fruit shop and studied the surrounding territory; the trial commenced the following day.

After the wicked old perjurer had given his evidence and Spot was acquitted, Andrews was taken in a taxi, first to Perkoff's office, then to Hyde Park Mansions, where he was shown a magnum of champagne, then back to Perkoff's office. Finally, Macdonough took Andrews back to his flat in a taxi and gave him £25; on 24 September (the day after Spot's acquittal) he received a further £25.

This presented Greeno with the blueprint for a prosecution. Now, as well as the absolute need for independent corroboration, he needed to discover what anybody else had to say. This was essential, because anything said by that duplicitous old cadger Andrews required stringent verification.

★

Sparks, together with Detective Inspector Shepherd, saw Macdonough, who made a statement saying he had first met 'Father Andrews' in April 1954 and rented him a flat. Then – 'just by chance' – he had met Andrews again on 10 September, when he had told Macdonough that he had 'seen the dreadful fight in Soho'; later, again 'by chance', he had met Andrews outside the Cumberland Hotel, when once more the lapsed clergyman told him about witnessing the fight. And that was all. He had not, he stated, seen Andrews again until after the trial.

He changed his tune a little later, however, when he told Sparks, 'If it comes to a charge, we'll show Andrews up as such an old villain that no one will believe what he says. I'll give him "Father Andrews", the old turncoat.'

By now, the word was on the streets that Andrews had spoken to the police, and on 6 October Jack Spot and Rita caught the Irish Mail from Euston and sailed on the *Cambria* for Dun Laoghaire. They took a taxi to Dublin and joined their two children, who a week previously had travelled to Pierce House, a block of council flats in Townsend Street, Dublin, where they were being looked after by relatives.

After consultation with the Director of Public Prosecutions, warrants alleging conspiracy to pervert the course of public justice were granted by the Chief Metropolitan Magistrate, Sir Laurence Dunne. On 20 October, Goldstein was arrested at his home in Gore Road, Hackney and he asked, 'How many others have been nicked? They say you can't do Jackie again.' Later (and referring to Andrews) Goldstein said, 'Cut the dressing. He must have told you who was at the flat but you've only got his word. No one will take any notice of him and Glinski's *schtum*.'

The next day, Rita Spot was arrested in Dublin by Inspector Shepherd and Woman Detective Sergeant Shirley Becke (later Commander Becke OBE, OStJ, QPM), and after the warrant had been read to her, she replied, 'Conspiracy? How many am I supposed to have conspired with?' On the flight back, she said, 'I suppose this means the Old Bailey all over again with me this time, instead of Jack, but Moisha and the others said the old parson would give evidence for a few quid. I'd like to know who told you that he was at the flat.'

Although this was later disputed in court, Mrs Becke was not given a particularly hard time during cross-examination because

(a) it was not then the done thing to question the word of a woman police officer and (b) because the defence counsel may have been aware that the previous year she had married the Revd Becke MBE, a gentleman undoubtedly more saintly than his counterpart, the Revd Andrews.

Rita Comer, Morris Goldstein and Peter Macdonough all appeared at Bow Street Magistrates' Court on 21 October where Sparks sought and was granted a remand in custody, fearing that if granted bail, the prisoners would abscond or interfere with witnesses. Mr M. J. Hart-Leverton for Goldstein asked Sparks if it was true that apart from a £5 fine for a conviction for assault, twenty years ago, his client was a man 'without any record'?

Sparks rather cleverly replied, 'I am not fully conversant with the complete record at the moment. I would rather not speak of that. He is not a man of unblemished character.'

When Neville Coleman for Rita Comer asked Sparks if he had had any trouble tracing her, he replied, 'Not this morning'.

This left Schack and Glinski, the man referred to by Goldstein.

Coincidentally, whilst Greeno was in conference with the senior members of Scotland Yard, Christopher Glinski was arrested at his home at 46 Kendal Street, Paddington on an entirely separate matter; he was accused of being concerned in a conspiracy with two other men to obtain goods by fraud. Having appeared at Marylebone Magistrates' Court, he was released on bail and promptly changed his address to one at Burwood Place.

On 7 October Glinski was spoken to by Detective Chief Inspector Mannings and was told he would be put up for identification in connection with the conspiracy investigation, whereupon he replied, 'Will you send for my solicitor?'

Mannings did so, and whilst they were waiting, he noticed a newspaper clipping which referred to Spot's trial. He picked it up to read it and Glinski remarked, 'That won't prove I committed perjury', adding ambiguously, 'Everyone knows what you're after.'

He was later seen by Sparks, who told him, 'I've had you brought here as I suspect you were concerned with Mrs Comer, Moisha and Sonny [Bernard Schack] and the Revd Andrews and others in conspiring to give false evidence at the Comer trial.'

Glinski replied, 'Look, the trial is over. We've had advice. Now, you can do nothing about it. I never talked about the evidence of the parson and nobody can prove I did. Hubby Distleman was at Comer's flat and he must have been talking about me. I'll do him. It must be him because he's the only one who knows about me going to Comer's flat. Moisha won't squeal. I shall still beat you. I shall refuse to be put up.'

When his solicitor arrived, Glinski refused to take part in an identification parade. That being the case, the only other way of dealing with the matter was confrontation by the witness.

The matter of identification was an important consideration. On 20 September, the second day of the trial, a Mrs Barbara Maureen Smyth of Coppice Walk, Three Bridges, Sussex, arrived in a car to visit her father, who lived at Hyde Park Mansions, and started unloading luggage at about 9.40 am. She saw a number of characters, including Glinski, who were about to depart for the Old Bailey. Since Glinski had denied ever going to Hyde Park Mansions during his testimony at Spot's trial, if Mrs Smyth identified him as being there, this was crucial evidence. And when Mrs Smyth walked into the charge room, she did identify him, without a moment's hesitation.

Glinski was arrested by Sparks on 27 October in Bryanston Street, Marble Arch on a warrant alleging that he had committed perjury at Spot's trial. 'So what?' replied Glinski. 'Mr Beach, my solicitor, has told me to say nothing. I want him.' When charged, he replied, 'What I said at the Old Bailey was the truth.'

Bernard Schack, described as 'a donkey greaser' (yes, really!), was arrested on 1 November and joined the other three in the dock at Bow Street Magistrates' Court the following day to face the conspiracy charge. Glinski, on the other hand, had been remanded to the Guildhall Justice Rooms regarding the perjury charge. With hindsight, it might have been better to have further charged Glinski with conspiracy as well and for all the defendants to jointly stand trial; but although consideration was probably given to this course of action, for some reason it did not happen.

Committal proceedings commenced at Bow Street with Reggie Seaton appearing, as always, for the prosecution and informing the court, 'The main evidence in the present case emanates from the man, Andrews. He is, in fact, a self-confessed perjurer. He gave evidence as desired and has since admitted he was a perjurer and that what he said was a pack of lies.'

He further told the magistrate that in this case it was desirable in the interests of justice that Andrews should go into the witness box, since he was, of course, an accomplice and naturally it was most desirable to get corroboration, so far as was possible, of what Andrews had said. Seaton then set out the facts of the case and called Andrews to the witness box.

In a quavering voice, the octogenarian scrounger described meeting Macdonough at the Cumberland Hotel. 'He asked me in a kind way if I would like to make some money', he told the Magistrate, adding, 'I told him, of course I would.'

Andrews described the meetings and his attempts to familiarize himself with the scene of the fight. 'How were you to deal with the cross-examination?' asked Seaton.

'I was to tell all the lies I could possibly manufacture', replied Andrews, before adding, 'of which I am now thoroughly ashamed.'

'Did you give evidence at the trial on oath?' asked Seaton.

'Yes'.

'Was that evidence true?'

'No, it was not true. It was a lot of lies.'

Robert Edward Swan, the security officer at the Cumberland Hotel, stated that Andrews was a frequent visitor and that he had last seen him there with Macdonough on 15 September; and Mrs Smyth gave evidence that when she had visited her father at Hyde Park Mansions on 20 September, she had seen Rita Comer emerge from the flats and be joined by Schack, and saw Goldstein in the driving seat of a car. She also saw a man in clerical attire whom she identified in court as Andrews. That was quite enough corroboration for one day, and the four prisoners were remanded in custody until 8 November. On that date, Perkoff, Spot's solicitor, gave evidence that Andrews had called at his office on 15 September and made a statement into a recording machine for it to be typed later. Goldstein then arrived – he and Andrews had never met before, said Perkoff – and he did interrupt but not, said Perkoff, 'with regards to the facts'. He suggested that Andrews should attend the Old Bailey at the commencement of Spot's trial, but Goldstein pointed out that he might have to wait several days before giving evidence which could lead to him being intimidated by friends of Dimes.

'In view of what I had been told from time to time about Dimes and his friends', said Perkoff, 'I thought it would be a good idea for the Revd Andrews to attend my office until he was wanted.'

And when Perkoff was asked by Neville Coleman, acting for Rita Comer, if despite his extensive experience in criminal cases he was completely deceived by Andrews, Spot's solicitor agreed that he was. It sounded almost believable.

The four prisoners were committed in custody to stand their trial at the Old Bailey on 28 November.

Meanwhile, committal proceedings for Glinski commenced at the Guildhall on 4 November with Reggie Seaton prosecuting and solicitor Norman Beach appearing for his client. Setting out the case, Seaton told the magistrate, Alderman C.J. Harman, that Glinski had given evidence on oath that he had witnessed the fight in Frith Street, that Dimes was the aggressor, that he did not know Spot, or where he lived, or the whereabouts of Hyde Park Mansions, which he never visited – all of which was untrue.

After Andrews had given evidence, he was asked by Beach why he had given false evidence in the trial and he piteously replied, 'Because I was very poor and I was offered money.'

But when Beach asked where he had stayed the previous night, Andrews said, 'Do I have to tell?'

When the Clerk of the Court asked if there was any reason why he should not, Andrews replied, 'I am told if I am seen by some of the gang, I shall have my throat cut', and added, 'I don't want that to happen if I can avoid it.'

Perhaps unwisely, Beach blithely retorted, 'There's no need to worry about having your throat cut', since it implied that if that eventuality arose, he might be able to control the situation.

This was the perfect opportunity for Reggie Seaton to get to his feet and say, 'Yes, there is!' adding, 'There are reasons why he is an anxious man.'

Andrews went on to repudiate Beach's suggestion that the police had brought pressure to bear on him, or that the *Daily Sketch* 'was keeping him'. When Beach implied that Andrews' suggestion that he had seen Glinski at Spot's flat on three occasions was 'a recent invention', Andrews countered this by saying, 'I particularly remember now, he was very kind to the little girl there.' Since the 'little girl' referred to was undoubtedly one of Spot's daughters, this was something that Beach *definitely* did not want aired.

Mrs Smyth, who had identified everybody else leaving Hyde Park Mansions, was absolutely adamant that Glinski was one of them, but Beach saved himself for Sparks and tore into him, stating that all of the spoken conversations he had had with Glinski were untrue, that he had ('for some reason') shown favouritism to Dimes and that his actions were motivated by spite. Sparks not only repudiated these suggestions of impropriety but stated that until he had seen Dimes in the wounding case he had never previously spoken to him.

Beach had seriously annoyed the Clerk of the Court by ignoring his instructions regarding his line of questioning, so no one was particularly surprised that when Glinski was committed for trial at the Old Bailey, he remained in custody. In fact, due to his consistently dodgy behaviour, no one was particularly surprised when, a couple of years later, Beach was charged with conspiracy to pervert the course of justice. He was acquitted, and then another twenty years went by before a Disciplinary Tribunal of the Law Society struck him off the Rolls of Solicitors.

The trial of the four conspirators commenced at the Old Bailey on 28 November with legal heavyweights in attendance, both for the prosecution (led by the Solicitor General, Sir Harry Hylton-Foster QC) and the defence.

Reggie Seaton, this time junior counsel to his leader, took Andrews through his evidence once more, and once more the villainous old preacher admitted that he had lied his head off at Spot's trial.

'I was very poor and very hungry', said Andrews.

Seaton asked him, 'How were you off for funds?'

Andrews replied, 'I had not got any.'

'How did you manage?' asked Seaton.

Andrews sadly replied, 'That is a mystery to me.'

The pathetic picture which had been painted of the old scoundrel was only improved when Macdonough's barrister, Fredman Ashe-Lincoln QC (who was later arrested and fined for possessing a loaded Webley-Scott 7.65mm pistol) asked him, 'Do you ever tell the truth?'

'I do sometimes.'

'Very rarely, isn't that so?

'You say so.'

'What do you think?'

'I think I always pride myself on being an honourable man, which makes it more disgraceful than ever that I should have lied as I did.'

The relentless cross-examination continued the following day, but it is very difficult to insist that a witness has been telling lies when that person has immersed himself in sackcloth and ashes and agrees with practically everything that's being said. In fact, cross-examination may badly rebound on the accuser, which happened when Andrews said, 'I told the most terrible lies on that occasion. It is awful having your sins thrown at you after you have repented of them.'

David Weitzman QC, representing Goldstein, suggested, 'You do not believe in repentance, do you?'

This was fairly unwise, because Andrews riposted with, 'Even the repentant thief on the cross was pardoned', adding sorrowfully for effect, 'I have no pardon.'

There is a time and a place for everything and also a time for defence counsel to cut their losses, shut up, sit down and, in this case, allow other defence barristers such as Anthony Marlowe QC for Schack to ask Andrews how soon after the Spot trial had he repented. This allowed the impious old rogue to reply, 'You mean when did I come to my real senses? I cannot tell you the time. Have you never heard of a sudden conversion?'

But Weitzman did not shut up. He alluded to the suggestion that the *Daily Sketch* were paying Andrews' bills and asked if what he had said at the trial was true, this would not have been any use to the newspaper.

It brought a very snappy intervention from the judge, Mr Justice Ormerod, who knew his stuff, since just over a year later he would be promoted to Lord Justice of Appeal. There was only one suggestion there, the judge told Weitzman: that the *Daily Sketch* was paying his hotel bill to induce Andrews to fake the evidence he was giving at this trial.

'I'm not suggesting that', said Weitzman.

The sixty-five-year-old judge snapped back, 'I do not care whether you are or not – that is the innuendo.'

It had been continually put to Andrews that he had been promised that he would not be prosecuted if he gave evidence for the Crown, something which he steadfastly denied, but the matter was finally laid to rest when the Solicitor General asked Sparks, 'Did you, or anyone in your presence, ever indicate to Mr Andrews that he would not himself be prosecuted?'

'No', replied Sparks and went on to say that on every occasion that he had spoken to Andrews, his solicitor had been present.

The judge's sharpness was not confined to the defence; after it had been pointed out that Sparks had been seen speaking to Andrews – albeit innocently – whilst he was still in the witness box, he was asked not to speak to any police witness between the close of the day's hearing and the next day. 'You have heard what has been said', remarked the judge, adding witheringly, 'I suppose you realize that is your duty and you will observe it.'

The remaining police witnesses came in for the usual defence barrister's savaging: the veracity of the conversations with the accused, the accuracy of the notes in their pocket books, when they were made, who else had been present, and so on.

When the accused gave evidence, where it was possible to say without contradiction by a third party other than Andrews that they did not know each other and had never gone to Hyde Park Mansions, the Cumberland Hotel or Perkoff's office, they all did so. One matter that they all agreed upon was that there had never been any offer of money to Andrews (other than ten shillings given him by Rita Comer for a meal or a taxi) and no one had suggested to Andrews that he should give false testimony at Spot's trial.

In their closing speeches for the defence, Ashe-Lincoln for Macdonough advised the jury to 'look carefully and tread warily', Weitzman for Goldstein said, 'nothing Andrews said in evidence could be relied upon', Anthony Marlowe QC, MP for Schack said that because of Spot's acquittal, 'it would be a deplorable thing . . . by seeing some of that man's friends were punished' and

Mr A.P. Marshall QC for Rita Comer said that because Spot had been referred to in the newspapers as a King of the Underworld, 'I suppose people began to think that his wife must be a sort of queen of the underworld', which was a rather daring, if not a foot-shooting, comment to make.

After the judge summed up the evidence, it took the jury just one hour on 7 December to find the four defendants guilty.

Macdonough had just one minor gambling conviction, as well as owing various bookmakers £134, and he was sentenced to twelve months' imprisonment. Schack had three previous convictions, having been bound over for being a suspected person in 1931, received a fine of £1 for assaulting a bookmaker in 1939 and also the six months' sentence imposed on him and Spot for unlawful wounding in 1939; he, too, was sentenced to twelve months. The judge was unaware that Goldstein had been acquitted of the charge for which Schack and Spot had been convicted, but he had three convictions, one in 1938 for unlawful wounding when he was discharged on probation and ordered to pay five guineas costs, plus two more for gaming offences. Nevertheless, the judge told him, 'I am satisfied that you were the ringleader' and sentenced him to two years' imprisonment. Saying, 'There must be considerable sympathy for her', the judge fined Rita Comer £50 with the alternative of three months' imprisonment in default.

As the defendants dispersed, three to prison, one to the comforting arms of her husband who, on legal advice, had kept well away from the court, so the trial began of Christopher Glinski before the same judge and the same prosecuting counsel. Once more, Andrews was the prime prosecution witness and he repeated that he had seen Glinski on at least three occasions at Hyde Park Mansions, something strenuously repudiated by the defence.

Asked by Mr W.R. Rees-Davies MP, for Glinski, how it was that he remembered the name of Hyde Park Mansions now, when the previous Monday he had forgotten it, Andrews replied that he had been reminded.

Rees-Davies was on him like a shot: 'Who reminded you?'

To general laughter in court, Andrews humbly replied, 'I think it was his Lordship.'

But whilst Rees-Davies dismissed Andrews as 'a wicked old perjurer and a terrible old rascal' he had to tread rather more carefully with Mrs Smyth, who had no doubt that she had seen him with the newly convicted conspirators at the Cumberland Hotel. Glinski would later say that he did not possess a sports jacket or windcheater of the kind which Mrs Smyth had described, but was obliged to admit that whilst he was on remand in Brixton prison he had exchanged a brown or fawn suit for the blue one which he was now wearing.

No such niceties were extended to the police officers, for whom the gloves were now well and truly off. Detective Chief Inspector Jack Mannings, it was suggested, had, with Sparks, told deliberate lies to secure Glinski's conviction; when Mannings, not unnaturally, disagreed, Rees-Davies told him, 'I am suggesting *you* are the person committing perjury and you deliberately took this man under unlawful arrest to West End Central police station'; this brought forth another firm repudiation. Sparks received the same accusations and uttered the same denials.

In summing up to the jury, the judge mentioned that in the case for the defence there had been no mincing of words. He felt that he could not emphasize too strongly that there was no possibility of a mistake. Either the two officers were speaking the truth or it was a most deliberate lie on their part to manufacture a case against the accused.

Fifty minutes later, the jury returned, having accepted the latter part of the judge's comments and found Glinski not guilty; the possessor of what was described as the 'Polish Military Cross' (probably the *Krzyż Walecznych*) and the French *Croix de Guerre* for wartime service with the RAF, as well as convictions for receiving stolen property and common assault in 1951, tottered from the dock a free man. Three weeks previously, he had also been acquitted of conspiracy to cheat and defraud. Three years later, Glinski sued the police officer who had arrested him on that latter charge and was awarded £2,500 and costs. The police officer appealed against the decision, and in 1962 that judgement was overturned.

Back in 1955, Spot went off with Rita – they briefly commiserated with a tearful Mrs Schack regarding her husband's incarceration and she responded with two words to them, the second of which was 'off' – and jointly announced their intention to open a small café. Dimes took over Spot's point-to-point interests. Although the 'small café' did not materialize, peace reigned – for just five months. Then things would change, dramatically and horrifically.

CHAPTER 6

The Attack outside Hyde Park Mansions

Billy Hill's star was in the ascendant; Spot's was nowhere to be seen. He was a worried man, fearing retribution from the Hill/Dimes camps; but logically speaking, was there any reason for him to worry? Not really. Neither Dimes nor he had been convicted. Albert Dimes and Bert Marsh had got what they wanted, control of the racetracks, and they knew – as Spot did – that there was no one strong enough to wrest it from them. Spot might just as well been dubbed 'Norman No-Mates' – he had permitted three men to go to prison and his wife to be convicted on his behalf; no one wanted to back him.

Billy Hill was satisfied, too: he had his clubs to run and, of course, the two robberies he had set up in 1952 and 1954 meant that he never needed to want for anything again.

It was therefore the height of foolishness when, just after Christmas 1955, Spot hired hardman Joe Cannon to shoot both Dimes and Hill. Three youngsters were sub-contracted to help, and Spot supplied the guns. What happened thereafter is rather hazy: Cannon claimed that shots were fired, but this is disputed. Another version has it that the youngsters boasted about what they were supposed to do and word got out; they were then suitably 'spoken to', the guns were returned to Spot and that was the end of the matter, at least as far as Spot was concerned.

But it was not the end for Dimes, and certainly not for Hill. Spot had thrown down the gauntlet, the word was on the streets about what he had planned and if he could get away unpunished then rival gangs would see it as a very definite sign of weakness on the part of Messrs Dimes and Hill.

So whilst Spot's fears might have been illogical previously, now he had real concerns. Whereas nine years previously Peter Beveridge, the head of No. 2 District's CID, had summoned him regarding the proposed confrontation with the White faction, now it was Spot who went, cap in hand, to see Beveridge and plead for protection. But in fairness, in the absence of any credible evidence there was nothing Beveridge could do – Spot could not really admit to planning the murder of Hill and Dimes – and as the early months of 1956 went by, Spot grew more and more apprehensive, with good reason.

During the evening of 2 May, Spot and Rita were returning to their flat at Hyde Park Mansions with a friend, Paddy Carney, when cars screeched to a halt and a number of men – the figures are vague, but there might have been a dozen or more – leapt out and attacked them.

'I screamed', said Rita later, 'and my husband pushed me against the railings and got in front of me. Someone pushed me down, trying to get at my husband. They started whacking him. One had a shillelagh and another had a big instrument; I don't know if it was a cosh.'

There was indeed a cosh; in addition, there was a shillelagh, which Rita later identified as the one she had given to Billy Hill, a present from Ireland. There was also an iron bar, a knife and a razor as this band of heroes, kicking, punching, beating and slashing, tore into Spot, cutting his face wide open; Rita, too, was punched and bruised, receiving a blow to the shoulder from the shillelagh.

It required the expertise of Dr Robin S.B. Ling at St Mary's Hospital, Paddington to insert seventy-eight stitches into Spot's face and left hand, an awful lot of bandages to hold his body together and a transfusion of two pints of blood, half a pint of blood plasma and a pint of plasma substitute; and now, Spot named names to the police.

He made two statements. In the first he said, 'Among others who were setting about me were Billy Hill, Albert Dimes, Bobby Warren, Falco and Frankie Fraser . . . these are the people I can remember.'

In the second statement he said, 'The man who cut me with the knife was the man I know as Frankie Fraser, he cut me on the face. I am prepared to give evidence against them. Bobby Warren struck me on the head with a piece of iron. All these men are known to me.'

Rita, too, provided the police with a catalogue of the attackers.

Hill and Dimes were brought in and both were unconcerned; their respective alibis appeared copper-bottomed and watertight, and although Hill was detained for seven hours, they were both released without charge. The same applied to 'Big Tommy' Falco, an associate of Hill's and a driver for Albert Dimes who had been shot at when he visited a racetrack; there was insufficient evidence to charge him and he, too, was released. A little later, there was what purported to be an attack on Falco in the most mysterious circumstances, of which more later.

The first of the gang to be arrested and charged was Robert Warren, aged twenty-eight, on 4 May. There was certainly bad blood between him and Spot: in 1947 Spot had given Warren's brother Johnny a ferocious beating. This in turn had led to another mob-handed confrontation, which resulted in a villain named Billy Goller getting his throat cut (one of the participants was Johnnie Carter – he appears later in the book); since it seemed likely that Goller would expire, this caused some concern amongst the combatants. Luckily, a soothing poultice of £300 was applied to the incision and peace reigned once more.

Warren was asked to participate in an identification parade, did so and was promptly picked out by Rita Spot. At Marylebone Magistrates' Court Detective Superintendent John 'Jock' McIver, the former schoolmaster from the Highlands requested ('in his thin, piping voice', according to Nipper Read) a remand in custody from the magistrate, Mr Walter Frampton, and got one.

McIver, meanwhile, put the word about that 'the heat was off' and that in any event Francis Davidson Fraser was not among the people he was looking for. This worked. In the first instance, Fraser had gone to Brighton; he later moved to Ireland, where Hill had rented a house for him. When Hill erroneously told Fraser it would be safe for him to return, he did so; however, as Fraser stepped off the plane at Heathrow, there was a reception committee waiting for him which, according to 'Nipper' Read, he acknowledged with 'a look of fury on his face'.

Thirty-two-year-old Fraser never looked very happy unless he was hurting someone; at that time he had fifteen previous convictions, several of them for violence, including a razor-slashing and attacking a man with a broken bottle, and had twice been certified as insane – hence his soubriquet 'Mad Frankie'.

He was identified by Rita Comer as one of her husband's attackers at an identification parade held at Paddington police station on 12 May, and when he appeared before Mr Geoffrey Raphael, at Marylebone Magistrates' Court on 14 May he was remanded in custody after Superintendent McIver told the court that when charged, Fraser had replied, 'I am entirely innocent of this charge.' Unfortunately, prior to that he had also told the police, 'Look here, you know I was in it, but you have to prove it and I am not saying anything more.' It is often the shock of arrest, for example after landing at Heathrow airport believing everything to be safe, that prompts psychotic razor-slashers to make incriminating comments such as that.

But when Fraser next appeared at that court he was in company with Robert Warren, and the court was told that there had been 'certain intimidation of witnesses', as indeed there had. Rita told police that she had received letters and telephone calls threatening her with disfigurement and her children with kidnapping if she continued to assist the police.

'Warren lies in prison at this moment', roared Marrinan with a fine disregard for accuracy, since his client was in the dock no more than a few feet away. He then vilified Rita Comer for her inaccurate testimony, adding that whilst she was a woman of fortitude and loyalty to her husband, 'One must not allow that to deflect one's knowledge from the truth'. Coming from a lawyer as crooked as Marrinan, that was a bit rich.

Now, despite Marrinan's ardent appeals for bail, Fraser and Warren were both committed in custody to the Old Bailey for the attack on Spot – and that was just the end of round one.

During the trial at the Old Bailey before Mr Justice Donovan, Fraser and Warren pleaded not guilty to causing grievous bodily harm with intent to do so, and Jack Spot went into the witness box to say that neither of the two defendants had been among his attackers. His decision to do so was possibly influenced by the fact that Billy Hill had arranged for a dozen or so men whom Jack Spot had previously cut (including Jimmy Wooder) to be seated in the court's public gallery and to gaze malevolently down on the witness. In addition, Billy Hill and several of his cohorts took up temporary residence at Rex's Café, opposite the Old Bailey, to scowl at and generally attempt to intimidate anybody likely to give evidence at the trial.

However, when Marrinan cross-examined Superintendent McIver, he scored a couple of own goals. At the Magistrates' Court, when Marrinan had asked if Dimes and Hill were present at the attack on Spot, it had appeared that the police were satisfied that they were not. But on asking McIver the same question once again, the officer replied, 'Well, at one time, I thought I was quite happy about that. Since then, there have been enquiries made which might show one of them could have been.'

That was bad enough, and Marrinan wisely refrained from asking, 'Which one?' But then, when he asked whether Rita Comer had named a certain person who had allegedly taken part in the attack, McIver truthfully replied, 'No. It was Mr Comer who had named that person.' It came a little too late for Marrinan, who should have remembered to study the evidence rather than rely on his own booming rhetoric, because the cat was now well and truly out of the bag. When a witness says one thing in a statement and then completely contradicts it in the witness box, that witness can be cross-examined and the whole matter aired before the jury.

The judge demanded to see Spot's statement and then immediately recalled him to the witness box. He read out the pertinent, damning passages and demanded, 'What is the explanation of your evidence on Thursday?'

Comer replied, 'Those names were read out to me. That is the second day I was in hospital.'

So apart from seeing Jack Spot's scars and hearing rather unconvincing denials as to his attackers' identities, the jury also heard positive identification from Rita Comer and an equally damning statement to police from Fraser upon his arrest. This, of course, was denied, and when Fraser went into the witness box he stated that at the time of the attack he was working until 10.30 pm at a bookmaker's office in Brighton, calling three witnesses in support of his alibi.

One of them was Sammy Bellson, a bookmaker, although Fraser would later say that when he was asked in court the colour of the telephones in Bellson's office, Marrinan slipped out of court to brief his answer to the alibi witnesses. Quite apart from that, Bellson was not the most satisfactory of witnesses, since he had a number of convictions for being a suspected person, being on enclosed premises for an unlawful purpose and attempting to steal women's coats; two of these offences merited imprisonment with hard labour. Matters became even less satisfactory for Bellson less than two years later, when he was convicted, together with two very crooked Brighton police officers, of conspiracy and was sentenced to three years' imprisonment.

Another witness was Paddy Carney, who although he made himself scarce on the night of the attack had tarried long enough to be able to tell the court that he was sure that neither Fraser nor Warren were amongst the attackers.

'That was a very unkind thing to do,' Rita Comer called out; but since Carney was halfway through giving his evidence, she was severely admonished by the judge for doing so.

Despite Marrinan telling Marylebone Magistrates' Court that Bobby Warren had 'a complete account of his movements and a complete answer to the charge', whatever they might have been, the jury at the Old Bailey never got to hear them, because Marrinan called no evidence on behalf of his client.

In his closing speech for the prosecution Reggie Seaton declared:

> Comer is in effect saying, 'This is nothing to do with the law. This is my affair. I am the man who was hurt and I say it was not these two men.' You might wonder why it is we are all here and the answer surely is this: if you are going to have in the West End of this great metropolis a gang of rascals who indulge in this sort of thing and who, when they think fit, because they do not like the way somebody else is carrying on his business, get together and use knives and commit grave assaults on a person or persons they do not like, then it becomes more than a matter for the injured person.

Marrinan told the jury that the only evidence against Warren
was that of Rita Comer's identification and not to pay the slightest
attention to the evidence Spot, whom he called:

> That vile, cut-throat gangster, that corner boy of the low-
> est ilk, who prided himself on being king of the under-
> world – the scum of the earth . . . the sweet-faced lit-
> tle Mrs Comer who comes into court, a tearful wife and
> mother. This is a woman who was prepared to go and live
> with a gangster and have a voluntary association with him.
> It is not the case of a woman marrying an honest man for
> better or worse and then sticking to him. Is it possible to
> convict Warren on the evidence of Mrs Comer when she
> was convicted herself of conspiracy to commit perjury, by
> procuring false evidence from an old clergyman?

Summing up, Mr Justice Donovan told the jury:

> Comer is clearly a man who said one thing one day and
> something else the next. But if Comer had said nothing in
> the witness box to incriminate the accused, the situation
> was entirely different when one considered Mrs Comer
> because she said the two men were there. This much is
> clear. One side or the other is doing their best to deceive
> you by hard lies. They are doing their best to see that a
> wrong verdict is returned by you. You will probably ask
> yourselves, what has Mrs Comer to gain by inventing
> a false story? If her story was false, what repercussions
> might she expect in this world of violence in which she and
> her children had been living for some time past and from
> which she has said she would give anything to escape?
> You may think you have been taken from your usual
> avocations to deal with a pretty unsavoury lot of people,
> who indulge in the activities of horse racing, employing
> race-gang warfare, people who you may think contribute
> nothing to the community except trouble and cause more
> trouble than they are worth. The civic value of the man
> Comer is neither here nor there. We are dealing with a
> very bad case of violence in the public streets in this city.
> It matters not at all who was the victim here – whether
> the best or worst of citizens. Everybody is entitled to the
> protection of the law, and everybody expects violence of
> this kind to lead to the punishment of those responsible,
> if apprehended. If this sort of thing is allowed to spread,

it would not be safe for any of us to walk the streets, let alone the racing fraternity.

After an hour and fifty minutes on 15 June 1956 the jury returned verdicts of guilty on both men. Marrinan declined to give any mitigation for Warren, saying that he intended 'to take another course' (he meant by appealing), and Mr John Richie, the barrister for Fraser, told the judge, 'It is manifest that there are behind this great forces who had made use of the two defendants', adding that, 'Fraser is weak, mentally.'

Detective Inspector Cornish provided details of the prisoners' backgrounds, including the fact that although Warren had five previous convictions, none were for violence. In passing sentence, the judge stated:

> I am not going to punish you for your criminal records; you have been punished for your past crimes and it would be unfair to punish you again. Neither am I going to distinguish between you. I had intended to impose a longer sentence on you, Fraser, but I am affected by what I have heard about you. This was an extremely wicked offence.

Both men were sentenced to seven years' imprisonment.

Meanwhile, enquiries were still being pursued to track down and arrest more of Jack Spot's attackers. And within a couple of weeks, 288 miles away across the Irish Sea in the Emerald Isle, events would be set in motion which would involve two more of the gang and the intervention of two of Scotland Yard's toughest and most tenacious detectives.

CHAPTER 7

Revelations in Dublin

Thomas Marius Joseph Butler had less than seven years service when, in 1941, as a detective constable he was posted to the Flying Squad. A brilliant young detective, he would spend the war years with that elite crime-busting unit under the charismatic leadership of the very tough, red-haired Scot, Detective Chief Inspector Peter Beveridge. A small man – he was just one and a quarter inches over the minimum height requirement for the Metropolitan Police – Butler was a workaholic and when he was promoted to detective sergeant (second class) after five years service with the Flying Squad, he had accrued a total of eighteen commendations for smart police work. Posted to 'G' Division in the East End, he kept his links with the Flying Squad; the Yard's ultra secret Ghost Squad had just got underway and this unit needed reliable men to carry out the arrests that their informants had suggested; Butler was one of them.

But on the day that Butler left the Flying Squad, a newcomer arrived to fill his vacancy; his name was Detective Constable Jasper Peter Vibart, an ex-soldier who had come to notice after arresting eleven people for housebreaking and receiving. Vibart's service on the Flying Squad would last almost exactly twelve years, and during that time he would be promoted to second-class, then first-class detective sergeant. Utterly fearless, he specialized in tackling dangerous criminals, two of whom were the very violent Arthur Frederick Parkyn and Harold Berlinski, wanted for inflicting grievous bodily harm on a police officer. When he was charged with attempting to murder Vibart and two other officers, Parkyn replied, 'I didn't think it would be as bad as that' – but it was, and he was sentenced to twelve years' penal servitude, with Berlinski receiving seven. The case added to Vibart's growing list of commendations which, by the time Butler returned to the Flying Squad on 2 August 1955 as a detective inspector, totalled twenty-eight.

With ten squads making up the Flying Squad, Butler, now forty-three years of age, took over the running of No. 1 squad, and Vibart joined him.

The pair took on the underworld together; when Butler was commended for arresting 'a troublesome safeblower', so was

Vibart. It happened again in a case of robbery and once more after they arrested two violent criminals; when they nabbed 'a persistent criminal' they were again commended, as they were for their ability in a case of robbery with violence. And all these accolades were collected within the space of just four months; Butler and Vibart were making a name for themselves in the underworld. Just one inch taller than his counterpart and forty-one years old, Vibart could in no way be described as Butler's twin – but nevertheless, the nickname bestowed on them was 'The Terrible Twins'. When they were called upon to assist in the razor-slashing Spot case, no one was particularly surprised; and quite a few criminals had cause to be worried.

Working under instructions from Superintendent McIver, Butler and Vibart flew to Dublin on 27 June 1956 where they liaised with Detective Inspector Philip MacMahon, a member of Eire's police force, *An Garda Siochána*. The Yard detectives were in possession of warrants issued by London Magistrate Mr Raphael on 23 June for the arrest of two men – on description, only – for the attack on Spot. This meant that when the warrants were executed, the persons arrested could be questioned as to their identities, during the course of which questioning all kinds of revelations might come to light.

On the evening of 28 June arrests were carried out at a public house in Morehampton Road in Dublin's Donnybrook district by members of the *Gardai* who were, as always, armed. One of the men arrested was William Patrick 'Billy-Boy' Blythe, a thirty-nine-year-old costermonger (or barrow boy) from Myddleton Street, Clerkenwell, EC1. If the descriptive warrant portrayed him as a bald-headed, satanic midget, this would have been a reasonable representation of 'Billy-Boy', who, like Fraser, was a former army deserter. He was the possessor of eleven previous convictions, including one for cutting a Flying Squad officer in the face whilst resisting arrest, for which he was sentenced to three years' penal servitude, and another, also for causing grievous bodily harm, two years later, for which he had similarly been sentenced to three years' penal servitude. Described by Reggie Kray as 'a cold, calculating, vicious rogue' (which many might think was rather like the pot calling the kettle 'grimy-arse'), Blythe, since release from prison in June 1950, had of course been a pillar of the community.

The second man to be arrested was Robert 'Battles' Rossi, a thirty-three-year-old asphalter from Sapperton Court, Gee Street, Clerkenwell. He had previous convictions for shopbreaking and receiving but none for violence. Both men were taken to Dublin Castle.

Much of the conversation which took place at the arrest and shortly thereafter would later be strenuously denied by the prisoners. Blythe denied, for example, that he had said, after Butler had cautioned him, 'You can all go and fuck yourselves. They came at me with guns tonight. I only wish I had one. I would have blown holes in the lot of them.' Similarly, he would later challenge the fact that when Butler told him he would be detained and taken back to London as soon as practicable, he had replied, 'You cunts are nicking everyone. You've even nicked Spotty for something he hasn't done.' This was an interesting comment – and it merits a whole chapter to itself later on.

But the prisoners were not taken to London, 'as soon as was practicable', because on Saturday, 30 June an application was made at Dublin High Court for a conditional order of habeas corpus for the two men, alleging that the arrest warrants had not been property made out. Garrett Brennan, Deputy Commissioner for the Eire Police, told Mr Justice Murnaghan that he had endorsed the warrants for execution in Dublin since he had reason to believe that the persons described in the warrants would be found there.

'Don't rush matters', the judge told Mr G. Clarke for the Attorney General, 'and don't press me to deal with the matter today'; he then adjourned matters until Monday 2 July.

And on that date, Mr Justice Murnaghan did indeed order the release of the two men. However . . . by that time fresh warrants, properly made out in the prisoners' names, had arrived in Dublin.

Blythe and Rossi were brought into an office at Bridewell, where Butler was present, as were Marrinan and Mr Curneen (their solicitor), and they were told they were free to go. As they left, they were followed by the police officers, MacMahon, Butler and Vibart, and it was then that Butler heard Marrinan say to Blythe, 'They are all outside and they are going to nick you again. If I were you, I should make a dive for it.'

Blythe, buttoning up his overcoat, replied, 'Too fucking true'.

MacMahon tried to get past Marrinan, who apparently blocked his way, but the officer seized hold of Blythe on the steps and in Butler's words 'took steps to restrain him' – although it was later alleged that MacMahon had 'struck him several blows'.

Whatever the truth of the matter, it was also said that Blythe had told MacMahon, 'If I get you in London, I'll fuck you up', although it was also suggested that Blythe's words were 'I'll cut you up.' It was all slightly confusing, although Blythe's general meaning was fairly plain. The men were then taken back into the entrance hall of Bridewell, with solicitor and barrister threatening habeas corpus and contempt of court.

Marrinan, referring to the alleged assault on Blythe, told MacMahon, 'I'm ashamed to be an Irishman when I see a thing like that.'

MacMahon crushingly replied, 'You get back to London.'

But why was Marrinan there in the first place? Both prisoners not only had solicitors, they also had leading counsel. It was later revealed that Marrinan had gone to Dublin following a meeting with a journalist from the *Daily Express* at a restaurant in Old Compton Street, Soho. Also present was one Albert Dimes, as was Franny Daniels (who had participated in the 1948 London Airport robbery but escaped arrest). Marrinan would later explain that he had been asked to go to offer evidence in the habeas corpus proceedings, in order to prove that the warrants for the arrest of Blythe and Rossi were based on invalid information. Right. However, to act in proceedings a barrister has to be instructed by a solicitor – not that this really mattered, because none of the explanation was true. Marrinan had been instructed by Billy Hill, whom all the men at the meeting saw at his flat at Barnes, where Marrinan received a sizeable bursary from Hill and a further £20 from Dimes, and a plane ticket to Dublin was booked.

The son of a Royal Irish Constabulary officer, Patrick Aloysius Marrinan had studied law at Queen's University, Belfast and had been convicted and fined for harbouring uncustomed goods in Liverpool in 1942. A greedy and unscrupulous racetrack gambler, he practised as a barrister in London, where he made the acquaintance of Billy Hill. By 1955 he was on far friendlier terms than was considered desirable for a barrister to be with the man who proclaimed himself 'The Boss of Britain's Underworld'. He constructed defences and invented alibis for Hill's men, and it is no exaggeration to describe Marrinan, as one detective put it, as being 'as straight as a dog's dick'.

And apart from these matters, there was one more strike against the Hill/Marrinan association that was going to cause a lot of trouble for the crooked counsel in the very near future. During 1956 the Home Secretary had authorized warrants for the calls to 159 telephones to be intercepted. One of them related to Billy Hill's telephone; consequently, everything said between him and Marrinan was known to Tommy Butler.

Meanwhile, back to Dublin's Bridewell. Butler now demonstrated his own brand of trickiness. He had had enough of Eire's judicial procedures; more proceedings were being threatened – an unsuccessful application was made for a Sergeant James Bell to be committed for contempt of court for failing to promptly release the prisoners – and although a booking had been made on an 8.45 pm flight from Dublin to London, this was cancelled. Instead, the prisoners were driven by the Gardaí to the Eire/Ulster border (with, it was said, four large policemen sitting on a wildly struggling Blythe) where they were met by officers from the Royal Ulster Constabulary. They were driven to Belfast Gaol, put into a prison van and taken to Nutt's Corner Airport, where they were placed on a BEA flight to London. Upon arrival at Paddington police station, both men refused to stand on identification parades; Superintendent McIver therefore confronted them from their cells with Rita Comer who, when asked if she recognized the prisoners as being amongst the men who attacked her husband, on both occasions replied, 'Yes'.

This led to an outburst from Rossi who exclaimed, 'You're wrong – I never saw that woman in my life.'

Upon being charged with the attack, Blythe replied, 'It's ridiculous.'

Rossi said, 'I want you to state I'm innocent' – which given McIver's status would have been problematic.

Both men appeared at Marylebone Magistrates' Court and were remanded in custody until 11 July, when it was ruled that Rita Comer need not provide the description which she had given to the police of two of the men who had attacked her husband; this was a legal decision which prompted Marrinan's rhetoric to go sky-high:

> If the Crown wishes to hedge and hide behind technicalities in this matter, I say now, whatever the consequences to me, that it is a disgrace, an absolute disgrace to justice! Two men are standing here charged with a very serious offence for which they can be sent to prison for life, in an atmosphere of horrible prejudice; and if the Crown wishes to deprive them of any opportunity of testing the accuracy of witnesses . . .

It was at this point that the magistrate, Mr Raphael, interrupted Marrinan's flow of grandiloquence, observing with the quiet urbanity with which many stipendiary magistrates were blessed, 'It doesn't seem to be an occasion to ventilate a protest.'

Evidence was given by Rita Comer, who again identified the men in court and said that on the night of the attack she had seen Blythe bending over her husband 'sort of digging things into him' and that Rossi had 'had a few whacks at her husband'.

She was predictably and scathingly attacked by Marrinan, as was Butler regarding his testimony; Marrinan was assisted by

The three faces of Jack Spot:
Somnolent (*above*), scarred (*below left*) and scared (*below right*).

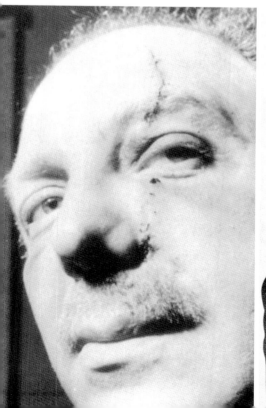

Zoe Progl.

Fay Richardson (*below left*).

Tommy Smithso

The Hunted:

hilip Ellul.

Bernie Silver.

The Hunters:

ommander Bert Wickstead QPM

Det. Sgt. John Lewis (*left*)
and Det. Sgt. Bernie Tighe

Jack Spot at the races.   Billy Hill.

Albert Dimes and his wife Rosie celebrating after his acquittal.

Jack Spot and his wife Rita after her conviction for perjury.

Revd Andrews.

Bernard Schack.

'Mad Frankie' Fraser

Patrick Marrinan.

Bobby Warren

'Big Tommy' Falco.

'Scarface Jock' Russo.

Johnny Rice.

DCS Bert Sparks.

DCS Ted Greeno MBE.

DCS Tommy Butler MBE.

Det. Supt. Peter Vibart QPM.

Rossi, who jumped to his feet, telling the magistrate, 'Sir, I have never said any such words', and by Blythe, who asked, 'Sir, can he say anything he likes?'

It appeared that he could, and the pair were remanded in custody for one week; but by the time that remand arrived, they had been joined in the dock by one William Edward 'Ginger' Dennis, a thirty-one-year-old car dealer from Royal Road, Kennington. He had been arrested on 15 July by Tommy Butler, who had tracked him down to a bungalow in Brighton. As he started to search the premises, Mrs Dennis picked up her hand-bag and went to leave the dining room. Butler stopped her, searched the handbag and found two letters addressed to her at Brighton which caused her to exclaim, 'Oh, please, don't find those! Give him a chance!'

The letters were certainly incriminating, because as they left the premises, Dennis said to Butler, 'Can't you bang those letters back to her? It's worth half a hundred to you.'

It might well have been, but once the offer was refused, Dennis said, 'With those, I've got no chance, as they'll put me out there with the other two.'

When Dennis was invited to take part in an identification parade, he replied, 'If this is a straight ID, Spot's old woman won't pick me out.'

It was, and she did; when Dennis was charged, this man who had three previous convictions for shopbreaking and storebreaking replied, 'I'm innocent.'

The shillelagh which had been used in the assault and which had been found on a rubbish heap in the centre of Dorset Square about a quarter of a mile from the scene of the attack was helpfully produced by Sidney Frank Wheeler, a gardener of Ouseley Road, Balham – and with that, the trio were soon committed to the Old Bailey to stand their trial.

The trial was held in front of Mr Justice Cassels, then aged seventy-nine, a stern old gentleman whose legal career had been interrupted by the First World War, where he fought on the Western Front, achieved the rank of captain and was twice mentioned in dispatches.

Inevitably, Reggie Seaton led for the crown and described the events on the night of 2 May when Jack Spot and Rita managed to ascend just the first three steps leading to their flat before the savage attack commenced. Rita identified Billy Hill as being there, as well as Blythe and Rossi; in Dennis's case, the piece of cloth covering the lower part of his face had slipped down as he attacked her husband, causing her to scream at him, 'I'll know you – I'll know you!'

Cross-examined by Malcolm Morris for Rossi, Rita Comer stated that the attack was not altogether unexpected. 'Someone had told my husband he was going to be "done up"', she said, and when she was asked if she would agree that she might be mistaken in her identification of the three men in the dock, the answer was an emphatic 'No'.

Jack Spot was brought into court, and the doctor who had treated him at St Mary's hospital pointed out his injuries. After evidence of the arrests, it was the turn of the defence, with Blythe going into the witness box first.

Denying that he had taken part in the attack, Blythe said he had known Jack Spot since 1947 and had seen his wife 'on three or four occasions'. He had known Billy Hill for a number of years and Rossi since he was a schoolboy, but knew Dennis 'not too well'. Blythe told the jury that on 29 May he had gone to Ireland 'for a rest' and stayed in a house in Dublin owned by Billy Hill, who paid all the expenses; he was later joined there by Rossi. But it was when he was being cross-examined by Reggie Seaton regarding his admissions upon his arrest that he came into his own. Picking up the Bible in the witness box and pointing dramatically to Butler and Vibart, he shouted, 'Those are the men who have framed me! It's all lies! Every word they've said is lies!' In case he thought that he might not have put his case across to the jury sufficiently force-fully, he added, 'They've taken the oath on this Bible and may the curse of God be upon all of them!'

The following day, it was Rossi's turn and he too denied having anything to do with the attack on Spot. The night before the attack, he told the courtroom, he had been to a boxing match and on the night of the assault he had gone to the Empress Club, where he set-tled a bet made with a friend the previous evening and had stayed until 11.15 pm.

Rossi denied saying to Inspector McMahon, 'How did you trace us here?' And when it was put to him that he had told Tommy Butler, 'I told Blythe I knew Hill would give us away when he knew the law was getting near to him', Rossi replied, 'If I said that, I ought to be before a psychiatrist and not before a judge', adding 'I never said anything like that, I swear that on the life of my two children.'

Asked if he had said, 'The game is up', Rossi replied, 'I never use that expression; it reminds me of something out of Sexton Blake.'

Rossi had denied ever seeing Rita Comer before, so when Seaton asked, 'Why did you object to appearing on an identification parade if you never took part in the attack and had never seen Mrs Comer in your life?' Rossi replied, 'Knowing what

Mrs Comer is from past experience, I wanted a fair identification. I've read quite a lot about her. I remember a case where she bribed a parson.'

After two hours of deliberations the jury returned to court on 15 October, the seventh day of the trial, to tell Mr Justice Cassels that they could not unanimously agree a verdict on the charge of inflicting grievous bodily harm with intent. The judge sent them out again, saying that they must find one way or another, and after a total of almost three and a half hours the jury returned a verdict of guilty on a lesser charge of unlawful wounding in respect of all three men.

In mitigation, Gerald Howard QC for Blythe said his client had kept out of trouble for five years: 'Bearing that in mind, I ask the court to deal with him as leniently as possible.'

Malcolm Morris said that Rossi was not a man of violence, and Kenneth Richardson for Dennis said that he had no convictions 'even remotely connected with violence'.

Asked by the Clerk of Assizes if the prisoners had anything to say before being sentenced, there was a predictable outburst from the dock. Dennis protested, 'There were people on that jury who obviously found us not guilty and then they were bullied into finding us guilty after they had been out for another one and a half hours. How can they find us not guilty first, and guilty afterwards? I am innocent.'

Rossi also asserted his innocence, and then Blythe shouted, 'I have said I am innocent; I am still innocent. The police have framed me. When I said that, I could not tell you the reason why. Now you have heard the reason read out. They have framed me on this charge but I am entirely innocent.'

In passing sentence, Mr Justice Cassels – reputed to be a 'brusque' judge – said:

> If men like you get tough with other people, you will be made to realize, if you come before a court, that the law can get tough with you. This was an outrageous assault upon a man who was never able to defend himself against you three and the others who were with you. It may be that you did not know that he was likely to be wounded, it may be that you were merely taking a part because you thought you could give him a bang or two, but in the course of that attack, Comer received wounds which necessitated seventy-eight stitches and he was undoubtedly very badly wounded. You took a part in it and now you have to pay the penalty.

He then sentenced Blythe to five years' imprisonment and Rossi and Dennis to four years each.

It is interesting to note that the maximum penalty for inflicting grievous bodily harm with intent – of which the three prisoners had been acquitted – was life imprisonment. For the offence of unlawful wounding – of which they had been convicted – the maximum was five years' imprisonment, which was what Blythe had received. Had he been convicted of the more serious charge, given his previous convictions, would his sentence have been double? I rather think it would.

Hearing the commendation which the judge bestowed upon the police officers – it was later endorsed by the commissioner (Butler's thirty-third, Vibart's thirty-fourth) – can hardly have been music to Blythe's ears as he was dragged off to the cells shouting, 'It's a mockery of justice!'.

And what did he mean when he told the judge that he could not previously say why the police had framed him but now 'the reason had been read out'?

Simply this. When Superintendent McIver told the court of the prisoners' previous convictions, together with the circumstances of them, he mentioned Blythe's conviction for cutting a Flying Squad officer in the face, requiring the insertion of twenty stitches, after he went to arrest him for being an army deserter.

The Flying Squad officer's name was Peter Vibart.

★

Three weeks later, the Lord Chief Justice refused Fraser and Warren leave to appeal against their convictions, and ten weeks after that, Rossi, Blythe and Dennis similarly had their leave to appeal refused, despite their counsel, 'Khaki' Roberts QC, stating that the jury's verdict had been 'monstrous'.

'Billy-Boy' Blythe never served his full sentence. On 18 February 1957 he was taken from prison to Walton Hospital, where he died following an emergency operation after a duodenal ulcer had burst.

His funeral, six days later, was organized by Billy Hill, and twelve Rolls-Royces led the way from his address at Myddleton Street to St Mary's Roman Catholic Cemetery, Kensal Green. The floral tributes alone cost £1,500; one of them read, 'The End – to Uncle Bill' and another, 'At Rest, Bill – from Billy Hill'.

Thus Billy Blythe was laid to rest. However, events had got underway in London which Patrick Marrinan would find anything but restful.

CHAPTER 8

A Busted Brief

As it turned out, Patrick Marrinan was to commit professional suicide. As soon as the trial of Blythe and Rossi was finished, he made a complaint of perjury against Butler and Vibart. There had been a great deal of damaging publicity regarding Marrinan's actions, and the day following his official complaint the police hit right back, complaining about his conduct in Dublin; the matter was then passed to the Attorney General, and in January 1957 Marrinan was summoned to a meeting with the Bar Council. Sir Hartley Shawcross presided over the three-man committee, and after informing a shocked Marrinan of the existence of the telephone intercepts, the committee decided the affair was so serious that it would have to be referred to the Masters of the Bench at Lincoln's Inn. In a later letter to the Bar Council, Marrinan wrote:

> Please do not believe that I would have any personal association with these horrible criminals. Necessity forced me to be caught up with them, particularly Hill . . . I have erred in allowing myself to be imposed upon by worthless people, but one thing I did not do was to tell Blythe to avoid arrest. There is no profession I love more than the law. Now this dreadful thing has come along, accusing me of dishonour . . . If it is within your power to recommend suspension rather than expulsion, in the name of humanity, I ask you to do so . . . my mind is in turmoil.

But penitent or not, Marrinan had still not learnt a much-needed lesson. Two days before his summons before the Bar Council, 'Gypsy' Riley, Hill's paramour, was involved in a fight in the Miramar Club during the course of which a certain Arthur Ranns was blinded in one eye by having a table lamp shoved into it. A woman who was in his company was also attacked. When Riley was arrested and charged in March with inflicting grievous bodily harm on the unfortunate Mr Ranns, it was Marrinan who unsuccessfully applied for bail and then went on to defend her. At a remand hearing, although Detective Inspector Evans told the magistrate, Mr Geoffrey Raphael, that 'witnesses had been intimidated', the witnesses' memories, despite their having picked Riley out of an identification parade, astonishingly became defective, and the case was discharged.

Of course, the magistrate was unaware that later Riley would crow, 'I done her good and proper – I was surprised she was able to identify me afterwards', but the fact that Marrinan was still carrying on his association with Hill and Riley could have done him no favours whatsoever.

On 27 June 1957 Marrinan was called before the Benchers of Lincoln's Inn sitting as a disciplinary body, and it was alleged that he had associated on terms of personal friendship and familiarity with Billy Hill, Albert Dimes and other persons in a manner unbecoming to a gentleman and a barrister. It was further alleged that this association was for the purpose of soliciting and obtaining professional work; that he gave legal advice to Blythe or Rossi without being instructed by a solicitor; and that he attempted to obstruct Detective Inspector MacMahon in the execution of his duty, including by saying to Blythe, 'They are all outside and are going to nick you again. If I were you, I would make a dive for it', or words to that effect.

Rather recklessly, Marrinan asked for the hearing to be in public and for details of the intercepts on Hill's phone line in which he featured to be read in court.

They took some explaining, as did the fact that Hill had arranged for a flat to be made available for Marrinan at Seaforth Lodge, Barnes in the same block of flats that he was living in. Marrinan denied referring on the telephone to Hill's partner as 'Gyp' and similarly refuted the claim that he referred to Hill as 'Billy', telling the Benchers rather unconvincingly, 'He is known as Mr Bill Hill.' The reason why Marrinan could dispute these matters (and many more) was that he had discovered the original tapes had been destroyed.[4]

The enquiry, which included evidence from police officers, continued until 2 July 1957. The Benchers expressed some doubt that Marrinan had obstructed Inspector MacMahon or that he had shouted a warning to Blythe but were unanimous that with regard to the first three charges he had been guilty of conduct unbecoming to a gentleman and a barrister. Consequently, he was disbarred and expelled from the Honourable Society of Lincoln's Inn.

---

[4] Or, more likely, re-used. This was common practice when tapes were used to record intercepted telephone conversations and there was no reason why not; they were never intended to be used for evidential purposes.

Within five days of his expulsion, Marrinan began hitting out in all directions, providing copy for Sunday newspaper, the *People*. Previously, it had been Jack Spot whom Marrinan had described in court as being 'that corner boy of the lowest ilk'. Now it was Hill's turn to be described in print as 'a cockney corner boy whose every other word was a curse . . . he is a notorious character'. Although Patrick Aloysius Marrinan had been heavyweight boxing champion of the Irish Universities, this was nevertheless a foolhardy thing to say; fortunately, Hill appeared to find the spectacle of Marrinan's public humiliation amusing, rather than his words warranting a 'striping'.

In October that year Marrinan appealed the decision before Mr Justice Barry; it did him no good at all. And in February 1962 Marrinan alleged that Butler and Vibart had conspired to publish defamatory documents about him to the Director of Public Prosecutions, the Central Criminal Court and the Benchers of Lincoln's Inn. At the High Court, Mr Justice Salmon kicked this set of unfounded allegations into touch as well.

After the failure of this appeal, all parties left the Royal Courts of Justice and walked into the Strand. Marrinan shuffled away, his reputation deservedly in tatters. The two police officers were met by a Flying Squad car, which conveyed them back to the Yard, Butler to the Flying Squad office, where he was now the superintendent, and Vibart to his office in Criminal Intelligence, where he held the rank of chief inspector. The following year, 'The Terrible Twins' would be immersed in the Great Train Robbery investigation and would go on to further accolades and advancement: Vibart to the rank of detective superintendent and the award of the Queen's Police Medal, Butler to detective chief superintendent and an MBE.

And Marrinan? He returned to Ireland. He became a solicitor.

CHAPTER 9

A Bloody Interlude

Before we leave the blood-letting in which Spot, Hill and Fraser were involved, there is another matter which needs to be slotted in to the story; out of necessity, it has had to be taken out of the chronological sequence of events and it involves, amongst others, 'Mad Frankie' Fraser.

We know that Fraser was cruelly tricked into believing that all was well regarding the attack on Spot; hence his return to Heathrow from Ireland on 12 May 1956. However, the assault was not the only charge he faced.

Fraser was at that time wanted on warrant, together with Ray Rosa and Richard 'Dicky Dido' Frett, for razor-slashing, then attacking with a hammer and, coincidentally, a shillelagh, thirty-two-year-old John Frederick Carter. The three men lay low in Manchester, with Fraser later going to Ireland.

Carter came from a South London crime family. His own criminal career had commenced at the age of twelve, and he had a whole series of convictions for assaults, including razor-slashings; his lengthiest sentence had been one of five years' imprisonment for stabbing 'Whippo' Brindle, a member of a family related by marriage to Fraser. In fact, Fraser had attacked Carter whilst they were both serving sentences, and lately Carter had threatened Fraser; so there was no love lost between them.

On 15 April Carter and his wife Tina had been in the Tankerville Arms public house, Goda Street, Lambeth, when four men rushed in. Carter fled through the bar and out of another door, but he was attacked in the street by the group and slashed; his face required the insertion of sixty stitches. Nevertheless, he managed to wrest a piece of sharpened steel from one of his attackers and then fled once more, pursued by the gang. After running some 200 yards, Carter got into a yard, then a house in Hutton Road, SE11 where he gained access to the bathroom; but the gang forced their way in and attacked Carter once more with their weapons.

On 9 May Rosa and Frett were arrested; they were picked out on an identification parade by Mrs Carter, as was Rosa by John Carter – Frett he already knew. But by the time Fraser had been charged with that offence and the three men appeared at Bow Street Magistrates' Court on 28 May, matters had changed considerably.

On that date, Mrs Carter nervously stated that she could not be sure if it had been those three men who had attacked her husband. Since there was no evidence of identification against Fraser, Mr E.C. Jones, counsel for the prosecution, did not ask for Fraser to be committed for trial; the case against him was discharged.

Frett and Rosa were committed to the Old Bailey and stood trial before Mr Justice Donovan. In the witness box Carter described the attack but stated that he did not know either of the two men and, furthermore, would not swear that either of them had attacked him.

The judge asked him, 'Tell the jury frankly, has something happened since the identification parade to make you not want to give evidence against them?'

Carter replied, 'Nothing has happened at all.'

And when Carter's wife said that she had picked out two men on the identification parade who looked like her husband's attackers but she did not know for sure, it was the perfect opportunity for that exquisitely bent brief, Patrick Marrinan to bellow, 'Are you prepared to swear positively that either of the defendants was present at the attack?'

Tina Carter duly answered, 'No'.

Another witness equally unable to identify any of the gang was Leslie Henry Benson, into whose house Carter had fled, followed by his attackers.

Frett denied any involvement in the attack, stated he knew neither Jack Spot nor Billy Hill and stated, 'There's a big feud going on in South London between Carter and the Brindles. Carter comes from the racing family.' Rosa similarly denied attacking Carter, saying that he was in Brighton at the time.

Summing up for the prosecution, Reggie Seaton told the jury, 'Carter now says neither of these men attacked him. You might ask yourselves if perhaps something has happened to make him a little reticent about identification.'

Patrick Marrinan must have felt that, with victory almost in his grasp, he could afford to be generous, because he told the jury, 'It could be said if gangs could go about cutting people up and then by some means of another their victim, after first identifying his assailants quite positively, could be given to entertain doubts in the witness box, then a very ugly situation was developing and it could lead not merely to a breakdown of the criminal law but to all law.'

Weasel words indeed. But in his summing up the judge had this to say:

> It may well appear to you now that there is a great deal
> more to this case than Carter's uncertainty in the witness

box. If gangs can cut people up and then, by some means or other, their victims – after first positively identifying them at an identity parade – are given to entertaining doubts in the witness box, then a very ugly situation is developing; and it would lead, not merely to the breakdown of criminal law, but all law.

Nevertheless, within an hour, the jury returned guilty verdicts in respect of both men and heard something of their backgrounds. Each had eight previous convictions. Frett and another man had been in a car in Chiswick and when another motorist remonstrated with them he was slashed across the face with a razor; in November 1950 at the Old Bailey Frett was sentenced to three years' imprisonment. Eighteen months prior to Frett's conviction, Rosa had appeared at the same court. He had found a man in bed with his (Rosa's) wife, and had slashed him across the face and body with an open razor; he had collected three years' corrective training.

Passing sentence, Mr Justice Donovan told them, 'I have not the least doubt that there are other and very wicked persons behind you but the tools of those persons must realize that if discovery follows, punishment will be condign.'

And this charmless pair went down for seven years apiece. Fraser, of course, was one of those 'very wicked persons' and felt able to later brag about his part in the attack, in print. No prosecution followed.

It is possible that following Rosa's and Frett's release each refused to go anywhere without the other, in case they missed out on the opportunity of simultaneously disfiguring one of their victims. It is also a possibility that from the confines of their cells they might have wanted to send Fraser a postcard saying, 'We had a slashing time – wish you were here.'

In fact, there was no need for a postcard, because he had already arrived, just five days previously.

CHAPTER 10

A Revenge Attack

B illy Hill and Albert Dimes were furious that Fraser and Warren had been sent down for seven years on 15 June 1956 for the attack on Spot and they decided upon a very foolish reprisal – to frame Jack Spot for an assault at a time when they had no idea of his whereabouts. For all they knew, at the time of the intended attack Spot could have been taking tea with the Commissioner of the Metropolitan Police – an unlikely scenario, I admit, but it shows the absurdity of the plan, not one that one would normally associate with a person of Hill's intelligence and strategic ability. In fact, the foolishness went further than that: the newspapers had reported that Spot and his wife had been receiving police protection and it was quite possible that Spot would thus have a very effective alibi at the time of any alleged attack. But if Spot could be framed, the advantage to Hill would be enormous. At this time, Blythe and Rossi were safely tucked away in Eire and the 'Ginger' Dennis arrest was still one month away; they, plus any of the other gang involved, might or might not be arrested. If, however, they were, it would be extremely helpful for Spot to be in custody on a serious charge; what would his credibility be worth then, whether he gave evidence against them or not? And how would this affect Rita's testimony? Not only was she already a discredited witness, due to her involvement with the Revd Andrews' conspiracy, but the fact that her husband was no longer around to protect her might well result in her refusing to give evidence against anybody else arrested for the attack.

So the risks were great but so were the potential profits; all that remained was to find a person to be slashed – willingly – and who was able to stand up in court, point to Jack Spot and say, 'That's the man who cut me.' Where could such a person be found?

Enter Victor 'Scarface Jock' Russo, a diminutive Glaswegian hardman, then thirty-eight years of age. With twenty-four convictions to his name, nine of them for violence, he had himself been the subject of vicious attacks. Shot and knifed twice, he had also suffered a broken jaw, leg, arm and shoulder and was the possessor of several feet of scar tissue around his face and body.

On the day after Fraser's conviction, Russo was in Frith Street, Soho, when he saw Hill, Dimes, Anthony John 'Johnny' Rice aka

Ricco, and Franny Daniels – and Hill suggested that for 'a monkey' (£500) plus all the expenses incurred for the resultant plastic
surgery, Russo should submit to being cut and then blame Spot
for it. Russo initially told Hill the plan could not possibly work
but eventually agreed to participate. Hill handed over the £500,
Russo promptly returned to Glasgow and telephoned Hill, saying, 'Thanks for the monkey, you dirty rat. If you ever come to
Glasgow, we'll send your body back in a sack!' And although this
was completely out of character for Hill, he did absolutely nothing
about it.

Quite apart from Hill's cock-eyed scheme to frame Spot, why he
should have picked on Russo as the victim and co-conspirator was
odd, to say the very least. True, they had known each other since
1940, but not as good friends, and although Russo and Dimes
were cousins they were certainly not close family. Russo claimed,
for some obscure reason, to have loosed off a shot at Hill in a nightclub in 1942. He had teamed up with Spot at the end of the war,
when Spot was testing out the club scene in Manchester, where
on a couple of occasions Spot had helped Russo financially. And
there had been a confrontation in a club between Russo and Hill's
brother Archie, who together with old-time villain John 'Dodger'
Mullins had unwisely mocked Russo, interrupting his courtship of
a certain 'Manchester Maisie'. Russo then followed them into the
club's lavatory and cut them both severely. When a quartet of Hill's
followers subsequently cornered Russo, he had taken the wise pre-
caution of arming himself with a carving knife, and the would-be
cutters fled in disarray from the tiny but terrifying 'Scarface Jock'.

Perhaps Hill thought that with so much damage inflicted upon
his body Russo wouldn't mind another stripe or two; but whatever
the case, Hill now had to find someone else dim-witted enough to
allow himself to be embroiled in such a crazy scheme as well as getting disfigured. Russo was out of the running, at any rate for now.

Thomas Joseph 'Big Tommy' Falco seemed to fit the bill admi-
rably. He had been regarded as a 'strong-arm man' in the Hill camp
and he had great difficulty in reading and writing. He had also been
named by Jack Spot as one of his attackers, as had Johnnie Rice,
a six-feet-four former boxer and physical training instructor. Both
had been questioned by the police regarding their involvement in
the attack but both had been released through lack of evidence.

But the story they now told the police was this: as they were
leaving the Astor Club in Lansdowne Row, Berkeley Square at
between 2.10 and 2.15 on the morning of 20 June, they turned
into Fitzmaurice Place, where Falco was approached by Spot who
slashed him in the left arm, saying, 'This is one for Albert.'

Rice's recollection was slightly different; the words he heard were, 'This one is for Albert Dimes.'

However, both men were in no doubt whatsoever that their attacker was Jack Spot, who ran off up the street towards Berkeley Square, where they heard a car start. Falco was taken to St George's Hospital, where Dr Ewen Crichton Bramwell examined the foot-long wound on Falco's arm, concluded that it had been caused by a sharp instrument arched in a downward movement and inserted forty-seven stitches. Had the wound been caused by an open razor, tied back by string and discovered three hours later in Fitzmaurice Place? It could have been, because Eric Dermot Sweet, the principal scientific officer at the Metropolitan Police Laboratory was able to say he found traces of blood on it.

So that was the story that Falco and Rice told the police – but not until nearly eleven hours after the alleged attack.

Detective Chief Inspector Jack Mannings from West End Central police station who was in his twenty-fifth year of service took up the investigation. He was a tough detective who had served for four and a half years with the Flying Squad; amongst the fifteen commendations bestowed on him by the commissioner was one, together with a £2 award, for arresting a suspected person who had assaulted him armed with an imitation firearm. With him was Detective Inspector John Du Rose, a leonine-looking, cheroot-smoking, forty-five-year-old detective who had arrived at West End Central just two weeks previously.

Having taken the two men to West End Central and obtained statements from them, Mannings spoke to Spot, asking him about his movements during the previous day and night. Spot replied that he had been watching the races at Ascot on the television all afternoon and then, during the evening, had gone out to get some sandwiches for himself and his wife. After they had eaten they had gone to bed and remained in the flat until he left at 12.40 pm on 20 June.

No one had seen Spot leave the block of flats. Police Constable 314 'D' George Howlett (later Commander Howlett OBE, OStJ, QPM) was one of the officers posted on night duty to Cabbell Street for, as he told me over sixty years later, 'the purpose of safeguarding him [Spot] in view of the fights and disputes involving other so-called gangsters, primarily Billy Hill. My recollection is that I was alone, that it was in the summer and a very warm night . . . I can see myself there, now, patrolling in the street only; I did not go into Hyde Park Mansions.'

There was no reason for Howlett to have gone into Hyde Park Mansions; his brief was to keep gangsters out of the block of flats, not try and catch Spot leaving the premises – besides, there were porters in attendance. But neither the porters, PC Howlett nor any of his contemporaries (who included random CID officers) saw Spot leave Hyde Park Mansions during that or any other night, for the simple reason that he did not. In fact, the only time PC Howlett saw Spot was very shortly afterwards, when he was languishing in the cells at Paddington Green police station.

The next stop, the following day, was Bow Street Magistrates' Court, where the magistrate, Mr R.H. Blundell, signed two arrest warrants. One was for Jack Spot, the other on description, presumably for the driver of Spot's getaway car; certainly, according to Falco and Rice, there was nobody else present at the assault.

Mannings then drove to Hyde Park Mansions, where he spoke to Rita Comer; Spot was not there. In fact, he had gone to see Detective Inspector Fred Cornish at Paddington Green police station in connection with a completely different matter. It was there that Mannings caught up with him and said, 'At 2.10 am on June 20, Tommy Falco was slashed across the arm at Fitzmaurice Place. This afternoon, he went with Johnny Rice to Bow Street Court and obtained a warrant for your arrest.'

He then read the warrant out to Spot, who replied, accurately, 'I'm innocent. This is a frame-up.' Spot was then driven to West End Central and en route he told the officers, 'This is a diabolical liberty. I'll get ten years for nothing.' Upon being formally charged at 4.43 pm, he replied, 'Not guilty. It's a deliberate frame-up.'

Kept in custody overnight, Spot appeared at Bow Street Magistrates' Court on 22 June and before going into the dock he told Du Rose, 'You see what they do for me? I should have named the twenty of them. I could have done.'

With Rita Comer sitting in the public gallery, Spot's solicitor, Ellis Lincoln, made a very good try for bail. Mannings agreed that Spot had gone to Paddington Green of his own volition in respect of another matter, but when he was asked, 'Do you know the position of Mrs Comer with regard to herself and threats which have been made against her?' Manning replied, 'No'.

'Do you know Mrs Comer has been threatened?' asked Lincoln.

Mannings replied, 'She has told me so.'

'I take it one of the reasons you are opposing bail is that he will not appear in court?'

'There is always a possibility that a man may abscond on such a serious charge.'

Not having got much change from Mannings, Lincoln now called Cornish, hoping for a little compassion. Cornish told the court that he had been shown letters by Mrs Comer which had threatened her and that she had also received threatening tele-phone calls. Lincoln stated that she had been in great fear, living alone in the flat with her two children, and asked, if it were possi-ble, should Spot be granted bail, for police to be on special duty at the flat whilst he was there. In that way, said Lincoln, Spot could still attend the hospital where his injuries were still being treated.

Cornish cautiously replied, 'This might be possible, with the consent of my superior officer', but Mr Blundell, the same magis-trate who had issued the warrant, was having none of it, and Spot was remanded in custody for a week.

When he reappeared on 29 June before the Chief Metropolitan Magistrate, Sir Laurence Dunne, it was for the purpose of commit-ting him to the Old Bailey for trial.

Mr E.C. Jones for the prosecution outlined the case to the court, stating that when Spot was seen by the police he had made a statement saying that he was nowhere near the scene of the crime.

Falco was called and stated that he and Rice had gone to the Astor Club at midnight and had left at about 2.15 am. 'Rice said he would drive me home,' he said, 'but as he lives a long way away, I said I would go home by cab and we parted at the top of the steps into Curzon Street As I went to turn right, this man Jack Spot – I know him as Jack Spot – came from the right. I don't know where he came from, but he said, "This is one for Albert" and I saw some-thing, bright. I felt blood and gripped hold of my arm, where it was cut. I turned away and the next moment, I saw Johnny Rice coming to help me.'

Falco was then cross-examined by James N. Dunlop, Spot's counsel, who asked him, 'You say you are a commission agent; are you also a driver?'

'Yes'.

'Do you drive for Albert Dimes?'

'I work for him, but not full-time, only when we go to the races.'

'Am I being naïve if I ask if Albert Dimes pays you a fixed salary?'

'When he wins at races', replied Falco, 'I get wages.'

'You know what Comer says about this charge?'

Falco replied, 'I can't read a lot. I've been told he says it's a frame-up.'

'And', persisted Dunlop, 'that the whole of the evidence you are giving is a complete fabrication?'

To this, Falco, with a complete disregard for his fate on judge-ment day, replied, 'I am a good Catholic and I don't take an oath to tell the truth unless I am telling the truth.'

The next witness was Johnny Rice, who although he was deeply involved with Hill's bookmaking enterprises always described himself as a metal dealer, trading as J & J Spares, Evelyn Road, Richmond, Surrey. He did so on this occasion when, after being permitted to write down his address, he told the court he was a steel merchant and went on to corroborate Falco's account.

Cross-examined, he was asked by Dunlop, 'For services of some sort, do you receive money from one Billy Hill?'

Rice replied, 'No, sir'.

'Would it be right to say you drive for Billy Hill?'

'No, it is wrong.'

'You are known to very many people, aren't you?'

'Yes sir, but not in the racing world', was Rice's reply.

'In the steel world?' asked Sir Lawrence Dunne, which Rice also denied.

The rejection of an association with the racing world was a rather reckless remark for Rice to have made; it would rebound on him badly at the forthcoming trial.

Mannings gave evidence of arrest and then Dunlop asked him this: 'Have you in your possession a statement taken from another person in which there is revealed a plot for something to be done in which Comer would be incriminated – and that statement is still in existence?'

'Yes', replied Mannings.

'And in the story or plot, is there something very similar to the circumstances with which we are now dealing?'

'Yes', replied Mannings. 'Similar'.

'The crux is that Comer should be implicated?' asked Dunlop. Mannings again replied, 'Yes'.

It must have become obvious that cracks of a considerable width were appearing in the prosecution's case. Perhaps production of that mysterious statement could have stopped the case there and then; but it wasn't, and it didn't, and Spot was not only committed to the Old Bailey for trial but once again refused bail.

The trial, before Mr Justice Streatfield, got underway on 16 July 1956; Reggie Seaton (who else?) prosecuted and a real heavyweight QC, Victor Durand, appeared for Spot.

In outlining the case to the jury, Seaton stated that Spot's clothing had been examined but no traces of blood were found; he suggested that Falco's jacket had absorbed the spurting blood (and that was probably the case).

Falco entered the witness box and gave evidence similar to that which he had provided at the lower court, adding that he had known Spot for seven or eight years.

Asked by Durand the present whereabouts of Billy Hill, Falco told him he had 'No idea', adding, sulkily, 'I'm not his keeper.'

'Are you swearing there is no connection between you, Dimes and this person I call Billy Hill?' asked Durand.

Falco replied, 'No relationship'.

'By Tuesday, June 19', asked Durand, 'was there in existence a plan for somebody in a list of names I have mentioned to you to be slashed and for Comer to be blamed for it – for someone in your gang to be slashed and for Comer to be blamed?'

'I have never heard of any plan at all', replied Falco, who was then asked why he had not told the police immediately that Comer was his attacker.

'There were no police about at the time', he replied.

Now Durand, terrier-like, tore into Falco: 'If you had told someone and the telephone had got busy and the police had gone round and found Comer in bed, that would be the end of the case against him. I am suggesting that you dared not have the police going round to Comer's address within minutes of you having been slashed.'

Falco did himself no favours with his answer: 'I wanted to deal with it in my own way. I didn't want to go to the police.'

'What is your own way?' the judge demanded to know.

'The same way as he had done it to me', replied Falco.

This answer infuriated Mr Justice Streatfield: 'And so it goes on, this ridiculous sort of warfare. One man slashes another . . . you won't put your worst enemy away but you will slash him.'

Rice was next in the witness box and he agreed to the description of his occupation as 'metal dealer'. Unfortunately, he had been photographed taking bets at Brighton races two weeks earlier which prompted the judge to ask, 'Is that a sideline from the steel business?'

Rice was obliged to answer, 'Yes', and furthermore, that he had bought the pitch from Jack Spot, whom he had known for fifteen years; and that there was no doubt in his mind that it was Spot who had cut Falco.

'It has been suggested that you and others have put your heads together to bring a false charge against Comer. Is there any truth in that?' asked Reggie Seaton.

'I would not risk the liberty and lives of my children and wife and myself to do a thing like that', replied Rice virtuously.

But cross-examined by Durand, Rice was asked if he knew a man named Victor Russo. 'You mean "Scarface Jock", that is the only way I know him', he replied.

'He was in your car that Saturday morning with Billy Hill, Dimes and you. During the conversation, Hill said, "We want someone to take a stripe from Spot, nick him, he's got to get some bird".'

'I don't know anything about that', responded Rice.

Leaving the best bit till last, Durand asked, 'What does "we want someone to take a stripe from Spot" mean?'

'I would say "cut him"', replied Rice, and with the jury quite obviously wondering what on earth was going on, that remark brought the first day's excitement to a close.

★

The following day, Jack Spot entered the witness box and denied knowing about or having anything to do with Falco's slashing. He told Reggie Seaton that he had been unable to work since the 2 May attack on him and that he had been living on his savings of £1,500 in a Post Office account in his wife's name. He agreed that he had told the jury in the trial of Warren and Fraser that he did not know who his attackers were and said by way of explanation, 'That's because I was afraid I would get beaten up again.'

Spot agreed that in 1954 he had been fined £50 for an offence of grievous bodily harm (he described the attack on Duncan Webb as 'just pushing a man') and fined £20 for possession of a knuckleduster; his conviction for unlawful wounding in 1939 he artfully substituted as 'an offence against the blackshirts' – rather than Nat Simmons being ripped with a razor or Hymie Jacobs being bashed with a bottle.

Rita Comer gave evidence that she and her husband stayed at home during the night of the attack and that he did not leave the flat until later the following morning. In fairness, this was not the most convincing of defences even if it was true.

But the next witness for the defence was a wild card in the form of Victor 'Scarface Jock' Russo (described by the *Daily Mirror*'s Cassandra as 'a hacked-up rat' and 'a mutilated gorilla'), who gave detailed, electrifying evidence. He stated that on 16 June he had not only met Johnny Rice (who was driving a Buick) as well as Falco, Dimes, Hill and Franny Daniels, but that they had gone to Peter Mario's restaurant in Gerrard Street (where Henry Cooper had met his future wife, who worked there as a waitress) and discussed a plan. It had been suggested that Russo should submit to being slashed in the face, the arm and the stomach. And when Russo raised the problem that Spot might well have a cast-iron alibi, Hill replied, 'I'll get Kye-Kye to find out.'

This was the nickname of Nathan Mercado, who traded as a bookmaker under the name of 'Sid Kiki' and who lived in an opulently furnished apartment in the same block as Spot and his wife. But why would he wish to assist in such an undertaking?

Well, perhaps because it was rumoured that he had alerted Frankie Fraser & Co. on the night when Spot and his wife had been attacked outside Hyde Park Mansions – although this was subsequently strenuously denied by Mercado. But the plot was full of holes: how could Mercado (or anybody else) say with certainty where Spot would be at any given time to coincide with Falco being slashed?

Russo told the jury that eventually (after accepting £500) he had told Hill that he would have nothing to do with the scheme; but after he had read in a newspaper that Spot had been arrested, he had gone to the police.

This raises the following question: having obtained Russo's statement, and in the light of Spot's repeated denials, why did the investigating officers not pull in everyone named by Russo as being in Peter Mario's restaurant? Yes, it was important to lock up a gangster like Spot in the first place, given the testimony of two alleged eye-witnesses, but given Spot's denials plus Russo's evidence, surely it was paramount to ascertain if there had been a conspiracy to pervert the course of justice on a grand scale, one that involved a number of criminals, not least two of Soho's leading lights, Billy Hill and Albert Dimes? Well, for whatever reason, this was not done, and the defence rested on three witnesses, all of whom had previous convictions and in Rita's case, one for actually perverting the course of justice in order to get her husband off the hook. Would the jury believe them?

Reggie Seaton asked for permission to call three witnesses to rebut Russo's accusations. The first was William James Kennedy, a coal miner, who told that court that whilst he was serving a sentence in Barlinnie Prison, Glasgow, he had been told by Russo that he had 'rowed himself into the Spot case' and that he was going to say that the whole thing was a 'get-up'. It's difficult to see how this helped the prosecution. Russo had certainly 'rowed himself in' because he had gone to the police and told them that the whole thing was indeed 'a get-up', courtesy of Hill and the others.

The next witness was Billy Hill, who was allowed by the judge to write down his address. He stated he had known Spot since 1947 and admitted he had thirteen convictions, adding that 'they were all for stealing', conveniently forgetting his two convictions for robbery. He denied that Fraser and Warren were his henchmen, and when Durand suggested that Hill had described himself as 'The King of Soho', he replied that that was what a newspaper had called him.

'What title do you take for yourself if it is not a kingdom or a dukedom?' asked Durand and must have been delighted when Hill replied, 'The Boss of the Underworld'. Quite apart from that cocky answer, Hill did himself no good whatsoever in the witness box. He slouched, spoke in monosyllables and answered questions before they were properly put. It was a performance guaranteed to alienate him from the jury, and so it did.

The third witness was Albert Dimes, who stated that he knew Falco, Hill and Rice, as well as Russo, whom he had known 'for about ten years'. He denied, as had Hill, suggesting that Falco should be wounded so that Spot could be blamed; and that was the end of the second day of the trial.

On 18 July, Reggie Seaton appeared to have grave misgivings when he summed up for the prosecution, saying:

> It has been suggested that certain people were attempting to prostitute the law, to bring about their criminal desire. The prosecution has no desire that anyone should frame the law to their own ends in order to achieve revenge. The only issue in this case is: did Comer wound Falco?

In his final speech Victor Durand told the jury that they might well consider their peace of mind had been violated by the idea of 'The Boss of the Underworld' using the High Court for his own ends. Referring to the evidence of Hill ('a miserable little character') and Dimes, he asked, 'Was it likely that they would come forward and say there was a frame-up?' and suggested that the court had been deceived by both witnesses.

The whole matter was now passed to Mr Justice Streatfield who said:

> We all know what we have read and heard, that there has been, unhappily in London at any rate, something like gang warfare going on and heartily sick of it all respectable people are becoming. People slash one another by way of revenge with razors and otherwise beating them up. These things are a disgrace to modern life in this great city. We only wish something could happen to stamp it out and assuredly, it will be, because commonsense prevails in the end and law and order in the end is always established.
>
> In connection with that gang warfare, the name of Jack Comer (or Jack Spot, as some people know him) has been mentioned before. First, do not allow your minds to be prejudiced merely because you thought that, in one capacity or another, he had been mixed up in a previous brawl. Secondly, you now know that it has always been Comer's defence in this case that he is quite innocent and

that it was a frame-up; in other words, that the injuries to Falco were caused by some other person he does not know. It may even have been staged for the purpose of fixing it upon Comer, so that he might suffer the penalty of the law. That is the defence but, members of the jury, you may think that the very existence of gang warfare may be a factor which lends colour to the possibility, at any rate, that this is in truth, a frame-up. On May 2, Comer was apparently attacked in the presence of his wife, outside his flat by a number of men. On June 15, two of those men, Warren and Fraser, were sentenced in this court to seven years' imprisonment by Mr Justice Donovan. They had been found guilty of wounding Comer, and Comer and his wife were called as witnesses. One understands now that two other men have been brought back from Ireland and yet a fifth man has been arrested. The two men having been sentenced on June 15, it is now alleged that Comer did exactly the same thing to a man, five days later. You might think it very unlikely that a man who had suffered himself, and had seen two other men suffer the severe penalty of the law, should himself, within a matter of days, do the same thing.

It took the jury just twenty minutes' deliberation to acquit Jack Spot.

There were calls in Parliament for Hill to be prosecuted, and the Director of Public Prosecutions demanded an enquiry, but within a month the whole affair fizzled out.

So who had cut Falco's arm? It seems likely it was Johnny Rice; and in the same way it seems unlikely, given the outcome of the trial, that Falco received any recompense from Billy Hill or anybody else.

CHAPTER 11

Gangsters – Exit Left

It's time for a clean sweep – this book is getting cluttered up with some of the dross of the underworld, so we need to get rid of them and allow a little more room for others of their ilk.

We'll start with Johnny Rice, because the law had not quite finished with him. Less than twelve months after Spot's acquittal, Rice appeared, once more at the Old Bailey, this time in the dock, and once more with Reggie Seaton prosecuting. Rice was found guilty of receiving stolen vehicle registration books and obtaining three books of petrol coupons by false pretences. In mitigation, his defence counsel stated that Rice was 'in fear of his life' from gangsters, especially one Billy Hill, whose name had been mentioned during the trial. The officer in the case, Detective Sergeant Vibart, when asked if he thought that Rice had been 'largely used by others', replied that he thought that was so, but added that he did not believe that Rice was a frightened man. Notching up his fifth conviction, Rice was sentenced to twelve months' imprisonment, but even then he did not learn from his experiences: in 1962, once more at the Old Bailey, he was convicted of conspiracy relating to car registration books. He was one of five men found guilty (another was a Scotland Yard detective sergeant), and his punishment was five years' imprisonment.

As for Tommy Falco, he apparently clashed with the Kray Twins and was shot and wounded by them, following a dispute at the racetracks. He died some years later.

Victor Russo returned to Main Street, Coatbridge, Scotland, and died there in 1982.

Before he succumbed to cancer in 1971, Albert Dimes was said to have known the identity of the murderer in 1967 of 'Scotch' Jack Buggy, who had previously fallen out of favour with Billy Hill. In fact, Franny Daniels, confidant of both Hill and Spot, was one of two men acquitted of Buggy's murder in 1974; Daniels died eighteen years later.

No one expected Jack Spot to rise phoenix-like from the ashes of his Soho empire and he did not disappoint them. He had not paid the damages owed to Duncan Webb and, as Jacob Colmore, he attended bankruptcy proceedings on 21 February 1957 in which he filed a statement of affairs showing liabilities of £1,321 and assets of £125.

The senior official receiver disproved much of what Spot had to say, to which Spot plaintively replied, 'I have been beaten up to such an extent that I cannot give the correct answers. I have been beaten up terrible.'

Blaming Duncan Webb (who died the following year) for his misfortunes, Spot said, 'I would have been better off if I went to prison for three years', adding, histrionically, 'Then I wouldn't have been beaten up by twenty-five men.'

Less than a year later, he was granted his discharge from bankruptcy, subject to a suspension of six months, but not before he and Rita were evicted from their flat at Hyde Park Mansions, and Spot, wishing to visit his wife's family in Canada, had been refused entry to the country. Rita opened the Highball Club in Bayswater which was first wrecked by a gang then set on fire, something which had been arranged by Reggie Kray, or so he said.

Spot appeared in court for the last time on 6 February 1962, when at West London Magistrates' Court he was fined £12 for stealing meat from his employer. Spot and Rita drifted apart; she died of cancer in 1988 and he followed her to the grave seven years later while living in a residential home.

It's time, too, to bid farewell to Billy Hill. He still immersed himself in criminality, some of his contemporaries received the odd wounding and although he and Gypsy lived from time to time in Cannes and Tangier, Hill made his permanent home at 4 Windsor Court, Moscow Road, Bayswater. He ran clubs that featured distinctly dodgy card games, but his relationship with Gypsy fractured after both of them had extra-marital affairs with partners considerably younger than themselves, including a liaison with a black singer for him and one with a native of Tangier for her. Hill died in 1984 – either impoverished or as rich as Croesus, whichever version you prefer – and Gypsy died twenty years later.

'Battles' Rossi was later questioned about the death of boxer Freddie Mills and was charged with the contract murder of Beatrice 'Biddy' Gold in 1975. He was acquitted.

I saw Bobby Warren in the 1970s when I wanted to speak to him, purely as a witness to a crime in which he had no criminal involvement. He refused to say one word to me.

Bernard Schack emerged angry and embittered from his twelve months' imprisonment for falsifying a defence for his friend Jack Spot. Spot, known for his parsimony, had refused to support Schack's family, and the men never spoke to each other again. According to Spot, after Moisha Goldstein finished his two-year sentence for the same offence, he chummed up with the Kray brothers and 'taught them everything they knew'. It's true that the twins did align themselves with Goldstein, although he later died alone, impoverished and frightened.

Sid Kiki – who may or may not have fingered Spot – went on to become a police informant; his testimony helped convict a three-man blackmail ring who between them collectively possessed nineteen convictions and were sent away for a total of twelve years. Kiki's betting shop was later burnt to the ground.

Pasquale Papa – Bert Marsh, as was – died in 1976, tremendously well respected in the Clerkenwell area. A few years ago, I had lunch with an upstanding pillar of Italian society from that area who bemoaned the present day lack of law and order in the district, saying, 'What we need is someone like Bert Marsh to sort things out!'

At the time, the name meant little to me and I asked, 'Isn't he dead?'

'Dead?' replied my companion. 'Of course he's dead! D'you think we'd be having all the trouble nowadays if Pasquale Papa was still alive?'

Food for thought.

As for the rest? Christopher Glinski features again, later on, as to a far greater extent does Frankie Fraser. And although he is left centre stage, Billy Hill will have a small walk-on part in the next bloody chapter – as will the Kray Twins – when three men were convicted of causing grievous bodily harm to a dead man.

No, honestly.

CHAPTER 12

The Pen Club Murder

Dorset Street in Spitalfields was known in Victorian times as 'the worst street in London', and with good reason; just 400ft long and 24ft wide, it was full of common lodging houses which catered for the sleeping arrangements of 1,200 men per night. It had also been the scene of several murders, including that of Mary Jane Kelly, courtesy of Jack the Ripper, in 1888. Perhaps in an attempt to dissociate it from its tarnished past, the City of London Corporation changed its name to Duval Street in 1904; it made little difference.

Before Duval Street was turned into a lorry park to service Spitalfields Market in the 1960s there was one more murder, and it happened during the early hours of Sunday, 7 February 1960 at the Pen Club.

To set the scene, we must first introduce William David 'Billy' Ambrose, who at the time of the murder was thirty-one years of age. By the time he was eighteen Ambrose had started to box professionally and in the following three and a half years he had won thirty-one of his thirty-four bouts; he was considered, with considerable justification, to be a contender for the middleweight championship of Great Britain. He won on points in an eight-round match against Bob Cleaver at the Arena, Mile End in 1952, but this win was his last professional fight, because his licence was suspended.

The reason for the abrupt termination of such a promising career was as follows: on the evening of 18 November 1952 Ambrose was one of six masked men armed with truncheons who broke into Conway Stewart & Co., Copperfield Road, Stepney, attacked, tied up and gagged Walter Morgan, the security officer, and helped themselves to 2,970 fountain pens valued at £1,500.

Ambrose and another man stood trial, as did Ambrose's mother for receiving, after 2,229 of the pens and the impedimenta used for opening the safe were found at her home. Fifty-one-year-old Mrs Sarah Jane Ambrose was later acquitted, but despite the introduction of a defence witness who claimed that although he had participated in the robbery, Ambrose and his accomplice had not, both prisoners were convicted and sentenced to five years' imprisonment.

Ambrose's incarceration commenced in Wormwood Scrubs
prison, where he was briefly reunited with Reggie and Ronnie Kray
– at various times they had all trained at Govier's gym. The twins
had been apprehended after being absent without leave from the
army and in the course of their arrest they had assaulted Police
Constable Roy Fisher. The magistrate had commended the officer,
who also received a modest bursary of 7s 6d, and awarded the
twins one month's imprisonment. Although Ambrose was just five
years older than the Krays, they regarded him as 'an old boxer, who
had been somebody, a celebrity' and they graciously dispensed
some tobacco and boxing magazines to him.

Ambrose's stay at Wormwood Scrubs was hardly longer than that
of the brothers; he escaped from the prison's hospital wing and was
on the run until, recaptured, he spent the rest of his sentence at
Dartmoor. There he settled down to serve his sentence and reflected
upon the spirited, albeit unsuccessful, attempt by the well-meaning
friendly witness to get him and his co-defendant off the hook. When
his next bit of criminal chicanery came round, it would be Ambrose
who would be the one offering a helping hand to absolve other criminals from blame. On that occasion there would be the assistance of
a number of others – including the Kray brothers.

★

It has been said that the Pen Club was named after and financed
with the spoils from the Conway Stewart robbery, but whilst this
is a possibility it does seem rather unlikely, since only 741 fountain pens with a value of £374 were not recovered. The Pen was
one of ninety-two such clubs in the Stepney area, none of which
were respectable. Its owners were Billy Ambrose and his associate
Jeremiah Callaghan (who, it was rumoured, had also participated
in the robbery), but they were not the licence holders.

The wartime Regulation 55C had permitted the police to object
to people of bad character managing licensed premises, but this
rule was scrapped in 1952. Now any person could fill in a form,
devise some rules, list the names of a few proposed members, take
it all to the Clerk of the local Justices and, for the princely sum of
five shillings, be granted a licence. Drinks could then legally be
served for nine hours out of every twenty-four, the hours to be
determined by the licensee. It was an utterly shambolic system,
although very little has changed with regard to the regulation of
licensed premises today.

So although Ambrose or Callaghan could have been the
licence holders, their names would undoubtedly have attracted

the attention of the police, with the possibility of uncomfortable enquiries being made in respect of income and expenditure.

The club had changed hands just three weeks previously, and Ambrose acted as doorman/bouncer. It was managed by a Mrs Fay Sadler whose husband, Alec Sadler, was nowhere to be seen. Blonde, thirty-six-year-old Mrs Sadler also managed a club at 17 Moor Street, Soho and she was better known to the authorities under her maiden name of Fay Richardson because of her conviction, four years previously, for larceny and false pretences, acquired when she had been the paramour of the late Tommy 'Scarface' Smithson.

How much longer this state of affairs would be allowed to continue was debatable. Despite the fact that Reggie Kray described the club as 'not being renowned for being a trouble spot, in fact, quite the opposite', there had already been two police raids the previous week and a third one had been planned for the week following the murder. In fact, two days prior to the murder, the club had been visited by representatives from the Society of Juvenile Probation Officers, to be told by Mrs Sadler, 'I can see you're looking for dens of iniquity but you won't find anything here.'

The club occupied two floors and on the night of the murder both were crowded. The juke box was playing and Fay Sadler was serving behind the bar when Selwyn Keith Cooney, in the company of his friends Joan Ellen Bending and Johnny Simons, walked in. Cooney – he was also known (certainly to Ambrose) as Jimmy Neill – was a promising middleweight boxer and he managed the New Cabinet Club in Gerrard Street, Soho which was owned by Aggie, the separated wife of Billy Hill; Joan Bending was a barmaid at the club. Simons had a bad criminal record: possessing offensive weapons, assaulting the police, larceny, taking and driving away cars and wilful damage.

Shortly afterwards, four more people entered the club: they were James Laurence 'Jimmy' Nash, a member of a notorious North London crime family of eight brothers, his girlfriend, Doreen 'Redhead' Masters, Joseph Henry Pyle and John Alexander Read; the three men were all former boxers.

Several versions existed of the lead-up to the confrontation, as well as what occurred thereafter, but because of the amount of detail involved it is more than possible that the following scenario was what initially brought Cooney into conflict with the Nashes.

Several weeks prior to the murder, Cooney had been driving his Vauxhall Victor in Hyde Park when the car collided with a vehicle driven by 'Blonde Vicky' James, the girlfriend of Ronnie, one of the Nash brothers. She admitted liability but confessed that she was uninsured, so she suggested that Cooney should get his car repaired and send her the bill. This he did, sending her a rather modest invoice for £2 14s 9d. She, however, refused to pay and then, perhaps by chance, on the night prior to the murder, Cooney went to a drinking club in Notting Hill. There he saw 'Blonde Vicky' in company with Ronnie Nash and two other men. The resulting conversation was rather lively, and Ronnie Nash and his two companions attacked Cooney. Outnumbered he might have been, but not outclassed; he fought back and although he collected a black eye he also flattened Nash with a left hook.

And now, twenty-four hours later, came the dénouement: one version had it that Jimmy Nash walked over to Cooney and struck him with an unidentified object which broke his nose, saying, 'That will teach you to give little girls a spanking'; whereupon Cooney replied that he had no idea what Nash was talking about.

Another account was that Simonds heard Nash say, 'You're the bastard I've been looking for' and 'I want you, you had a go at my brother.' The latter version does have a certain ring of authenticity to it.

A further version had Cooney shouting, 'Fuck Ronnie Nash. Fuck all the Nashes. If Ronnie or any of the Nash brothers want it, if they want to mess with me, they can have it any time.'

It was at this moment that Jimmy Nash walked up to him and said, 'Hey, my name is Jimmy Nash and you're talking about my brothers.'

This elicited the reply from Cooney, 'I don't give a fuck what your name is', and then the battle royal commenced.

However, since this final version of events was provided by Joey Pyle some considerable time later, it can be viewed with a certain amount of scepticism.

In any case, Nash continued the attack, knocking out two of Cooney's teeth, while Pyle and Read joined in the beating-up; then Billy Ambrose's wife, Betty, shouted, 'He's got a gun!'

There was immediate pandemonium as the crowd tried to disperse; Ambrose pushed his way through the throng and Bending and Simons would both later say that it was Nash who pulled out a gun and shot Ambrose at point-blank range in the stomach.

Mrs Ambrose screamed, 'You've shot my husband!'

Cooney shouted, 'Don't let him get away!'

Then a second shot was fired, hitting Cooney in the head. Some of the crowd attacked Nash and his associates; Simons hit Read over the head with a bottle, and the three men and Masters fled from the club, escaping in two cars.

Cooney had died instantly; Ambrose was grievously wounded and had also been struck on the head, but nevertheless, he, Callaghan and Simons dragged Cooney's body down the stairs and deposited it some way from the club. Ambrose then drove himself the three miles to his home at Brock Place, Glaucus Street, Poplar, and examined the wound; although he later told a court, 'I felt a bit of pain but not a terrible lot', he decided that the best place for him was the London Hospital. He drove to the hospital and when spoken to by the police told them that he had been shot by an unknown assailant outside a club in Paddington the name of which escaped him.

Meanwhile, Sadler – no stranger to killings, since three of her boy-friends had been murdered – cleared up the bloodstains and mess at the club. When she was later seen leaving the London Hospital, she claimed she had been visiting her friend Billy Ambrose and, giving the police a false name, stated she knew nothing about a shooting.

But it was not too long before the police began to build a strong case for murder, which at that time still attracted the death penalty. Although there was no trace of Nash, the other three, Masters, Read and Pyle, were arrested.

When Masters was seen by Detective Inspector James Driscoll at her home address in Parkhill Road, Haverstock Hill, later that morning and asked if she had been at the Pen Club between mid-night and 2.00 am, she replied, 'Pen Club? I don't know the Pen Club. I wasn't there. I came home at 1.00 am this morning – what's it all about?'

Told that she was alleged to have been at the club when one man was shot and another killed, she replied, 'I would rather not say anything at the moment.'

Masters changed her tune after Driscoll found a woman's pale blue raincoat with spots of blood on it, a bloodstained towel and, inside her crocodile skin handbag, a certificate from Hampstead hospital bearing the name John Read.

Regarding the towel, Masters said, 'That's what I wiped the car seat with. I didn't want to get them into any trouble and I don't want to get involved myself.' She then made a statement in which she admitted taking Read home with her and then on to hospital.

When Detective Superintendent Millington told Read and Pyle that he had just seen Cooney's body in the mortuary, Pyle replied, 'What will happen to us?', whilst Read claimed, 'I didn't do any shooting.'

Although Simons failed to identify anybody, both men were positively identified by the two women, Sadler and Bending; the latter also identified Masters. When Pyle was unhesitatingly picked out by Sadler, he immediately said, 'You didn't see me shoot him', to which she agreed, 'I didn't see you shoot him.'

Pyle and Read were detained in separate cells at Commercial
Street police station. It did not prevent them from conversing with
each other, although they did have to shout. The noise attracted
the attention of Police Constable Ronald Spiers, who felt com-
pelled to record snatches of the conversation:

(Read)   'They all know who done it, you know. Don't make a
            statement saying you know the Nashes.'

(Pyle)   'I told them I know Ronnie.'

(Read)   'I think they know I know them. If we can get out, we
            might be able to get in touch with Jimmy.'

(Pyle)   'I never knew what the row was about. He [referring to
            Nash] never walked in there and shot straight, did he?'

(Read)   'No'.

(Pyle)   'They can't say we were concerned in the matter, can
            they?'

(Read)   'No. We never done any shooting. Three or four tried to
            get going into Nash. I said, "Turn it up, boys". It was a
            ruck and that was that.'

(Pyle)   'It's horrible because you don't know what they're
            going to do you for.'

(Read)   'No. It's a fucking worry.'

(Pyle)   'I'll lead a quiet life after this.'

(Read)   'You're telling me.'

(Pyle)   'I never knew they could do us for being concerned,
            did you? We never got into this, with that stabbing on
            the Common.'

Pyle then referred to a man named Harris being stabbed to death
and another man named Marwood.

(Read)   'Yes, all that gun business is fucking silly, isn't it? I
            mean, they were only having a ruck to start with.'

(Pyle)   'He'll get life, you know.'

(Read)   'Who?'

(Pyle)   'Jimmy'.

(Read)   'They might top him.'

Later in the conversation, Pyle said, 'I won't go into any more clubs'.

Read replied, 'Nor will I, Joe. I was thinking last night they topped the three of us. If they topped me, my wife would be fucking happy.'

At this, there was general laughter, which suggested that Mrs Read might not find the matter of her husband being hanged by the neck until he was dead as hilarious as all that.

Charged with the murder of Cooney, Masters made no reply, Read replied, 'Nothing to say' and Pyle rather gormlessly said, 'Is it concerned in murder?'

In the meantime, the police were searching for Nash. As *The Times* reported in their 9 February 1960 edition:

> The police are anxious to interview a man who may be armed and who may be able to assist them with their enquiries. A detailed description of this man was sent from Scotland Yard to every police station throughout Britain, yesterday. The alert was centred in London, however, because the wanted man is a Londoner and is in fact well known to many Metropolitan Police officers. His associates and places he habitually visits, including many public houses and drinking clubs are also well known to the police.

Two days later, Nash, in the company of his solicitor's legal representative, Emmanuel Fryde, walked into City Road police station at nine o'clock in the morning, with Fryde loudly proclaiming, 'I understand you wish to see this man, James Lawrence Nash, in connection with a shooting affair last Sunday morning at Stepney when a man was shot dead. I want you to understand he denies any kind of a charge at all. He is not guilty and acting on legal advice he is not making any verbal or written statement.'

Nash, like the other three prisoners, was charged with murder. However, there had already been a great deal of activity behind the scenes.

★

Freddie Foreman, 'The Godfather of British Crime', would later say that to save all four from going to the gallows, negotiations were started, with him acting for Billy Ambrose and the Kray twins for the Nash family, in order to try and ensure there would be no further ill-feeling. Reggie Kray said that following the shooting, Nash & Co went to the Kray address in Vallance Road asking for help;

whether or not they immediately visited 'Fort Vallance' is debatable, but in any event they got help, because Ambrose was quickly visited during his month-long stay in hospital by Reggie Kray. He paused only to acknowledge the presence in an adjoining bed of Bernard Schach, alias 'Sonny the Yank', who at fifty-eight was over double Reggie Kray's age and whose jaw he had courageously broken the previous evening, as well as head-butting him, for daring to refer to him as 'son'. Kray wanted to know from Ambrose the names of the witnesses; Jimmy Nash was visited by the twins whilst he was on remand; and Fay Sadler was just one of the witnesses 'invited' to the twins' Double R Club. One by one, the thirty-six customers in the club who had volunteered their services as witnesses started to change their minds about what they had seen and heard.

At the preliminary hearing at Thames Magistrates' Court on 8 March 1960, the magistrate, Leo Joseph Anthony Gradwell DSC, RNVR, cleared the court after he felt that Joan Bending was giving her evidence nervously, believing that she would speak more confidently if the public were absent – a wise move.

'Ambrose was shot first, then Jimmy', she told the court. 'Then next thing I remember, I was downstairs in the street.'

During the following hearing, Ambrose (referring to Cooney as Neill) told the court:

> I was talking to my wife when somebody pulled Neill round. There seemed to be a bit of a scuffle. When I turned round, I saw blood on Neill's nose and he was staggering. Someone cried out, 'He's got a gun.' I turned round and tried to get the gun from a man. I asked the man to give me the gun and I got pushed at that time. I heard a bang and felt a burning pain in my stomach. I then got a blow on the head and it seemed to be a free-for-all. Five or six were fighting. A man I know as Jerry Callaghan pulled me round to go out. As I was going out, I saw Neill on the floor. I went home and found I had an injury on the head and a bullet wound in the stomach. I tried to patch myself up and went by car to the London Hospital.

The magistrate asked him, 'Did you see the people that came into the club?'

'No, Sir,' replied Ambrose. 'I wouldn't say I saw them for sure. It was dimly lit.'

'There must have been a moment when you were able to pick out someone as the probable holder of this gun', persisted the magistrate. 'If a number of people came in and suddenly started to row, you would have an idea of what they looked like, wouldn't you?'

'If I was looking for them', answered Ambrose disingenuously.

'Look around this court', said the magistrate, 'and tell me if there is anyone you can see that was in the club that night.'

Ambrose obliged, slowly and theatrically surveying the court before returning his gaze to the magistrate and replying, 'I cannot see anyone. It would be unfair for me to say I can.'

Someone who would have been able to assist with the identification of the guilty parties was thirty-six-year-old Mrs Frances Sadler, aka Fay Sadler, otherwise Morgan, also Davies, née Richardson, but as the court was told, 'She had not been seen for the past eleven days' – hardly surprising, since she was ensconced in Ireland.

Mr C.G.L. Du Cann, barrister for both Nash and Doreen Masters, was plainly unhappy about the evidence of the conversation overheard by PC Spiers, because if the prisoners were to be charged together, that evidence against Nash would be heard by the jury.

'That evidence is clearly not evidence against your client', said the magistrate. Du Cann replied, 'I am not complaining against you, Sir, but the evidence might appear in a place where the jury could read it.'

'A jury would get a strong warning from the judge', replied Mr Gradwell soothingly, 'and it's his last words, I find, that always have an effect.'

'We know how dangerous that could be, despite that warning', remarked Du Cann unhappily.

★

Even though he had deliberately failed to identify Pyle and Read, it was obviously thought that there would be no harm in Johnny Simons being reminded how unwise it would be to engage in any further dealings with the police. Shortly after the non-identification, Simons was attacked by a gang of thugs in a Paddington café; he was ruthlessly slashed with razors in front of a group of terrified women and children and his wounds required twenty-seven stitches.

The day after the exchange between Du Cann and the magistrate, on 16 March, Simons, who until now had made himself unavailable, suddenly came forward. The reason was this: on that date his girlfriend, a twenty-two-year-old model named Barbara

Ibbotson (who was not connected with the case in any way), was walking along Wardour Street when a car pulled up and she was dragged inside; her face was slashed with a razor and she was told that there was more to come unless she revealed Simons' whereabouts. She went straight to the officer in charge of the case, Detective Superintendent Roly Millington, and after her wounds were treated at St Bartholomew's Hospital she was joined by Simons at Commercial Street police station; both of them were then smuggled away to a secret address.

Simons appeared at Thames Magistrates' Court on 21 March. During his account of the disturbance, he said, 'I saw Nash open his coat and go for something stuck in the top of his trousers, but Ambrose had his back to me, so I couldn't see everything. There were words spoken between them and then Ambrose copped it in the guts. I heard the shot. Ambrose sort of fell back to the bar. His old woman screamed her old man had been shot.'

Asked by Oliver Nugent, counsel for the Director of Public Prosecutions, 'Did you see what had hit him?'

'Yes', replied Simons. 'A small gun'.

'Who had it?' asked Nugent

'Nash'.

Simons went on to say that Nash went out of the room but then returned, shouting 'Do you want some, too? Get out of the way!'

Simons then told the court that he had attended identification parades and had seen Pyle and Read there but failed to pick them out. When Nugent asked why, Simons provided a one-word answer: 'Scared!'

After legal submissions, Doreen Masters had the murder charge against her dropped; the magistrate wished to consider a charge of her being an accessory after the fact, but Du Cann stated that whilst she had tried to bind Read's wounds before taking him to hospital, this could not be construed as 'comforting, harbouring or relieving' him.

'It seems that if you drive someone away in your car, you are assisting him', suggested the magistrate, but Du Cann rather cleverly countered this by saying, 'If you say that a person who binds up wounds is guilty, you could indict the Good Samaritan.'

'I would never say that!' gasped Mr Gradwell and, rather unhappily discharging Doreen Masters, nevertheless committed the three men to stand their trial at the Old Bailey.

The police searched thirty addresses for Fay Sadler and on 2 April her photograph was published in all the national newspapers (although possibly not the Irish ones) asking for the public's help in tracing her, but without success. This led police to apply to a judge on 4 April for the earliest possible trial date but it also led Miss Ibbotson into a false sense of security. Believing herself safe, she returned to her home address three weeks after the initial attack on her. This was a mistake: three men broke into her flat whilst she was in the bath and slashed her face again, which required twenty-six stitches. She left London the following day.

Simons was now given round-the-clock protection, as was Joan Bending; the same sort of safeguard was not deemed necessary for Billy Ambrose.

And that was the end of round one. In the few weeks before their trial commenced, a great deal more dirty work was carried out.

CHAPTER 13

The Pen Club Murder – The Trial

On 21 April 1960 the three men stood in the dock at the Old Bailey charged with murder and various other counts pertaining to violence. Twenty-eight-year-old Jimmy Nash, who despite being a member of a family said to have been involved in violence and extortion, had just two convictions. One was for stealing cash from a vending machine when he was seventeen. The second came two years later when he was undergoing his National Service (he was apparently described as being 'good non-commissioned officer material'); probably the conviction, for stealing poultry, came after that recommendation.

Next, Joey Pyle, who at twenty-five had just the one previous conviction, for stealing a car. Like Nash he had boxed, having had, according to his biographer, 'twenty-four professional fights'. Official records note just six, the last on 10 June 1958 when he was knocked out by Maxie Beech at Wembley Town Hall, so it seems likely that eighteen of his fights were fairground bouts.

The third defendant, John Read aged twenty-eight, was of good character; his father was a police station sergeant and was said to be 'heartbroken' at the situation his son was in. Read had had thirty bouts as a middleweight; he was good enough to have confronted Dick Tiger on two occasions and had won twenty-two fights, fifteen of them by knock-outs. His last fight was on 5 February 1959, and it was a pity that he had started collaborating with Pyle in running the Floral Club instead of pursuing his promising career in the ring.

Victor Durand QC for Nash unsuccessfully applied for a separate trial for his client, and the trial got underway before Mr Justice Gorman. The first witness was Joan Bending; when asked by Alastair Morton for the Crown who had shot Cooney, she was unequivocal: 'It was Nash.'

The following day, Johnny Simons took the stand. Telling the court that he had heard Nash say to his friend Cooney, 'I want you, you had a go at my brother', he also stated that Nash had had a gun in his hand.

Victor Durand suggested, 'Ambrose must have seen what you say you saw? Simons was just as definite in his answer as Bending had been: 'Ambrose saw the gun. He saw it all, if he would only open his mouth and tell the truth.'

But as well as the defendants' high-powered legal team, there was additional help to bring about an acquittal. The Nash brothers were in the public gallery; so were the Callaghan brothers; representatives from Billy Hill's gang were present; and so were the Kray twins. Bending and Simons were intimidated as they left court. A juror was seen to nod at the head of the Nash family, Billy Nash; when his background was investigated he was found not only to have a conviction but also to be related by marriage to a gang of violent East End criminals. The Flying Squad was called in, and after the juror left the court, a man who had been seen previously in the company of the Kray twins joined him in his car; the juror subsequently made some incriminating comments to the Squad officers. And one of the women jurors visited her husband who, like the three defendants, was on remand in Brixton prison. Her husband told the prisoners that his wife was on their jury, had decided that Nash was guilty of murder and then, helpfully, provided them with his wife's address. And as if that were not enough, Reggie Kray in his often unintentionally hilarious memoirs recalled that whilst he 'watched the jury intently, trying to contemplate their thoughts' he was rudely made aware that he was being kept under observation by Detective Inspector Peter Vibart, then of the Yard's newly-formed Criminal Intelligence Branch, who had no doubts whatsoever as to which direction Reggie Kray's thoughts were moving in.

After three days, and a weekend of intensive enquiries and observations by the detectives, the trial was dramatically halted. The judge stated that he had been provided with information which 'makes it impossible for this case to be continued for trial before this jury'. The jury was duly discharged, and on 27 April Alastair Morton told Mr Justice Diplock that in the new trial he would not offer evidence against Pyle or Read on charges of the murder or being accessories after the fact; however, they were still to be tried on charges of causing grievous bodily harm. When the retrial commenced on 2 May 1960, eight jurors were challenged by the Crown; the judge stated that he did not want 'a weekend to intervene' and warned jurors not to speak to anyone about the case, 'not even your wives'.

When Nash gave evidence, it was essential to make it clear that there was no premeditated reason for he and his three companions to be visiting the Pen Club that night – certainly not to seek a confrontation with Cooney. In fact, it would be sensible to say that he had never heard of him under the name Cooney or Jimmy Neill. So he told that court that he had gone to the North London Penton Club with Doreen Masters where by chance they had met Pyle and

Read. Masters suggested they go to Barney's in Aldgate for supper, but on the way they decided to go to the Pen Club.

Nash told the jury that in the first-floor bar of the club Cooney had beckoned to him:

> I took no notice at first because I didn't know him, but he beckoned to me, again. I went over to him and he turned his back on me. I pulled his sleeve, wondering what it was all about and he turned round and before I could say anything, he started to have a go at me. He said, 'So you're another of those fucking Nashes?' I said, 'What's it all about?' and he said, 'You're a lot of fucking gaolbirds, you, Ronnie and the rest.' Then he referred to Doreen Masters. He asked, 'Who's the bird with you? A bit of easy money for you, I suppose.' By that, I took it he was suggesting that I was living on her, so I hit him on the nose with my right hand.

Under Victor Durand's expert tutelage, Nash told the court that he had nothing in his hand when he hit Cooney, stating that he had been a pretty good boxer in the army ('I won the Tripoli welterweight') and that he had suggested to Cooney that they should go outside and fight, man-to-man. However, he had been surrounded by five or six of Cooney's associates and although he was blocking a lot of blows, 'I was really worried about Doreen.' He did hear someone say 'He's got a gun', but that person was not him, since he had never possessed one. He was going down the stairs when he heard a second shot but he never saw Cooney after he had hit him.

It was a clever, well-constructed defence and it all depended on whom the jury believed.

Summing up for the Crown, Senior Treasury Counsel Mervyn Griffith-Jones told the jury:

> It is perfectly true that Read and Pyle and Doreen Masters were all originally charged with the murder of Cooney but they have been acquitted and now have nothing to fear on that charge. All three were in that room at the Pen Club and you may think they must have been only a few feet away from Nash. Who better than they to tell you whether or not Nash was responsible for the shooting? Two of those witnesses are available in this building. Doreen Masters is at her flat, as far as we know. Where are they?

But as the cunning Victor Durand told the jury, 'If you take the view that this case remains a mystery, then let it remain so.'

The following day, the judge, in summing up to the jury, told them this:

> You may have felt as you listened to this story of witnesses disappearing, of what you may feel was surprising lapses of memory on the part of those who have been called, that there are sinister implications here and that you have had a glimpse of an underworld which has its own code of loyalty or its fear. But if you felt that, you must not visit it upon the accused. He is being tried for murder, not for the company he keeps.

It took the jury just 100 minutes to acquit Nash of murder at 1.35 pm; he showed no emotion at the verdict, as his brothers cheered and Joan Bending burst into tears; at 2.20 a new jury was sworn in to try the three accused on a fresh indictment in which they were accused of causing Cooney grievous bodily harm.

It was then that what Joey Pyle would later describe as 'a surprise witness' came forward. David Sammons was not really a surprise – he had given evidence at the Magistrates' Court and at Nash's murder trial – but his testimony was surprising. His evidence changed dramatically; he said that Simons had remained on the upper floor of the bar at the Pen Club when the three defendants had gone downstairs and therefore could not have witnessed the shooting.

Mr Justice Diplock tore into him and, referring to Simons, demanded, 'You knew that he had given evidence that he was in the first-floor bar at the time of the disturbance?'

'Yes'.

'Did you tell anyone that you knew he was not in the downstairs [first-floor] bar?"

'Nobody'.

'You realized, if you were right, that Simons was telling a pack of lies?'

'I did.'

'And you knew that it was in a murder trial?'

'I did.'

'And that Simons' evidence, which you knew to be untrue, might result in a man being hanged?'

'Yes, I realized that.'

'And yet you say you told no one?'

'No one'.

'Why not? If it were true, why not?'

'It is true. When I read it, I was rather shocked, to be quite honest. I also read afterwards that the jury had been dismissed and there would be a retrial and I knew I would have a good opportunity of telling the truth at the retrial.'

'You thought you would be able to volunteer the truth at the retrial, did you?'

'Yes'.

'Did you say anything about it when you gave your evidence in chief at the retrial?'

'I'm not familiar with the words "in chief".'

'Did you say anything about it while you were being examined by Mr Griffith-Jones?'

'No'.

'When did you intend to volunteer it?'

'When I was asked. Then I would have volunteered it.'

'Supposing no one had asked you, what would you have done?'

'I would have seen my solicitor or I would have had to see the prosecuting counsel.'

'Why didn't it occur to you to do that before the second trial if you knew your story was true?'

'I'm not familiar with court procedure. I'm lost in these surroundings.'

'It didn't occur to you, knowing that Simons was not there [on the first floor] to tell anyone?'

'I thought it would be best kept to myself until it could be told to the prosecution.'

Sammons also stated that Joan Bending was so drunk she had to be assisted down the stairs. But again, he had also not mentioned this previously, and when this was put to Bending, she replied, 'Sammons is a liar.'

When Simons was questioned about Bending's capacity for alcohol, he told Durand, 'She could put back as much as you would care to buy her', which elicited the caustic reply, 'I hope I will never be in your circle.'

And when Durand suggested that Simons had remained on the second floor of the bar whilst the shooting was going on, Simons replied, 'No, I'm telling you the truth. I'm not being paid, like some people.'

It was unclear if he was referring to Durand, Sammons or any of the other witnesses.

Summing up, the judge, referring to witnesses in the case, told the jury:

> Ambrose, you may think, does not help you very much. You
> may think he wasn't trying to help you. David Sammons
> had said that Joan Bending was drunk and Johnny Simons

was in the second floor bar at the time of the disturbance on the first floor. He said that for the first time last
Monday. You may think there is no room for mistake and if
he is lying, you may think the evidence of Simons of what
happened in the first floor bar when the blows were struck
is uncontradicted. None of the accused has gone into the
witness box to tell you anything different. You will examine
Simons' evidence on its own merits. Did it bear the ring of
truth under probing and skilful cross-examination? Has he
been shown after he has given evidence now four times to
have varied his account of what he saw? Is there any possible reason why he should be guilty of so wicked a fabrication, because if Sammons is right, it must be a complete
and wicked fabrication against men against whom he had
no previous grudge?

After retiring for an hour and a quarter, the jury found Nash guilty
of causing grievous bodily harm to Cooney and he was sentenced
to five years' imprisonment. In passing sentence, the judge told
him:

> You have been found guilty on abundant evidence of a
> brutal assault upon a man who is now dead in a drinking
> club frequented by crooks. And as a result of the fight you
> started, there was such a panic that two men were shot.
> An example must be made of you and people like you.

As Nash was led off to the cells, James Cooney, the murdered
man's father, cried out, 'He killed my son; and I will kill him, that
is a certainty', leaving Nash's barrister, Victor Durand, to murmur
with almost unbelievable unctuousness, 'That very outburst illus-
trates the strength of feeling that is to be seen in the currents that
swirl about us', piously adding that he hoped that the Pen Club
would 'not operate again'.

Read and Pyle were acquitted of the same charge but were both
convicted of being accessories after the fact; passing sentence on
Read, the judge told him:

> You have been a professional boxer. You went to this
> drinking club, the resort of crooks and when Nash made a
> brutal attack on another man, you, as the jury have found,
> tried to prevent justice from taking its course. You and
> your like have got to learn that you cannot do that. I take
> into account you have been in prison for three months
> and have had hanging over your head a capital charge.

Telling Pyle 'You are in exactly the same position' and having heard that they were 'easily led', the judge sentenced each of them to eighteen months' imprisonment.

The trial, which had cost £20,000, was over, and with the dock now empty of miscreants, the judge told the jury:

> I have no doubt you have been shocked to learn the sort of thing that is going on in this city. Perhaps the most shocking thing of all is that some of these witnesses, and I have no doubt that you thought so with me, were scared, scared to tell the truth. It is a perfectly shocking thing.

It was these remarks that the firebrand Labour MP for Northampton, Reggie Paget (later Baron Paget of Northampton QC), alluded to on 26 May during a House of Commons debate when he asked the Home Secretary, R.A. Butler (later Baron Butler of Saffron Walden KG, CH, PC, DL), whether 'in view of Mr Justice Diplock's observations from the Bench, he will institute a public enquiry into allegations as to intimidation of witnesses and jurors in the Pen Club trials?'

The answer was short and succinct: 'I do not think a public enquiry would be appropriate.'

That was a pity. It is difficult to imagine a more serious miscarriage of justice in a murder trial, and the perpetrators later had the gall to publicly boast about what they had done and how they did it.

By their own accounts, Freddie Forman and Reggie Kray were responsible for much of the skulduggery which went on before and after the Magistrates' Court appearances and the subsequent trials; and it begs the question, why did they do it? Was it because they thought that the three men were innocent? Certainly not. Was it because they were close associates? Again, unlikely. And yet the machinery was put in place to frighten some witnesses, injure others, nobble juries, provide lying witnesses and carry out wholesale intimidation, as well as providing a range of top class Queen's Counsels for the prisoners' defence.

The answer is this: they were not demonstrating that they were above the law; they were setting out the fact to their fellow East Enders that they *were* the law. So when the Kray empire was smashed up, eight years and a few more murders later, it came not a moment too soon.

Referring to the Pen Club affair, Foreman said, 'It's a pity that politicians and heads of state can't settle their differences as effectively as we did.'

This is an interesting comment, because it fits in quite well with the claims frequently made by him, the Krays and other gangland glitterati, who would assert, 'Well, wimmin could walk the streets in safety in them days.'

Mind you, that wouldn't have included Fay Sadler, who had been frightened off to Ireland and who later departed from London, saying, 'Cooney's death was the end for me.'

Nor, I expect, Joan Bending, who also left the capital. 'I'm turning my back on the life I've known', was her parting remark.

Then there was the forty-five-year-old woman juror whose address was provided by her charmless husband to the three men accused of murder. And – oh yes – Simons' girlfriend, once attractive Barbara Ibbotson, who retired to Yorkshire with her ruined face, which required one less stitch than her boyfriend had.

So apart from those isolated instances, London's East End in the 1960s was a veritable haven of safety for women.

★

All three men were refused leave to appeal, with Mr Justice Hilbery commenting on 21 January 1961 that there was 'an abundance of evidence' to secure their convictions.

Chief Inspector Leslie Jones visited Fay Sadler's club at Moor Street, Soho; of her, there was no trace. The local magistrate, Mr Barker, granted an application to strike off Mrs Sadler's club but he was glumly informed that a new club was in existence at the same address, having been registered at the same court.

The Pen Club was closed and boarded up. But the Shamrock Club, which immediately backed on to the Pen Club, was opened just after the murder. It was raided and on the same day it was closed it opened again, this time as the Ricardo Club. The police only became aware of this after they were told by a social worker.

Irene Curzon, 2nd Baroness Ravendale CBE took a passionate interest in these matters; the sixty-four year old peeress steamed into 'one of the hottest strip-tease clubs in London' situated just 150 yards from the Pen Club looking for 'a lost girl from Newcastle'. The proprietor – described as 'oily and cautious with excuses' and said to have been connected with the Pen Club – had opened the present premises one week after the closure of the Pen Club. But despite the Baroness's apparent disgust at the revolting behaviour which went on at this and other strip-tease clubs, she could be accused of double standards. She had a penchant for sleeping with married men, including the celebrated pianist Arthur Rubinstein on his wedding day, as well as her brother-in-law, the notorious Fascist, Sir Oswald Mosley.

Billy Hill apparently offered to organize (but not necessarily fund) a spectacular gangland-style funeral for Cooney along the lines of those provided for Tommy 'Scarface' Smithson or William 'Billy-Boy' Blythe; the offer was flatly rejected by his dignified parents. Jimmy Nash was twice attacked in prison, apparently losing half an ear in one of these encounters. Johnny Simons was provided with a new life in Spain but returned disenchanted after three months. He visited Cooney's parents in Leeds but at that city's bus station he was attacked by three men who slashed him once in his arm and twice on his face, leaving a two-and-a-half-inch cut by his ear; twenty-seven stitches were required to sew him back together.

★

This little episode considerably strengthened Billy Ambrose's position in the underworld. Not only had he maintained the skilful series of rebuttals in court demanded by the East End lowlifes, he had actually assisted the defence of those charged with attempting to murder him. He was 'staunch', wasn't he? One of the chaps. In fact, the tributes went further than that: he was a 'diamond geezer', and there could be no greater accolade than that on the slippery streets of Stepney.

Foreman hinted that Ambrose and Callaghan were employed by him carrying out 'pavement jobs' – armed robberies. The two of them later bought up betting shops in Stepney. And when the Great Train Robbery was pulled off in 1963, Ambrose's name was one of eighteen on Tommy Butler's list of possibles, but he was eliminated from the enquiry.

In the mid-1970s he came to the attention of the Yard's Serious Crime Squad after he moved into a rather prestigious house in Sandown Road, Esher, Surrey, just across the road from Sandown racetrack. Since these properties fetch anything from £2m to £3.5m at the time of writing, and because he was now driving a Rolls-Royce Corniche, he really could not expect to blush unseen. Whatever business he was involved in was definitely dodgy, and he was duly arrested and charged with being the leading light in a firm of international swindlers. Known as 'The Hungarian Circle', they used London as their base and carried out frauds world-wide; it was claimed at the Old Bailey that 'they had the ability to bankrupt a small European country'. Ambrose filled the public gallery with his thugs, who scowled at the jury – old habits die hard – and he was acquitted. His leading accomplice went down for fifteen years. Billy Ambrose died in April 2009, aged seventy-nine; his wife Betty, who stayed with him during the bad times as well as the good, followed him to the grave four years later.

Joey Pyle became as well known to the law-abiding public as had Billy Ambrose; that is to say, hardly at all. But he became one of the underworld's most prolific members and had his fingers in any number of dodgy pies, being involved with protection, loan-sharking and drugs. Time and again he was arrested; in 1972 he was acquitted of possessing a gun, and seven years later he was cleared of conspiring to pervert the course of justice in the murder trial where John Bindon was accused, and acquitted, of murdering fellow gangster Johnny Darke.

Pyle had links with the US mafia and in 1987 he was charged in connection with a £5m cannabis smuggling plot; he was released after a witness for the prosecution refused to give evidence. In 1992 he was convicted of drug trafficking after a retrial (during the first trial jurors had received death threats to induce them to return a not guilty verdict) and sentenced to fourteen years' imprisonment. He appealed, received a fresh trial and in 1995 was again convicted, although his sentence was reduced to one of nine years' imprisonment. He died in February 2007 of motor neurone disease.

The year after the Pen Club case, Victor Durand QC was suspended from practising for three years by the Masters of the Middle Temple after admitting concealing evidence during a trial. Naturally, he appealed. Naturally, the suspension was reduced to twelve months.

William John Kenneth Diplock QC, who as Mr Justice Diplock presided over the murder trial, was later elevated to the peerage. Thirteen years later, he was responsible for founding what became known as 'Diplock' courts during the IRA offensive in Northern Ireland: trials were heard in front of a single judge, without juries being intimidated by the garbage in the dock and their supporters, or bamboozled by smart-arse lawyers; I witnessed several and thought they worked very well. However, I'm prejudiced; I like to see guilty people convicted.

CHAPTER 14

The Krays

It seems to me that about once a week another book is published about the Kray brothers; each one contains startling new revelations about them and previous facts which everyone thought to be gospel are debunked.

In outlining the history of the brothers Kray – briefly, I hope, because most Kray aficionados will be fully aware of what follows – any new disclosures will be few and far between. To grip your attention, I should love to impart to you that Ronnie Kray was the father of twenty-three illegitimate children or that Reggie was secretly married to Princess Margaret, but alas, neither would be true. Nevertheless, it is necessary to outline the accomplishments of the brothers to show how their preoccupation with gang warfare brought about their demise.

The twins – Reggie and Ronnie – were born within ten minutes of each other on 24 October 1933 in Bethnal Green. They were the latest additions to the family of Charles David and Violet Annie Kray, who already had a son, also named Charles, who was seven years older than his siblings; a daughter, Violet, born in 1929, died in infancy. By the time the Second World War arrived, the family had moved to 178 Vallance Rd; and even at this early age, it was clear that the twins would fight any of their contemporaries, as well as each other, at the drop of a hat. They came from a fighting family; whilst their father was not a violent man, his father was known as 'Mad Jimmy' Kray, a well-known street-fighter, whilst the twins' maternal grandfather was boxer Jimmy 'Cannonball' Lee.

Any parental control was minimal; their father deserted from the army and was away from home for long periods, while their mother doted on them (and vice versa) and refused to acknowledge any of their wrongdoing. So when Reg was arrested, aged twelve, for firing an airgun out of a train window, Violet was furious – but only with the police. Father Hetherington from the local church spoke up for Reg (as he would do on several more occasions) and he was placed on probation; however, a condition of the order was that he should attend the local boxing club in order to instil a little order into his life. In fact, both boys already trained at a lads' boxing club south of the river, so to have this made the a subject of an order suited Reg down to the ground; and where he went, Ron followed.

Boxing became a religion to them; a gym was fitted out on the first floor of Vallance Road and they trained incessantly. They fought as amateurs and also in fairground boxing booths; their fighting skills were honed in beating up anyone who crossed them and even people who didn't. They were now gathering an arsenal of weapons, including a revolver which they hid under the floorboards in their bedroom; their home was nicknamed 'Fort Vallance'.

In 1950 came their first serious confrontation with the law. Sixteen-year-old Roy Harvey and two friends were attacked in the street; Harvey had been punched hard on the nose, in both eyes and kicked all over his body, then mercilessly thrashed with a bicycle chain and left for dead. The twins were committed in custody from North London Magistrates' Court to stand their trial at the Old Bailey, but between committal and trial witnesses who had been appropriately 'spoken to' (a typist was told she would have her face slashed) suddenly lost their memories and the trial collapsed.

One of their contemporaries referred to them as 'A thoroughly evil pair of little bastards'. It was an epithet that was not undeserved.

The twins were seventeen when they became professional boxers, Reg, at five feet seven a lightweight and Ron, two inches taller, a welterweight. But a week after Ron's second bout he was arrested for punching Police Constable Donald Baynton on the jaw; hearing the news, Reg roamed the streets until he found the self-same constable and attacked him, too.

Aided and abetted by Father Hetherington, the local magistrate (probably believing with considerable justification that the brothers had had the living shit knocked out of them whilst in police custody) placed them on probation.

It is perhaps surprising that they were allowed to keep their licences during their five-month professional career, but they did and Reg won all seven of his bouts. At their final appearance, on 11 December 1951, all three brothers appeared on the same bill at Earls Court Empress Hall. Charlie, in the last of his eighteen bouts, was knocked out by Lew Lazar. Ron won four of his bouts and was disqualified in one – Bill Sliney (whom Reg had beaten twice) won on points.

If Billy Ambrose had imparted any words of wisdom to the twins in respect of National Service when they all trained at Govier's Gym, they failed to take them on board. Five years previously, when King and Country called him, Ambrose had decided that his fighting would be confined to the ring, rather than against His Majesty's enemies; he put on such a convincing display to the medical board that he was classified as 'a mental defective'.

Had the twins followed his lead – and to be fair, they could have been far more persuasive to the board than Ambrose regarding their mental capabilities – they would have saved themselves a great deal of hardship and could have continued their activities around Bethnal Green, happily slashing, shooting or maiming anyone they pleased.

But when they were conscripted into the Royal Fusiliers, the twins decided to take on the army. It was a fairly unwise course of action but it was symptomatic of the Krays. They went absent without leave time and again, assaulted non-commissioned officers and spent time in the glasshouse, until eventually they were court-martialled, sentenced to nine months' imprisonment in Shepton Mallet Military Prison and ignominiously discharged from the army.

Following their release in 1954, and for the next two years, the twins busied themselves, seamlessly taking over the Regal Billiard Hall, whereupon the violence there ceased as quickly as it had begun. Later, the Green Dragon Club became theirs, and shortly afterwards, the Double R Club opened in Bow Road In between times, they worked protection rackets and became 'thieves' ponces' – taking a percentage from the local criminals' illicit takings.

Reg kept his closet bi/homosexuality under control, but not so his brother; Ron was openly gay and gathered around him a coterie of effeminate young men who became his eyes and ears. Known as 'Ronnie's Boys', they collected and collated useful information for him. They were generally feared; to upset them could cause Ron to receive damaging false information which might be dealt with by a variety of weaponry, including red-hot pokers, a Ghurkha kukri (knife) or Ron's favourite, a cutlass. This last had replaced the open razor, since Ron now believed it to be 'babyish', saying, 'You can't put no power behind a razor'.

The Krays' gang was now increasing in size, and they recruited local tearaways who were looking for excitement; with Bobby Ramsey, they got it.

Robert Edward Ramsey, a former welterweight boxer, was the co-owner of the Stragglers Nightclub in Cambridge Circus. There had been some rowdy behaviour there, and Ramsey suggested to his partner, William 'Billy the Fox' Jones, that the twins might be able to offer a level of protection. This job suited the Krays down to the ground – not only would they have extra revenue coming in and be able, almost legitimately, to beat up troublemakers, but it also provided them with an avenue into the nightlife of the West End.

The trouble at the Stragglers soon abated, but trouble linked with Ramsey was now coming from a different quarter. 'The Watney

Streeters' were a disorganized gang of East End dockers who did not really represent a threat to the Krays. But trouble erupted between Billy Jones and one of the Watney Streeters named Charlie Martin, and Jones came off worse. The following night, Ramsey beat up Martin, and two nights after that, Charlie Martin and a considerable contingent of the Watney Streeters attacked Ramsey, punching, kicking and beating him with an iron bar.

Although this was a private quarrel, the twins were affronted because it was known that they were affiliated to Jones and Ramsey; to do nothing would be seen as a sign of weakness, but matters went further than that. Charlie Martin had been running a scam which Ronnie had found out about and he demanded 50 per cent of the profits; and Martin's payments had been dilatory, to say the very least. Therefore, Ronnie had decided to shoot him, and now (if any of Ronnie's insane acts required justification) the assaults upon his two associates provided an excuse for what was about to occur.

In September 1956 'Ronnie's Boys' made enquiries and ascertained that Charlie Martin and others of Ramsey's attackers were in the Britannia public house. Ramsey, driving his Buick, together with Jones and Reggie Kray and armed with a bayonet, a crowbar and a machete, roared down to the pub. The car behind contained Ronnie Kray, who was armed with a Harrington & Richardson 'Young America' double-action revolver chambered to fire five shots. This one was loaded with dum-dum bullets to cause the maximum damage to whomever they hit.

Perhaps Charlie Martin possessed a sixth sense (or more likely, he heard the screech of the cars' brakes) but he and his companions fled out of the pub's back door, leaving their drinks on the bar. And perhaps Ronnie Kray believed that Terry Martin, one of the four remaining people in the pub playing cards, was his adversary's brother, or perhaps he didn't care, but when he screamed, 'Come outside, or we'll kill you here!' it was Terry Martin who was dragged outside, where Ramsey kicked him and stabbed him twice in the back of his head with the bayonet – the wounds required eight stitches – and in his shoulder. Both the twins were involved in the assault; Reggie's jacket was soaked in blood.

The attackers left; there were still the rest of the Watney Streeters to be found and dealt with – and there was still Charlie Martin to be shot. As soon as the coast was clear, Terry Martin's companions conveyed him to hospital.

'I was an aid to CID working out of Limehouse', George Taylor told me, adding that at that time he and his partner, PC Freddie 'Mexy' Gamester, were night-duty CID which meant that they patrolled the whole of 'H' Division. 'A call came to the station indicating that a man had been admitted to the London Hospital suffering serious stab wounds. Fred and I went to the hospital and Fred persuaded the doctors to let him speak to the victim. The information gained led us to believe that the Krays were involved and the wounding had occurred outside a pub known as "The Ash Bucket" somewhere near Arbour Square.'

Taylor and his companion searched the area and found the Buick, which Taylor knew from a previous enquiry belonged to Ramsey, close to a billiard hall. Inside were Jones, Ramsey and the Krays – a search of the car revealed the miscellany of weapons and a search of Ronnie Kray revealed the mercifully unused revolver.

'Careful with it', entreated Ronnie. 'Can't you see it's loaded?'

Charged with inflicting grievous bodily harm, the four appeared at Thames Magistrates' Court. William Hemming appeared for Reggie Kray and requested bail, saying, 'One witness said both twins entered the public house while another said it was only one twin.'

'The difficulty is to know which one to give bail to', sighed the magistrate, Leo Gradwell, and to be on the safe side he remanded everyone in custody.

But now something went badly wrong – for the gang, that is. Terry Martin and the witnesses could not be straightened. At the Old Bailey, although Reggie Kray's initial explanation of the bloodstains on his jacket ('I 'ad a nosebleed') was changed to the possibility of blood being sprayed over him whilst watching boxers sparring, that, together with some clever defence work regarding the identity of the twins, was sufficient to bring about an acquittal in his case.

'A small dispute arose at the trial over the distance the car containing the weapons was from the billiard hall', George Taylor told me. It was a matter not previously discussed by him and Fred Gamester. 'I think I said about 200 yards; when the same question was asked of Fred, he replied, "As far as you could throw a cricket ball". After a short discussion, the judge (Sir Gerard Dodson) suggested we move on!'

Doc Blasker, who had a surgery in Docklands, could usually be relied upon to remove bullets and insert sutures without necessarily informing the authorities and he had known the twins from his days as an Amateur Boxing Association doctor. He was now called upon to provide a character reference for Ron, as was a local member of the clergy. Both were given short shrift by the judge.

So although Reg was free of the toils, the other three were not; and after Ronnie admitted unlawful possession of a loaded revolver, on 5 November 1956 he and Jones were each sentenced to three years' imprisonment. Ramsey's past now caught up with him. Although he had won thirty of his seventy-four bouts, he had received a pasting from Gillie van der Westhuizen during his final bout on 29 April 1947 in Johannesburg and at a loose end, still in South Africa, met up with Billy Hill. They had got involved in a fight, during which Ramsey had attacked his victim with a knife and a razor, slashing the back of his head and his buttocks which required the insertion of ninety-four stiches. Then, after Hill had skipped bail, Ramsey had been sentenced to five months' imprisonment – now he was sentenced to seven years.

Ramsey really was unlucky; he had already been knifed by Frankie Fraser and later would be savagely beaten up by his co-defendant, Ronnie Kray – the reasons for both attacks are unclear. It's only slightly amazing that he managed to outlive both the twins and died aged eighty-four in 2004.

★

Ronnie commenced his sentence at Winchester Prison but was later certified insane and transferred to Long Grove Hospital. Meanwhile, Reggie and brother Charles were running the Double R Club and making a resounding success of it. The club started welcoming celebrities: Dame Barbara Windsor, Jackie Collins, Queenie Watts. But Ronnie's plight pricked Reggie's conscience; being certified insane meant his brother might never be released. Instead of deciding this might be a blessing in disguise, he swapped places with Ronnie during a visit to the hospital; and during his six months of liberty, with Doc Blasker liberally supplying him with pills, the family finally and irrevocably came to the conclusion that Ronnie was not only as mad as a box of frogs but highly dangerous as well. Eventually, they gave him up to the despised police. He was not re-certified but was transferred back to prison and, now heavily dependent on Stematol, released in the spring of 1959.

As probationary Police Constable 398 'N', John Simmonds (later, head of the City of London's CID) patrolled the streets of Stoke Newington during the late 1950s. He and other uniformed officers were requested by the CID to report back on any activity in and around premises owned by local villains, so when he was passing such places he would take the opportunity to chat to the occupiers and, in police parlance, 'give his eyes a treat'. There was a spieler – an illegal gambling club – in Amhurst Road often used by taxi drivers, and Simmonds noticed that it was also frequented by 'two rather dapper brothers' who had moved into a block of art

deco flats in Cazenove Road and who drove a large black limou-
sine. As he told me:

> One night duty, I saw the limo drawing away from the
> club so I decided to pull them. The driver had all the cor-
> rect documents and they drove off; his name was Kray.
>
> A few days later, I was walking past the house of an
> old taxi cab driver I had got to know and he called out
> to me and asked me if I had pulled the twins, the other
> night. I didn't fall in straight away and then I realized
> he was talking about the black limo. I admitted I had
> stopped them and he said they were very angry about
> it. I expressed surprise, as I said to him they were very
> polite and I thought we had parted on good terms. He
> said, 'Maybe to your face, but you want to watch them;
> they're nasty people'. He used the spieler and obviously
> knew more than he was going to tell me.

Left to their own devices, Reg and Charlie could have stayed successful businessmen; crooks, certainly, but the violence could have
been kept to a minimum. They had proposed an alliance with
Albert Dimes and the Clerkenwell Italians which, given Dimes'
contacts with the US mafia, would have provided them with a toehold in the West End club scene. Ronnie ruined any such hopes at
the first meeting he attended with his brothers, telling their proposed partners that he didn't need any help from 'a bunch of cheap
Italians'; it looked as though plans for a profitable nightclub scene
were going straight out of the window.

'Curly' King, one of many known as 'The King of the Teddy
Boys', suggested to Ronnie, when referring to his skills at getting
an attack force together, 'You're just like a colonel.' Surprisingly
for someone who despised the army so much, Ron decided that he
liked the nickname and he was referred to thus ever after.

In the summer of 1959 Ronnie demanded a senseless confrontation with the Watney Streeters at the Hospital Tavern pub; he got
one, and Reg was with him as side-by-side they lashed out with
knives, knuckledusters and bicycle chains. The Watney Streeters
were routed, and when the police arrived to survey the blood-
spattered scene of broken glass, tables and chairs, the Krays had
vanished; there were no arrests.

With the twins' lifestyle spiralling out of control, Daniel Shay,
a car dealer who was beholden to the Krays, purchased an expensive briefcase from a shopkeeper named Murray Podro. Within a
few days he returned, told Podro he had been overcharged and

demanded £100 – that or a cutting in default. Podro informed the police, who were waiting two days later when Shay returned in company with Georgie Osbourne and Reg, who head-butted Podro in the face to reinforce the demand.

The Recorder of London, Sir Gerald Dodson – who had previously sentenced Ronnie to three years and had seen Reg acquitted – made Reg Kray's acquaintance once more at the Old Bailey. For the offence of demanding money with menaces, which carried a maximum sentence of life imprisonment, and knowing something of the Kray family's background, Sir Gerald dealt with the matter quite leniently – eighteen months' imprisonment each for Reg and Osbourne, three years for Shay. And with Reg safely tucked up in Wandsworth, this left Ron to do whatever he pleased.

★

In fact, Ron did not do very much. He dreamed his dreams of running an army of thugs throughout London and smoked incessantly; the profits from the Double R Club plummeted.

Reg, meanwhile, met two characters in Wandsworth who would later figure prominently in his and Ron's life. The first was Jack 'The Hat' McVitie, then serving seven years for robbery; the other was Frank 'The Mad Axeman' Mitchell, a huge, simple-minded, keep-fit fanatic with a ferocious temper, now serving a life sentence.

Appealing against his conviction, Reg was released on bail and with Ron made himself busy. They fell out with Perec 'Peter' Rachman, the slum landlord, and after he neglected to contribute to the Kray finances, his thugs were methodically beaten up. Johnny Hutton, a car dealer, introduced them to Leslie Payne – owing to his financial ability he would become known as 'Payne the Brain' – and they took over Esmeralda's Barn, a nightclub with a gaming room and restaurant in Wilton Place. They also found time to make their presence felt in the Pen Club murder before Reg's appeal failed and he went back to Wandsworth to serve the remaining six months of his sentence.

Ron was no businessman; he unwisely allowed credit to gamblers, and with violence creeping in, many of Esmeralda's Barn's clientele left to go elsewhere. Not that the club was losing money; a discotheque had been added, brother Charlie was assisting in the management and Ron, living in a pederast's heaven, was up to his armpits in dewy-eyed young men with long lashes. Then matters began to go badly wrong between the twins. Reg fell in love with a girl.

The object of his affections was Frances Shea; at sixteen, she was eleven years younger than Reg. She was completely unworldly, Reg was totally smitten and Ron loathed her on sight. Her father had run the gambling at the Regency Club in Stoke Newington in which the twins had an interest.

It was at this club that Mike Bucknole, then a fresh-faced eighteen-year-old police cadet, noticed the door lock was broken; when he looked inside he was confronted by a well-dressed, well-built man. Bucknole asked if he was the owner, and the man replied that he was. Bucknole now takes up the tale:

> [The man told me], 'We're not open, we've come to fix it and we're having a meeting'. I could see across the entrance hall that others, seated at a table, all 'hardened types', were now glaring across the room at me.
>
> 'Don't I know you?' said the first man. 'I saw you at York Hall a few weeks ago, didn't I? Don't you box for the Old Bill?'
>
> He was right, as just before Christmas, I'd boxed for the Metropolitan Police at York Hall, Bethnal Green on a Repton Boxing Club night.
>
> 'I remember you, you got some promise, you had a right paste-up with a tall boy from Brixton, enjoyed it, gutsy fight.'
>
> 'Thanks', I said.
>
> Then one of the seated types, named Reg, said, 'Leave it Ron, he's a lightweight kid', to which I replied, 'No, mate, I box at light middleweight!'
>
> They all laughed and I left.

Recounting the tale back at Stoke Newington, Bucknole was told the identity of 'Ron' and 'Reg' and advised to keep out of the Regency club in future!

But business was booming: more clubs in the West End were being minded by the Krays, long firm frauds were perpetuated, foolish and vulnerable people blackmailed. At the same time, the twins were busying themselves with charities: boys clubs, old peoples' homes and hospitals. Hardly a week went by without the *East London Advertiser* proclaiming their 'generosity'. This was a fallacy – others contributed to the charities, not the Krays. And all the time they were surrounding themselves with more and more celebrities from the world of politics, show business and sport.

But now cracks were beginning to appear in the façade. Esmeralda's Barn had started losing money and soon it closed; Ronnie's violent behaviour was getting worse, with brandings and knifings, not that that concerned him. He had his newly established flat at Cedra Court, Walthamstow, where he threw wild parties. They were attended by the good and the great and the old and bold – and also a peer of the realm by the name of Lord Boothby.

When the *Sunday Mirror* proclaimed, 'PEER AND A GANGSTER: YARD ENQUIRY' in July 1964, it was hinted that the Commissioner, Sir Joseph Simpson KBE, was conducting a witch-hunt against homosexuals, which he truthfully denied. *Mirror* readers were probably disappointed to discover that the photograph described as 'THE PICTURE WE DARE NOT PRINT', later published in the *Daily Express*, simply depicted Lord Boothby and Ronnie Kray sitting on a sofa, both fully dressed.

Boothby sued, stating, 'I am not a homosexual' (in fact, he was actively bisexual) and was awarded damages of £40,000; Ronnie Kray received just an apology.

But an investigation was conducted, not into homosexual practices but into the activities of the Krays. Detective Chief Superintendent Fred Gerrard was in charge and his assistant was the new Detective Inspector at Commercial Street police station, Leonard 'Nipper' Read.

Read, a three-times winner of the Lafone boxing cup, had joined the police in 1947 and was a tremendous all-round detective who had also carried out undercover work and had assisted with the investigation into the Great Train Robbery. He formed his own team, mainly from the 'G' Division Aids squad, and set to work investigating attacks carried out by the Krays, while working hard to uncover witnesses for their long firm frauds. Read had his successes; after six months' work seventy people had been arrested and committed for trial – but the Krays were not amongst them.

Then it appeared that Read had made a breakthrough. Hew Cargill McCowan, the son of a baronet, was the owner of the Hideaway Club in Gerrard Street He complained that the Krays were pressurizing him for protection money, and this claim was substantiated when one of their associates, Edward Richard 'Mad Teddy' Smith, arrived at the club and began smashing it up.

When he was ejected, he shouted to McCowan, 'You bastard! You know who I am – you know me and my friends! I'll be back to wreck the fucking joint!'

When McCowan complained to the twins he was blandly informed that all this could have been avoided by having one of their men on the door – in return for 20 per cent of the weekly profits. McCowan and his manager, Sidney Thomas Vaughan, both made statements to the police and Read decided to wait no longer. The twins and Teddy Smith were arrested and charged with blackmail.

Whilst they were in the cells at City Road police station, Mike Bucknole met Ronnie Kray for a second time. Kray asked him for a cup of tea and said, 'Still boxing at Repton?'

Bucknole told me, 'I told him no and thought, but you're still ducking and diving and bugger me, don't these villains commit faces to memory!'

Now that the twins were charged and remanded in custody, Read firmly believed that other witnesses would rush forward to give evidence, but he was wrong; not one of them did.

The twins tried repeatedly for bail, and Boothby campaigned on their behalf, all without success; but as always, strings and strokes were being pulled. Three days prior to committal, Vaughan was seen entering the twins' house in Vallance Road Immediately thereafter, two of the twins' gang emerged and set off in a car, only to return shortly afterwards with the local vicar, the Revd Albert Edward John Foster. Read had Vaughan brought into his office, to discover that he had declared in the presence of the priest that his former statement was a pack of lies and that McCowan had been paying him £40 per week to perjure himself at the trial. He repeated this at the Magistrates' Court but, incredibly, the case was committed for trial.

A man named Peter Byrne, a friend of Vaughan's, was attacked and slashed by four men, one of whom said, 'No – McCowan only wants him frightened.' He later gave evidence to that effect.

Manny Fryde, the solicitor who had triumphantly produced Jimmy Nash to the police for the Pen Club Murder five years earlier, now acted for the twins. On the second day of the trial, when McCowan was giving evidence (and giving it well), Fryde approached the judge, Sir Carl Aarvold OBE, TD, and in the absence of the jury stated that a witness had heard one of the jurors discussing the case with a police officer. He then identified the juror, whom the judge told to stand down.

The juror was flabbergasted. 'I would like to express an opinion on this', he told the judge, who replied, 'Please don't. Please leave the matter where it is.'

But the juror would not. 'As this aspersion has been cast', he persisted, 'I would like to know in what manner?'

However, the judge was adamant, and the trial continued with eleven jurors. This was a pity. He had not identified the witness or the detective and had not questioned the juror. Although Carl Aarvold was a well respected lawyer and judge, with an excellent war record in the Royal Artillery, he had permitted Fryde to thoroughly bamboozle him and had swallowed the accusation hook, line and sinker. The case for the prosecution was going too well and the juror had looked too intelligent; hence the accusation. When the angry juror was questioned by Read afterwards he stated quite unequivocally that he had not discussed the case with a detective or anybody else.

McCowan, meanwhile, was still giving persuasive evidence in the witness box; however, it emerged that he was homosexual and had given evidence in three other blackmail trials which centred around his sexuality.

Vaughan repeated that the twins had never threatened McCowan; in fact, he went further and stated that when McCowan wanted a man 'cut up' he provided Ronnie Kray with the man's name and address.

Next came the Revd Foster, who told the court that he had visited Ronnie Kray in Brixton Prison on the morning of 20 January and had later gone to Vallance Road In a story slightly at variance to that of the watching detectives, he stated that he had gone into a back room, where he saw Vaughan, Charles Kray and a William Noble, a police officer for twenty years and now an enquiry agent.

The Revd Foster told the jury:

> Mr Noble said, 'This young man [pointing to Sidney Vaughan] says he has given some evidence to the police about the Kray brothers which was not true.' There was a long conversation and Sidney was asked whether he had actually heard the Kray brothers actually demanding money and he replied that he had not. Mr Noble asked Sidney whether he was willing to give evidence in court and so perjure himself. Sidney said he was getting £40 a week financial aid and if he did not give this evidence, that financial aid was going to be cut off. He said the money was coming from someone whose name sounded like 'McGowan'. Sidney added that he had two flats to keep and a wife and child to support. Mr Noble also asked him if he was frightened that the Krays might take reprisals if he did give perjured evidence and Sidney said he was not frightened of the Krays at all.

In cross-examination, John Mathew QC for the prosecution assumed that the reverend gentleman immediately advised the penitent Mr Vaughan to tell this story to the police, but he did not – nor did he go to the police himself. And neither did the erstwhile copper, Mr Noble, who was called next. He corroborated the vicar's story and added that Charlie Kray had soothingly told Vaughan, 'Just tell the truth Sidney, that's all', with Vaughan replying, 'That's not so easy when you're dealing with McCowan', and adding for good measure that McCowan was a pathological liar.

In a particularly hilarious episode of the case, the judge told the jury, 'Do not make the mistake of thinking that Vaughan has been got at by the defence; that would be quite improper.'

After four hours deliberation the jury were unable to agree upon a verdict and a retrial was ordered eleven days later, this time before Mr Justice Lyell. Vaughan was not called, McCowan's evidence was trashed, great weight being placed on his homosexuality, and the case collapsed when, at the invitation of the judge, the jury found the three men not guilty.

An application for costs was refused, but the twins still had sufficient spare change to buy the Hideaway Club on the afternoon of their acquittal; they renamed it El Morocco.

The three brothers must have now assumed that they could walk on water. They arrived back in Bethnal Green to the sort of tumultuous reception that one associates with a returning and victorious premier league football team. They talked about suing the police for wrongful arrest, but never did so. They made all sorts of reckless promises about their immediate future, all untrue save one: Reg said that he and Frances would marry – and they did.

*

Having already helped the twins quite considerably, Father Foster officiated at the no-expenses-spared wedding of Reg Kray and Frances Shea on 20 April 1965. The glitterati of the East End turned out in their droves to congratulate the allegedly happy couple. After a joyless honeymoon in Athens they moved into a flat in Cedra Court, one floor below Ronnie's; they stayed there for just eight weeks before Frances returned to live with her parents. It was claimed that the marriage was unconsummated; Frances would later receive psychiatric treatment and there would be attempts at suicide.

Pat Pryde knew the twins from her time as the CID typist at Dalston; when she took tea into the interview room, she told me, 'They always stood up when I came into the room and took the tray off me.' She occasionally drank at the Regency Club, where, she told me, 'They treated me with respect.' She also met Frances Kray, whom she described as being very attractive: 'She was always like a nervous little mouse and so badly matched with her gangster husband. I always used to think of a lamb led to the slaughter when I saw her.'

And now we have to leave pretty, unhappy and ultimately doomed Frances Kray, together with her equally unhappy husband and her malevolent brother-in-law, (whom she referred to, behind his back, as 'a pig') and who had screamed at his sibling to 'throw that fucking woman out for good'.

We shall return to them later, but now it's time to introduce you to the brothers Richardson.

CHAPTER 15

The Richardsons

Throughout the pages of this book there have been tales of utterly sickening brutality and violence, from Billy Hill ('I'm one of the best chiv merchants in the business') stripping his victims with a razor, to the antics of Ronnie Kray, who delighted in slashing adversaries across his buttocks with a cutlass ('So they'll think of me every time they sit down').

But those cruelties are put in the shade by the depravity of the Richardson Torture Gang; witnesses told the court how Charlie Richardson presided at mock-trials where they were hit with a variety of what were colloquially referred to as 'blunt instruments' before being stripped, whipped with barbed wire, had their teeth pulled out with pliers, had cigarettes stubbed out on their bare flesh and their genitals connected to an electricity generator. Sometimes victims would be immersed in water to make the electric shocks more acute. And eventually, sometimes after a period of hours during which time Richardson would often munch his way through fish and chips, when the bleeding, terrified victim regained consciousness and was finally allowed home, he would be given a joking apology and what became known as 'a shirt from Charlie' to cover his partial nakedness.

Richardson's brother Eddie, who later – much later – stated that he derived pleasure out of inflicting pain, also admitted, 'Charlie liked to stretch things out.'

Mr Justice Lawton put things rather differently. Referring to the victims, he told Charlie Richardson, 'You terrorized them in a way that was vicious, sadistic and a disgrace to society.'

This is what happened.

★

When Charles William Richardson was fourteen, in 1948, his father abandoned the Camberwell family home, leaving him and his mother to bring up his two younger brothers and a sister. The father's desertion coincided with Charlie going right off the rails and he took to stealing lead and cars as a duck takes to water. Although he got friends to arrange a false alibi for him (probably not for the first and certainly not the last time) on a charge of stealing a car, it failed, and this ensured Charlie's admittance to

Approved School, one of those institutions where the authorities harboured an often forlorn hope of reform. Forlorn it certainly was in Charlie's case, since he escaped and committed further offences.

Charlie and his brother Edward George Richardson – 'Eddie' – both boxed at the Fitzroy Club, where Eddie fought, first as a welterweight, later as a middleweight.

By the time he was seventeen Charlie had acquired a lorry and commenced trading in scrap metal; a year later, he was called up for National Service. Like the Krays (whom he later met in Shepton Mallet), he fought against the system; he was sentenced to six months for assaulting a medical officer and dishonourably discharged.

Rather than have his brother endure the same rigours of National Service, when Eddie's call-up papers arrived Charlie carefully instructed him in the art of appearing to be mentally defective to the medical board; it worked.

Charlie was placed on probation for two years for receiving stolen metal and then, a year after his discharge from the army, he married Margaret Cheyney. The following year, 1956, he founded the Peckford Scrap Metal Company in New Church Road, Camberwell. He also met Roy Hall, a teenager who was stealing metal from his yard. He gave him a job there, and ten years later, a judge at the Old Bailey would tell Hall, 'Right from school you came under the domination of Charles Richardson and but for his evil influence you would not be here.' Eddie was initially also an employee at the yard, then a year later became a co-director.

Charlie was convicted twice more: in 1957 he was fined £80 for receiving stolen metal and in 1959 he was sentenced to six months' imprisonment for receiving stolen bacon.

Seven years after their marriage, and five children later, Charlie's wife walked out on him. He took custody of the children and moved in with Jean Goodman, with whom he had started an affair. She started work in the office, checking the books and sorting out administrative details. His company, which soon employed thirty men, was actually a front for receiving stolen property, as were many of his other business concerns.

Newcomers to the area were put straight. When John Barnes arrived on 'L' Division as a brand new detective constable, he was seen by a senior officer who told him, 'You've got a good record; you're going to Camberwell, boy. When you get there, you're to have no dealings with the Peckford Scrap Metal Company – IS THAT CLEAR?'

Barnes, who had just arrived from Cannon Row, next door to the Houses of Parliament, and had never heard of the company or its owners, replied, 'Yes, sir!' and was dismissed, having first been told, 'I drink Scotch!'

Bryan Woolnough told me that Charlie could always be contacted at his mother's address (she lived in a block of flats in Denmark Hill). 'When the CID needed to interview him, they just phoned for him, and he always turned up at the station, saying, "CID want to see me",' he told me. 'He was always well-dressed, spoke well and had the appearance of a businessman. He always appeared to co-operate and was always pleasant, a clever person.'

Woolnough recalled being the duty officer who called at Peckham police station to be told of a car being seen in suspicious circumstances during the hours of darkness; he discovered that the users of the vehicle had entered a branch of Sainsbury's and were just about to blow the safe. In those days a manual search had to be made for a vehicle's owner at the London County Council offices, and this took a considerable time. Woolnough told me:

> In those days, professional criminals had a system of maintaining regular phone contact whilst 'doing a job', and if a call was missed, their accomplices would know something had gone wrong. The men had no identification on them and said nothing for over twelve hours. Eventually, we were notified of the car ownership details. Surprise, surprise! It belonged to the Richardsons, but during the delay it had, of course, been reported stolen before we could take any action to implicate them in the crime.

Charlie was lucky on that occasion, but then he was arrested once more for receiving stolen metal; he jumped bail and fled with Jean Goodman to Canada, where he set up another scrap metal business. After eight months he returned to England, was recognized and arrested, but clever lawyers got him out of an embarrassing charge.

Charlie took Jean Goodman and his youngest brother, Alan, out for a speedboat trip on the Thames. Due to his stupid and reckless handling of the speedboat, it overturned, throwing them all into the water. Charlie and Jean Goodman survived; Alan did not. It was a passing pleasure boat that rescued them. Naturally, Charlie was in no way to blame; it was all the captain of the pleasure boat's fault.

His relationship with his brother Eddie was not always an easy one and was not helped by the presence of Jean Goodman. Charlie's children openly detested her, Roy Hall felt the same, and for a while Charlie and Eddie diversified and opened various businesses, most of which were long firm frauds.

The term 'long firm' (or LF) has been mentioned several times before in this book; it was a crime which was profitable to the Krays as well and the way it worked was this. A wholesale business would be set up, with a front-man as manager. Goods for which there was a ready market – washing machines, refrigerators, televisions etc. – would be ordered from various manufacturers, and as soon as they arrived the invoice was settled, immediately. This would continue for several months, with the manufacturers being paid on delivery of each shipment, giving them the impression that they were dealing with a reputable company. Finally, a huge order would be placed, the goods sold at knock-down prices and the front man would desert the empty warehouse, leaving the manufacturers with a colossal deficit. By the time it was reported to the police and investigated, months, sometimes years, would have passed; if the front-man was arrested, he would say nothing – and if he was convicted, he alone would go to prison for a couple of years. His silence would have been bought by means of a handsome bursary; or, more probably, by threats made against his family.

One such LF involved several thousand Olivetti typewriters; over a period of six months it was investigated by two officers from the Fraud Squad, one of whom was Detective Constable (and later Chief Superintendent) Max Vernon. He told me:

> We kept observations at Peckford Metals several times, noting the numbers of cars coming and going. On each occasion, we were followed back by Richardson's men, to see where we went. Eventually, we interviewed Charlie Richardson at Snow Hill police station, in the City of London. He was smarmy; seemed very much at ease and thought a lot of himself. He didn't have a brief and didn't answer many questions, most of which were 'no comment' on the contentious stuff. He was arrested and charged and was committed for trial from Bow Street He represented himself; he had no idea of what sort of questions to ask and made himself look ridiculous.

I asked Vernon his impressions of Charlie Richardson.

'I didn't like him at all', he replied. 'I thought he was a little shit.'

Since I knew Richardson was five feet ten and a half, I did question the first of these epithets, only to discover that there was some justification for it after Vernon admitted to being six feet four.

'However', he added, 'I wouldn't have liked to have got on the wrong side of him!'

Charlie – who held all coppers, bent or straight in the greatest contempt – did his best to ingratiate himself with the law; Eddie did not. By now, Eddie had married and moved into a house in Sidcup Road, Eltham, and it was there that Keith 'Chalky' White, a very new young copper at Eltham police station, was told by his sergeant – obviously to test his subordinate's mettle – to serve a summons on Eddie for running a red light. Having no idea who he was dealing with, White drove up on his Velocette motor cycle and when he told Eddie's wife the nature of his business, she shouted, 'Eddie, there's a young copper at the door who wants to serve a summons on you.'

The reply came, 'Tell him to fuck off!'

White responded that he would not leave until the summons was served, and this brought Eddie to the door saying, 'It'll take more than you, you cunt, now fuck off!'

White then told him that there was a radio on his motor cycle and if necessary he could call up 21,000 more coppers. This made Eddie laugh; he accepted the summons and then told the young copper once more to 'Fuck off!'

Back at the police station, White was asked if he'd served the summons.

'No trouble', was his reply. 'He was as good as gold!'

Eddie had branched out once more; he and Frankie Fraser, now released from his seven-year sentence for slashing Jack Spot, with the assistance of £5,000 courtesy of Billy Hill, set up a wholesale business in one-armed bandits, which they leased to club owners for a percentage of the takings and the tacit acceptance of protection.

Anybody who upset the Richardsons was subjected to a mock trial with Charlie Richardson as judge. The victims were punched, kicked, stripped, humiliated and jeered at by the gang. Toes were broken, one victim was knifed through the foot and yet another was nailed up under floorboards, made to eat excrement and then sodomized. And yet, amidst this degradation there was occasionally black gallows humour. Much later in court, when a witness gave evidence of his appalling mistreatment, one of the barristers told him, 'You are, thankfully, one of the few witnesses for the Crown not to claim you had electrodes attached to your genitals.'

'Oh, but they did use electricity on my testicles', was the reply. 'I didn't mention it because I thought they were trying to revive me!'

Matters came to a head in July 1965. Perhaps Charlie Richardson thought that James Taggart was, as he suggested, a police informer, or he owed Richardson £1,200, or perhaps these were just excuses for a session of exemplary depravity. Taggart was seen by a fellow gang member Alfred Berman in Richardson's office – naked, tied to a chair, in a pool of blood and with blood splattering the walls. He was hardly recognizable as a human being: his head, eyes and ears were all swollen and his body had been battered. Richardson was out of control, shouting, screaming and punching and kicking Taggart, whilst Fraser was hitting him with a pair of pliers.

After that terrifying encounter with Charlie Richardson and his cohorts Taggart, frightened of another, went to the police. And not the Metropolitan Police, either; he believed that the Richardsons had so many corrupt officers on their payroll that he drove to the headquarters of Hertfordshire Constabulary at Welwyn Garden City. The man he wanted to speak to was the assistant chief constable and the head of No 5 Regional Crime Squad; his name was Gerald McArthur.

★

Gerald Elwyn McArthur was then forty-nine years of age. Leaving his home town of Newport, Monmouthshire at the age of nineteen, he joined the Metropolitan Police in 1935 and became a member of the CID in 1939. Within two years he had volunteered for service with the wartime RAF; four years later, he was demobilized with the rank of flight lieutenant and resumed service with the Metropolitan Police. Promotions came in jumps of four years; by the time he transferred to the Hertfordshire Constabulary on 30 April 1964, he had achieved the rank of detective superintendent, taken a decisive part in the Great Train Robbery investigation and collected a mixed bag of commendations from the commissioner. He was a tremendous all-round detective – he had been congratulated for arresting receivers and shopbreakers, an armed criminal and gangs of crooks variously described as 'active' and 'violent'; when the Fraud Squad opened its doors in 1946, he had been snapped up. Those who committed offences of false pretences and fraudulent conversion or who conspired to defraud were also mopped up by McArthur. There was no aspect of criminal investigation in which he flagged, he was hugely admired by his contemporaries and there was one other crucial facet to his character: Taggart had gone to him because he knew that McArthur was a completely straight copper. It was a prudent move.

McArthur was appalled by what Taggart had to tell him. He made what enquiries he could to corroborate Taggart's story without arousing suspicion and then just before Christmas 1965 took his information to the Yard. This would not have been to Taggart's liking, but it was the nature of the beast. McArthur could see the wide-ranging ramifications of such an enquiry. The manpower, the equipment, the costs of such a massive investigation would be enormous; not something that could be borne by just one of the nine Regional Crime Squads or a single constabulary.

So he conferred with the Assistant Commissioner (Crime), Peter Ewan Brodie OBE, QPM, the CID Commander, John du Rose and the National Regional Crime Squad coordinator, Commander John Bliss, and the investigation commenced at Tintagel House on the Thames Embankment, well away from the Yard. Just twenty detectives, specially selected for their trustworthiness, were involved.

Gwyn Waters was a detective sergeant (first-class) attached to the Flying Squad – he described McArthur to me as 'Brilliant. Criminals were terrified of him' – who had suddenly been called in to see John du Rose. His initial reaction, as he told me, was, 'What have I done?' He need not have worried; he was one of the Metropolitan Police officers seconded to the enquiry because his honesty was beyond question.

Another was John Simmonds, who as a second-class detective sergeant was seconded from the Met to the No 5 Regional Crime Squad at Old Harlow in Essex in September 1965. He told me how, after a couple of months, he was summoned to McArthur's office – he was known as 'Mr Mac' – at Welwyn Garden City:

No explanation was given, just be there at 10.00 am. Mr Mac welcomed me into his office and then started to go over my police career and postings. He questioned my knowledge of 'names' of various villains, and then casually asked me what I knew about the 'Richardsons' from South London. I sussed out that this was the purpose of the meeting and was gutted that apart from vaguely knowing their names, they were a team that I knew nothing about. I apologised to Mr Mac saying that my contacts were basically North and North East London and I could not help him. He smiled at me and said that was what he thought but he wanted to make sure. He then swore me to secrecy and told me that he was about to undertake an investigation into the Richardsons and he wanted to build up a small team to investigate their activities. He said there were a number of witnesses who were prepared to assist him but only after the Richardsons were arrested.

I went with Mr Mac to an address in North London where we spoke to a potential witness. He was a professional man who had become embroiled with the Richardsons; he was extremely nervous and reluctant to talk to us. Mr Mac spent a long time talking to the man before he eventually agreed to make a statement and I wrote it down. The man had a medical background and had been 'required' by the Richardsons to treat a victim who had been tortured by them. The victim, according to the witness, had been systematically beaten about the head over a long period of time (some days) with wet knotted towels, the victim's head was swollen to twice its size but no skin had broken. The witness said that in all his years in medicine he had never seen such an injury and was amazed that the head could swell to the extent that it had. Mr Mac promised him that he would not be called to give evidence unless the Richardsons were in custody.

Over the next few weeks I met a number of other witnesses all speaking of barbaric acts of torture by the Richardsons while they were terrorized into working criminal scams on behalf of them. Some were just beaten up, others were subjected to a variety of body mutilations, including having electrodes attached to their genitals and finger and toe nails being ripped off with pliers.

The Richardsons seemed to prey on people who were already acting criminally and were therefore reluctant or unable to go to the police because they would have to implicate themselves. The Richardsons had a good nose for ferreting these people out and once they got their victim they then forced them to continue their criminal activity but took the proceeds from the victim leaving them to face the music when the police eventually caught up with them.

Sadly, the witnesses also mentioned that there were a number of police officers who were 'on the books' of the Richardsons. Hence Mr Mac's caution in forming his team.

Du Rose issued the strict instruction that if any member of the team suspected any officer of having corrupt relations with any of the Richardson gang, it was to be reported to him immediately. By the time the enquiry was completed, the squad had swollen to a total of 310 officers.

Many of the victims and witnesses in the investigation were on the wrong side of the law; therefore corroboration was essential. Curiously, one confirmation came from a distance of 5,638 miles away from London.

On 29 June 1965 a mining prospector named Thomas Holmes Waldeck was shot dead at his home in Melrose, Johannesburg, South Africa. He had been involved in a business deal with Charlie Richardson, who had invested £200,000, and Waldeck had made the mistake of swindling him. Retribution was required, and it came in the form of a Richardson gang member and fellow torturer, Laurence Johnny Bradbury.

Bradbury was arrested, convicted and sentenced to death. But he was reprieved, and when the Yard's Detective Chief Inspector Arthur Rees flew out to South Africa to interview him, Bradbury started talking. He did so for several weeks, and what he had to say was highly disturbing – and enlightening. It fitted in exactly with what Taggart had said six months earlier.

But while McArthur's detectives were cobbling together a blueprint for the Richardsons' prosecution, something happened which would herald the beginning of the end of their rule and it happened at a venue known as Mr Smith's Club.

CHAPTER 16

The Murder at Mr Smith's Club

When in August 1964 Eddie Richardson rammed a broken glass into the face of Peter 'The Greek' Joannides, who was managing the gambling tables at the Horseshoe Club in Southport, after he and Frank Fraser had paid the club a visit, he must, like many others of his ilk, have felt as though he was invincible after the local magistrates threw the case out. It was the same old story: witnesses were threatened, bribed and conveniently lost their memories. The deputy head of the Labour Party, George Brown MP (later Lord George-Brown of Jevington PC), together with former wartime SAS soldier, Captain Henry Briton Kerby MP, called upon the Home Secretary, Henry Brooke (later Lord Brooke of Cumnor CH, PC), to hold an investigation into the allegations by police of the intimidation of witnesses. However, Brooke – controversial and hugely ineffective (he had been a fervent supporter of Neville Chamberlain which speaks volumes for his character) – declined; but in any event, those who had changed their stories in court (one witness actually stated that Joannides was the antagonist) were hardly likely to change them back again.

What Eddie Richardson had done before – and got away with – he obviously felt he could do again. It happened nineteen months later at Mr Smith's Club – or to give it its proper title, Mr Smith and the Witchdoctor's Club – in Catford, South London in March 1966.

'It was originally known as the Savoy Ballroom, which was frequented at the weekends by many of the residents of Blackheath Road Section House, so it was always crawling with fit young coppers', Ron Cork told me. However, matters were about to change.

The club had been opened six months previously by the film star Diana Dors and initially it was well run, with gambling and a dance floor; when guests were requested to leave at 2.00 am, they did.

The head of the CID at Catford was the very well informed Detective Superintendent John Cummings; well informed because he had headed the Criminal Intelligence Branch, which had opened its doors six years previously. He had an extensive knowledge of criminals, especially the South London variety, and he still kept in contact with his successors at the Yard; what was more, he had heard that a move would be made to demand protection money from the club.

On the evening of 7 March, Richardson came to the club to discuss matters of 'security', as he put it. Amongst others who joined his group were Frank Fraser, Ronald Jeffrey, William Stayton, Henry Rawlins and Jimmy Moody.

Sitting, as it were, on the opposite side of the fence were Richard 'Dickie' Hart (who had just been released from a prison sentence), Harry Haward, Henry Botton, Peter Hennessy and William Gardner; the first two were armed, Haward with a sawn-off shotgun, Hart with a .45 Colt automatic.

During the evening the atmosphere grew more and more tense; more men arrived to take their places with one or other of the opposing teams, until there were approximately sixteen in all.

Two o'clock came and went; by three o'clock most of the staff had left and then Eddie Richardson told Haward and his team, 'Right, drink up – that's your lot.'

Not unnaturally, Haward disagreed and there was some agitated conversation before Peter Hennessy told Richardson, 'Ah, fuck you, you cunt. I'm going to help myself', and reached for a bottle.

As he did so, Richardson smashed his glass on the table – although a slightly different account was given by Janet Tripp, a croupier at the club. She stated, 'Richardson stood up and this blond fellow who had been sitting at the other table, swearing, stood up and he hit Eddie Richardson who fell backwards. As he fell, his fist which was holding a glass hit the table and the glass broke.'

But whatever the sequence of events, a battle royal now commenced; tables were overturned, chairs were thrown, glasses were smashed, Hart loosed off shots from his automatic, hitting Harry Rawlins in his left arm, and Haward was struck on top of his head with 'a blunt object'.

Hart dropped his gun and ran out of the club's rear entrance into Farley Road, closely pursued by Fraser and others. Ronald Jeffrey also arrived in Farley Rd; he collected a blast from a shotgun in his groin. Eddie Richardson, too, was hit by shotgun pellets in his leg and buttocks.

Stayton, who was found in a garden nearby, said in the second of two differing statements to the police, 'Hart was the only one with a gun and was the one who started the shooting. Hart shot Fraser in the leg outside the club.'

Matters were certainly confused; at some stage Henry Botton shouted, 'You're fucking mad, Frank!'

Frank Fraser lay moaning in a front garden, his thigh bone shattered by a bullet. He was found to be lying on top of an automatic pistol, the one used to shoot Richard Hart in the back. As he lay dying, Hart – whose jacket had been pulled down, thereby trapping his arms, before he was shot – had been kicked and a bottle had been smashed into his face.

Terrified residents telephoned the police to tell them of men fighting in the street and shots being fired. One of them was Andrew Henry Lowe, who was awakened by the sounds of shooting. He looked through his bedroom window and saw about twelve men, two of whom were holding guns. After a shot was discharged, Mr Lowe heard one of the men shout, 'God, you've shot him'. Another dragged an injured man by the arm towards Honley Road, threw him on the ground and, taking a gun from his waistband, pointed it at him. Mr Lowe heard him shout, 'Let me kill him – let me kill him!', and an unidentified man called out, 'Don't do that – that would be murder.'

Another resident, Mrs Margaret Beale, said, 'I was woken by bangs and saw two men dragging a third. One lifted him on to the other and they carried him towards Honley Road A dark-coloured Jaguar car parked in front of my house was driven away. I called the police giving them the number of the car.'

The car, driven by Moody, contained Richardson and Rawlins, who were taken to Dulwich Hospital, where the resident house surgeon, Dr Colin Alfred Tourle, saw Rawlins, whom he described as being 'shocked and ill from loss of blood and in danger of dying'. Eddie Richardson was arrested after having given the name 'George Ward', and the others followed.

At Lewisham Hospital the registrar, Dr Michael Cyril Pietroni, saw that Jeffrey had multiple shotgun pellet wounds in his thigh, groin and stomach; Fraser had been shot in the thigh with a larger bullet.

Richardson, Jeffrey, Haward, Moody, Rawlins and Botton were all charged with causing an affray and appeared at Woolwich Magistrates' Court; at a later hearing they were, incredibly, released on bail. Hennessy – who might be thought to have been the catalyst for what occurred and who the previous year had been acquitted of murder – was not charged because nobody named him. However, justice, in its roughest form was meted out some time later when he died after receiving multiple stab wounds. Patrick O'Nione ('a lovely guy') was acquitted of his murder; in turn O'Nione was shot twice, the second time fatally. Jimmy Davey was arrested for O'Nione's murder; before he could be charged, he died in police custody.

Meanwhile, Fraser and later Stayton (who had fled but was arrested on a Fugitive Offenders warrant in Gibraltar) appeared at Bow Street Magistrates' Court. Both were charged with affray and Fraser was additionally charged with the murder of Dickie Hart. When Detective Chief Superintendent Tommy Butler went to Lewisham hospital to interview Fraser, his solicitor, Fellowes, told him to ignore Butler and to put the headphones of his radio on.

Stayton was committed to be tried with the other six defendants; Fraser was committed for trial at the Old Bailey.

When charged with the murder, Fraser had replied, 'I'm completely innocent of this. It's perfectly ridiculous. I was not at the club. I had no gun. I took no part but I finished up a victim. I do not know who caused my injuries.'

That was all he did say; he had nothing to say at his trial and after legal submissions by the defence, Mr Justice Mocatta directed the jury to find him not guilty of the murder. However, on 24 June he was found guilty on the affray charge and, sentencing him to five years' imprisonment, the judge told him:

> This was an extremely serious and shameful affray but there is no evidence that you used or carried a weapon of any sort. Your record is a bad one and your last conviction was wounding with intent for which you were sentenced to seven years' imprisonment.

Meanwhile, Charlie Richardson was in South Africa, where he had already met and bedded the glamorous Jean La Grange, the wife of a business associate; hearing of his brother's plight, he resolved to return immediately to ensure that he would not be convicted and imprisoned. He could hardly be faulted for not trying hard enough, because he set to work with a will.

★

The trial of Eddie Richardson and his six co-defendants opened at the Old Bailey before the Common Serjeant, Mr Justice Griffith-Jones, on 1 July, one week after Fraser's conviction.

Approaches were made to the jury, but the judge directed that the case should continue, telling the jury, as judges always do, to 'put this out of your minds'. However, the judge ordered that the jury should receive police protection and stated:

> I propose to request the police to take every possible step, not only to discover who is doing this, but also to ensure that no other incident of this kind can occur.

The four-week trial ended on 26 July with the jury unable to agree on verdicts in respect of Richardson, Stayton and Moody in the September sessions. Haward and Botton were found guilty and the following day both were sentenced to five years for causing an affray, with Haward receiving an additional three years for being in possession of a loaded shotgun.

On 12 September the retrial of the three men started. After two weeks Stayton and Moody were acquitted but Eddie Richardson was found guilty of affray. Judge Aarvold told him, 'There was evil afoot in the club that night and you were prepared to play your full part in it', and sentenced him, like the others, to five years' imprisonment.

Neither Charlie Richardson nor Johnnie Longman attempted to nobble the jurors or suborn the witnesses at the retrial, nor did they attend court. They had been unavoidably detained. Six weeks previously, they – and quite a lot of other people – had been well and truly nicked and were now in prison, on remand.

CHAPTER 17

The Torture Trial

On 18 May 1966, in the lead-up to his arrest, Charlie Richardson had divorced his wife; he also obtained a flat for Jean La Grange. Two months later, their affair was discovered by Jean Goodman and after a tremendous row she flounced out of his life, forever, as she thought; in fact, their separation lasted exactly fifteen days.

Charlie maintained that the night before his arrest he was forewarned by a go-between or a bent copper – stories differ between him and his biographer, but at any rate he was expecting the police on the morning of 30 July 1966. The arrest, he believed, would be a fit-up; it would probably cost him a couple of grand to brush off this latest peccadillo. So when the police arrived, he could hear them downstairs and pretended to be asleep. As they entered his bedroom, embarrassed and whispering to each other, he appeared to wake up and smilingly demanded, 'And who the fuck are you?'

Then, according to his memoirs, he sat up in his pyjamas and contemptuously told them, 'The kettle's downstairs; mine's with two sugars.'

So that was Richardson's version of events of that momentous day. Did he receive advance warning of his arrest? I doubt it, although it's clear that he did have bent coppers on his payroll. But just for the record, what happened was this.

On the morning of the arrest, Gwyn Waters entered Richardson's house; the back door had not been locked, so he let in McArthur and Fred Gerrard, then went into the bedroom and shook Richardson, who was sound asleep, awake. He stripped off the sheet which was covering him, to find that he was just wearing underpants – 'And they were filthy', Waters told me. 'The whole house was filthy.' There were no smart, contemptuous remarks from Richardson; he was simply stunned.

He wasn't the only one; John Simmonds was one of those tasked to arrest Roy Hall and he recounted what happened:

> We were briefed in the early hours of the morning at Tintagel House; I was allotted to Detective Superintendent Vic Evans' team with seven other officers. I was partnered to a DC from Hertfordshire and I think Evans thought I was also from Hertfordshire. We went mob-handed to the address we

had for our target but he was not there. Evans had an 'intelligence' sheet of contacts and other addresses for our man and was proposing to visit them. There were two brothers of our target at the address; I spoke to one of them and he 'volunteered' where his brother was. When I told Evans he said it was not on his intelligence sheet and proposed to visit the other addresses first. As I was convinced that the brother had not lied to me, I persuaded Evans to let me and the DC from Hertfordshire to go to the address.

On our arrival the door was answered by a small boy; he said his Dad was in bed. We rushed upstairs to find our target in his vest and underpants; he launched himself at us like a rat trying to escape through the door. We threw him back on to the bed and after a struggle managed to handcuff him; the prisoner calmed down, we searched the house and in the lounge we found a fully loaded handgun clearly placed in a strategic location and I have no doubts had he not been handcuffed, the prisoner would have used it.

In a twelve-hour operation nine other people had been arrested and taken to West End Central police station. They were Jean Goodman (who would be charged under the name of Richardson), Albert John Longman, Derek Brian Mottram, Robert Geoffrey St Leger, James Thomas Fraser (the nephew of Frankie), James Henry Kensitt, Thomas James Clark, Brian Morse and Alfred Abraham Berman, and they faced sixteen charges – not all of them for the same offences – of inflicting grievous bodily harm with intent to do so, demanding money with menaces, conspiracy to defraud, robbery with violence and assault. McArthur had done his work well; and that was just for starters.

Charlie Richardson invariably described all the detectives with whom he had dealings as being bent, stupid, overweight, sweaty, with green, rotting teeth and foul breath; but no one even vaguely resembling that description entered his cell to cop a couple of grand and let him off the hook.

No. That same day, England won the World Cup against West Germany, and when the BBC's commentator, Kenneth Wolstenholme, uttered those prescient words, 'They think it's all over . . . it is now!' he might also have been referring to Charlie Richardson's reign of terror.

For the man who had been acquitted of receiving stolen goods on no less than fourteen separate occasions, it really was all over.

★

Now the job began of protecting the witnesses. As John Simmonds explained:

> These were not normal witnesses, i.e. run of the mill citizens who had witnessed an event and reported it to police, but witnesses who themselves had been engaged in criminal activities and were now giving evidence against other criminals. In the eyes of the criminal fraternity they were 'grasses' and were hated by all criminals. It followed then that, once their identities were known, the witnesses were at risk of attack by any criminal. In 1966 there was no witness protection system and we were thrown in at the deep end.
>
> Each witness was offered 24-hour police protection and depending on their location the nearest officer to them was assigned as their bodyguard. As I lived in Potters Bar I was assigned to Benny Wajcenberg, who lived in Edmonton. The arrangement was that during the week he had a uniformed constable outside his home from 6.00 pm to 8.00 am and I would take over from 8.00 am when he went to work to whenever he came home – very often nearer to midnight than 6.00 pm. At weekends he had 24-hour uniformed police cover.
>
> Although we were assigned as 'bodyguards' it was rather a joke, we were not armed and had no radio or telephone. Any concerted effort to take Benny out would have been child's play and of course I was obviously going to be taken out with him. In 1966 detective officers were expected to dress smartly, i.e. suit, collar and tie, so in my opinion any gangster coming looking for Benny would spot me as dressed like a detective and would have probably taken me out first. It took me about two days to realize my vulnerability so I quickly dressed to blend in with the location and started to 'work' on the premises as if I was an employee. Soon people visiting the premises assumed that I was a worker there and I did my best not to draw attention to myself.
>
> Being right in the East End my biggest fear was that, despite their known animosity, the Krays might still take out 'Benny the grass' on behalf of the Richardsons and gain kudos from it. I expressed this fear to Billy Ackerman, Benny's partner. Billy was a known associate of the Krays and thought they were great guys. He told me that the twins knew Benny was on their 'manor' and that I was

there and he said that I was safe from them as they were not going to help the Richardsons.

Guarding Benny was no picnic, I had a telephone call from the station officer at Edmonton police station one weekend complaining that Benny had climbed out of his bathroom window and gone into the local pub and got drunk while the PC was standing outside his house 'protecting' him. The first the PC knew of it was when Benny came rolling up the street, well drunk.

Benny liked his scotch and many an evening after work we reverted to the pub where he drank scotch as if it was going out of fashion. I limited myself to shandies and had to deliver him home, inebriated. Maria, his second wife, used to get very angry with him and accuse him of consorting with women and Benny always used to say to me, 'Johnny, never marry your mistress.'

Whenever he had business meetings away from Fashion Street I used to take him in my car; although I was in attendance on the premises I was very rarely au fait with the transactions, but I knew Benny to be a wheeler-dealer and sometimes we brought cloth etc. back with us in my car. I told Benny that if I ever found out he had put stolen stuff in my car I would 'nick' him. I think he recognized I was serious.

However, at the outset I had a personal briefing from Mr Mac who informed me that I needed to be very careful with Ben, there was an International Arrest warrant out for him and Mr Mac did not want him being arrested and deported before the trial. He had cleared this with the Director of Public Prosecutions and I was to ward off any zealous officer who may try to arrest Ben. Some months later two CID officers from City Road police station came into the premises at Fashion Street and asked for Ben. I showed out who I was and asked them what the problem was; they told me to mind my own business and I explained what the situation was. They said they were going to arrest Ben and threatened to arrest me for obstruction if I tried to stop them. I had no choice but to let them go. I immediately rang Mr Mac, who, as I understood later, rang the detective chief superintendent at City Road and he in person went to the back gate at City Road and as those two DCs drove in, the DCS stopped them, told them to 'fucking well take him straight back' and see him when they had done it. A short while later Ben came back with the senior of the two DCs who came up to me and asked what was going on. I told him it was none of his business and he should have listened to me at the start.

Security was very strict. Arthur Porter BEM was a member of No 4 Unit of the Special Patrol Group and he outlined the escort system for me:

> The system was that we paraded at 7.00 am, taking the car and two carriers to Vauxhall, to pick up the prison van and driver, then to Wandsworth prison to pick up Frankie Fraser, who was already serving time, then to Brixton for the rest of the bunch. There were also a couple of Traffic Patrol outriders. We then went 'on the blue' from the prison to the Magistrates' Court, during the rush hour in twelve minutes. One of the sergeants became the van sergeant with a PC on the back door of the van. There was some suggestion that there would be an attempt to escape from the van and firearms would be used, so we carried revolvers in a shoulder holster so they were out of sight. Whilst at court, the Unit provided extra cover and when proceedings finished, we would then make the return journey.

Amidst a large police presence, the accused appeared at Bow Street Magistrates' Court on the morning of Monday, 1 August, when pleas for bail were made.

'Advocates can renew their applications next week', said the magistrate, Mr K.J.P. Barraclough, adding, 'different considerations may then arise.' He remanded everybody in custody.

But upon their next appearance, as far as the defendants were concerned, matters had only deteriorated. More arrests had been made, and further charges were being considered by the Director of Public Prosecutions (DPP). And after Jean Richardson's further application for bail before a Judge in Chambers had failed the previous week, DCS Gerrard, when asked by her counsel, 'You know she has five children to look after?', was able to reply, 'I know that is not so' and went on to tell the court that they were Charlie Richardson's children and that she had not been looking after them for some time. Everybody was once again remanded in custody.

The prosecution started outlining their case for committal proceedings on 30 August 1966 at Clerkenwell Magistrates' Court. Four more prisoners were in the dock, which had been enlarged to accommodate two rows of them – the newcomers were Frank

Fraser, Eddie Richardson, James Moody and William Stayton – and sixteen police officers surrounded the dock. It took thirty-five minutes for Mr E.J.P. Cussen for the DPP to read out all the charges. The following day, the first of the prosecution witnesses was called; this was Christopher Glinski, who had given evidence in the Jack Spot trial eleven years earlier.

He stated that he had been attacked, an assault which caused him actual bodily harm, by Frank Fraser, his nephew James, Johnny Longman and Robert St Leger who also demanded sums of £350 and £200 with menaces. The men had pulled the curtains at his office at 190 Vauxhall Bridge Road before launching the attack in December 1965.

Glinski told the court that he had attended four identity parades which had been held at Brixton prison the previous Thursday to try to identify his attackers. 'I asked the officer if the man in the blue suit could say something', he said. 'He was then asked to say a date or something like that. That was James Fraser.'

This prompted an outburst from that defendant: 'You're a liar – why don't you tell the truth?'

Another of the prisoners – it was probably Frank Fraser – shouted, 'That's a blooming lie. I've never been there. He's an innocent man and you know he's innocent.'

However, Glinski's evidence in respect of St Leger was less than convincing, and after the lunchtime adjournment Mr Cussen offered no evidence on the charges relating to him. Although he was discharged by the magistrate, St Leger was remanded in custody in respect of another quite unrelated charge, one of conspiracy to defraud.

It was round about this time that there was a little trouble concerning one Francis Davidson Fraser. It is thought that there had been a problem with his walking stick, which the prison warders had taken away from him. He had complained, and when he was collected by the prison van the following morning, it had been restored to him. But he was in an unpleasant mood and having been locked in his compartment in the prison van he started banging on the partition with his stick. This prompted Sergeant Arthur Porter from No 4 Special Patrol Group and a constable to pull open the cell door and to exclaim, 'What the fuck's the matter with you?' Since Arthur Porter was a pretty tough character, awarded a British Empire Medal for gallantry for the arrest of a gunman, Fraser probably realized he was outmatched and apologized. However, this did not improve his mood.

On 3 September Taggart gave evidence, and a pretty horrifying account it was too. Bundled into his car after being attacked in Jamaica Road by Thomas Clark, Frank Fraser and Charlie Richardson, he was taken to an office in a warehouse in Bermondsey:

> I was attacked by feet and fists, by all three. After this attack, all my clothes were taken off. After Richardson made several phone calls, Fraser picked up a wooden pole, two inches in diameter and several feet long. He smashed it across my body and head until it broke. By this time, my body was a mass of blood and also my head and the walls and floor of the office were splattered with my blood. I was made to clean the walls and floor with my own under-wear. The men broke off for beer and sandwiches and then attacked me again. I wanted to remain conscious, because I assumed from the condition I looked in that if I became unconscious, then it might look a different matter altogether so far as these people were concerned; I assumed that I would automatically become a dead man.

Cue for an outburst from the dock: 'You bloody liar, you ought to be writing for the newspapers!'

Taggart continued, saying that Alfred Berman had interceded on his behalf, asking the others to stop, but 'It appeared that any suggestion Berman made was not agreeable to the others.'

It was later suggested that he would be freed providing he was willing to pay £1,000; Charlie Richardson then received a tele-phone call saying that his brother was arriving at the airport from Johannesburg and would have to be met, and he and Berman left the office. Taggart was left with Fraser, Clark and a man named Frank Prater; Charlie Richardson later returned with his brother and other people, men and women. When Taggart mentioned Frankie Fraser's name, it provoked Fraser to bellow from the dock, 'You liar! I have never seen him before in my life. It's like writing a James Bond book the way he's talking.' (This was rather at variance with the account Fraser gave much later, saying he *had* been there.)

Taggart completed his evidence by saying he was later allowed to dress and was helped to his car; the following day, his business partner was asked to sign two cheques made out to Berman.

At one point, Frankie Fraser seriously lost his cool in the dock; whilst the prison officers were attempting to contain him, Edwin Williams (then Police Constable 212 'N' and later detective super-intendent), one of the officers drawn from the 'N' Division boxing team ringing the dock, stepped in, helped subdue him and took him to the cells.

Williams told me, 'I turned to look at him as he sat on the cell's wooden bench, nursing an injury to his nose. He looked very small and not at all dangerous, more a case deserving of a little TLC. However, I was not inclined to provide it!'

Cyril George Green had first met Charlie Richardson when he had been released from prison in May 1964. By the time he gave evidence at Clerkenwell he was again in trouble, on remand on a charge of fraud, although the prosecution told the magistrate that at the appropriate time the charge would be dropped.

Green stated that he had gone to Charlie Richardson's office with Johnnie Bradbury; they had brought with them a bottle of whisky. Richardson was questioning Lucien Harris, from whom he wished to discover the whereabouts of Jack Duval, evidently without success. The whisky was poured over Harris, he was punched, stripped naked and then wired up to the generator. One of the men turned the handle of the box, causing Harris to scream, and he vomited; this treatment continued for about an hour.

This should have been a salutary lesson to Green regarding the type of people he was consorting with, but having received 'a final warning' from Charlie Richardson in respect of some misused cheques, he was set about by George Cornell in Richardson's office after he told him the police had been contacted. Cornell tipped him upside down on a chair and hit him across the head with a pair of pliers – 'Then he started hitting me with chairs and ashtrays, kicking me and punching me.'

'He's not here to defend himself!' shouted a woman in the public gallery, as indeed he wasn't. There was uproar in the courtroom and not for the first or the last time the magistrate ordered the court to be cleared.

Resuming his testimony, Green told the court that Cornell got on the telephone to Jean Goodman, telling him to 'send Roy round'.

Roy Hall had arrived carrying a pot of tea. 'Cornell said, "Give him a cup of tea",' said Green. 'I had it poured over my head; it was boiling hot tea. Hall made me sit in the corner with my hands on the floor and made me keep my eyes open. Then he kicked me about the body. He kept punching me. Hall made me take my shoes and socks off, then they tried to break my toes. They couldn't do it properly, so used pliers. The middle toes of my left foot were broken.'

★

The day's proceedings were concluded when Moody was charged with causing grievous bodily harm to a police sergeant the previous Saturday. 'My client was in fact violently attacked by the police',

The Two Firms:
(*Above*) The Kray Brothers - Reg (*left*), Charlie and Ron (*right*).
(*Below*) The Richardson Brothers - Charlie (*left*) and Eddie.

ACC Gerald McArthur MBE, QP

ACC Leonard 'Nipper' Read QP

The Beginning of the End of the Krays:
The Krays arriving at Bow Street Magistrates' Court.

The End of the Krays:
The investigation team at the trial's conclusion.
Trevor Lloyd-Hughes, who upset Reggie Kray so much, is shown, back row, 4th from left.

Charlie Kray (*left*), Reggie Kray and Freddie Foreman (*right*).

Joey Pyle.

Ron (*left*) and Reg Kray – fighting fit.

Three addresses of Kray significance:
(*Above left*) The Blind Beggar pub, where Cornell was murdered.
(*Above right*) Evering Road, where McVitie was murdered.
(*Below*) 'Fort Vallance', 4th door on the right, where several murders were planned.

Three of the Krays' victims:
(*Left*) Frank 'The Mad Axeman' Mitchell
(*Below left*) 'Jack the Hat' McVitie.
(*Below right*) George Cornell.

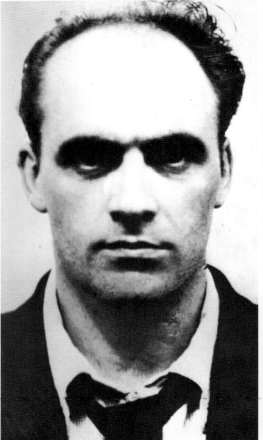

Four of the Krays' murderers:
(*Above left*) Ronald Bender. (*Above right*) John 'Scotch Ian' Barrie.
(*Below left*) Tony Lambrianou. (*Below right*) Chris Lambrianou.

 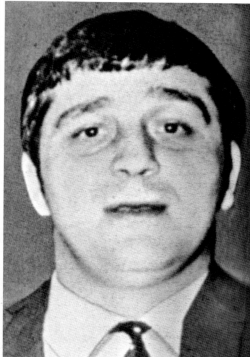

Sgt. Ken German
(Underwater Search Unit)
attempting to find the
'Richardson Torture Box'.

Reggie Kray at his
mother's funeral.

stated Moody's counsel, adding, 'He was hit on the head with a truncheon.'

Moody, who had in fact head-butted the officer, was quite aggrieved. 'I was bleeding from my head in the cells for an hour', he screamed from the dock. 'I had to have stitches' – but nobody (least of all the police) seemed interested in this latest miscarriage of justice because the press reporters were now under attack.

'You've applied for it, mate, and you'll get it', illogically shouted a supporter, and a woman tried to grab hold of another reporter; yet another was smuggled out of court by the police.

By Saturday, 10 September, further charges were preferred. Charlie Richardson, Jean Goodman and Brian Morse were charged with making false statements to procure passports and associated offences, whilst Richardson, Goodman and Derek Mottram were charged with possessing dangerous drugs. Mottram alone was charged with possession of ten forged $100 United States Federal Reserve notes, while Roy Hall was charged with possession of a stolen pistol and five rounds of ammunition and associated firearms offences.

Now it was the turn of Benjamin Coulston – who since 1958 had acquired eight convictions for dishonesty – in the witness box. Coulston was suspected of swindling Richardson out of a consignment of cigarettes valued at £600; this had been more than sufficient to have him brought to the scrap metal headquarters, threatened with a gun, stripped and then punched repeatedly in the face by Frankie Fraser. He was immersed in a bath full of water until the blood was washed off, before being returned to the office for round two.

Fraser now tried to extract some of Coulston's teeth with pliers – Coulston said that most of one of his teeth was removed and the rest of it came out in his hand – before an electric fire was moved up and down on his naked body. He gave evidence that all the toes on his right foot were smashed, as was his left big toe.

Next, members of the gang stubbed out their cigarettes on his body. When his arms and legs were bound with rope, his head was covered in a tarpaulin and he heard 'weights' and 'Vauxhall Bridge' mentioned, then was put into a van and driven away, he fainted.

He later recovered consciousness in the office, surrounded by the sniggering gang, who asked if he was all right. Richardson told him that he had discovered that someone else had stolen the consignment and laughingly apologized.

At hospital a fractured skull was diagnosed, and Coulston's wounds required twenty stitches. Recompense in the sum of £30 was pushed under his pillow by the Richardsons' father.

Eddie Richardson decided to conduct his own defence, when Coulston denied that he was a police informant. When Richardson asked permission to see his wife, the magistrate, Geraint Rees, told him, 'Subject to the regulations, you may'; but McArthur, concerned at any possible delay to the prison van convoy, told the magistrate that there would be an opportunity for her to visit her husband whilst he was on remand.

'Isn't the law that a man is innocent until he's proved guilty?' shouted Richardson, telling the magistrate, 'I wish you'd keep an open mind. It's an unsavoury sight looking at these other people.' He was probably referring to the other people present during visiting times at Brixton Prison rather than his co-defendants; but whatever the case, he was ordered to keep quiet.

Just before Christmas, William Stayton had the charges against him dismissed, as did Charlie Richardson and Roy Hall in respect of the allegations of actual bodily harm and demanding money with menaces regarding Christopher Glinski, the magistrate, Geraint Rees, declaring there was no case to answer.

Police Constable Kenneth 'Taff' Rees had had the unenviable task of guarding Frankie Fraser at Lewisham Hospital whilst he was recovering from his bullet wound. They played draughts, discussed the virtues of the Saab motor car (with which Fraser seemed obsessed) and said nothing about the case. Some time later, Rees had been attached to Traffic Patrol and now formed part of the escort group to court.

'Following the gates being closed at Bow Street, the prisoners were let out of the van', he told me. As Fraser emerged, he shouted, 'Hello, Taff – how ya doing?' and, as Rees told me, 'I nearly dropped my Woodbine!' He received a tap on the shoulder – 'Come inside!' – from a couple of grim-faced 'tecs who demanded to know the reason for this apparent chumminess. It was easily explained, and as a bonus, Rees later married the staff nurse whom he had met at Lewisham Hospital.

Between 24 and 27 January 1967 legal submissions were heard, and then the defendants were committed to the Old Bailey to stand trial on a variety of charges. All were remanded in custody with the exception of Jean Goodman, who had previously been granted bail in her own recognizance of £2,000 with two sureties in similar amounts. They faced a total of forty charges, committal proceedings had lasted 71 days and 250 witnesses had been called.

It was now time for the police to assemble their witnesses and ensure that the case for the prosecution was as watertight as possible, whilst some of the defendants ensured that the skulduggery which had already commenced continued with breathtaking impudence – as will be seen later.

*

The 'Torture Trial' commenced on 4 April 1967, and many of the defendants were upset when they realized that Mr Justice Lawton would be their judge. At fifty-six years of age, Lawton was a rather controversial figure. He had been selected as the parliamentary candidate for Hammersmith North for the British Union of Fascists during the 1930s, at which time he also converted to Roman Catholicism; he was later invalided out of the Rifle Brigade during the Second World War. A brisk, no-nonsense character, he was known for making comments in court which would send present-day adherents of political correctness into a swoon, for example when he spoke about the difficulties arising from dealing with 'gyppos and tinkers who invade a farmer's land'.

After hearing legal submissions, indictments were served and the number of charges for the first trial was reduced to twenty-two, a jury was selected and the next day, Sebag Shaw QC for the prosecution, outlined the case to the court. At the time of the trial, sixty-five-year-old Shaw was serving as Honorary Recorder of Ipswich and he was also a formidable prosecutor; he wasted no time on niceties, telling the jury, 'This present case is not about dishonesty and fraud; it is about violence and threats of violence. Not, let me say, casual acts of violence committed in sudden anger but vicious and brutal violence, systematically inflicted, deliberately and cold-bloodedly and with utter and callous ruthlessness.'

In an effort to show that this was not the case, the defendants were represented by twenty-five barristers, including ten Queen's Counsels.

The first witness for the prosecution was the very slippery Jack Duval, who admitted that he was currently serving a three-year sentence imposed on 8 November 1966 for a conspiracy to defraud which involved airline tickets; at the time of being sentenced, he was also serving a twelve-month sentence for making a false declaration to obtain a passport. Born in Russia in 1919, he stated that he had served in the French Foreign Legion for six months before being invalided out and arriving in England in 1947. He had used a number of aliases, including 'Jack Oliver', and had been convicted of fraud on a number of occasions.

Having met Charlie Richardson in 1960, Duval told the court that he had worked for him ordering stocks of nylons on credit in Italy; but after he had experienced what he referred to as 'a rough time' abroad he was taken to an office in Camberwell where Eddie Richardson punched him in the face and beat him with golf clubs; when Duval asked why he was subjected to this kind of treatment, he was told, 'You do as Charlie tells you to do.' Understandably, he told the jury, 'I was very frightened and felt bad.'

Nevertheless, Duval went back to work for Charlie Richardson in a travel agency where, over a period of two to three months, airline tickets were obtained on credit, with none of them being paid for. Later, in Italy, the same scheme was re-enacted and £20–30,000 was owed. Charlie Richardson arrived in Italy and provided him with a passport in the name of Rumble. He fled Italy to England via Lugano (where he stated he was again attacked by Eddie Richardson) and Brussels, but having reached the UK he received a telephone call from Charlie Richardson, who said, 'It's no use hiding yourself in Brighton, Duval. Do you want me to come and fetch you or are you going to come?'

He did come; and he stated that in September or October 1963 he was beaten, once more with golf clubs, by Eddie Richardson. It seems incredible that Duval continued to work for Charlie Richardson; perhaps it was an indication of the power that Richardson exerted over him or greed on Duval's part – and maybe a combination of the two. In any case, in the spring of 1964 Richardson sent him to Germany to order textiles, electrical goods and cutlery on credit on behalf of Common Market Merchants, of which Alfred Blore was the manager.

In June 1964 Duval and Blore were summoned to Richardson's office in Camberwell where, as soon as they arrived, Charlie Richardson punched Duval in the face; when he recovered consciousness he discovered that Richardson had relieved him of $200, his watch and a ring. Blore – who did not want to continue running the company under Richardson's orders – was being subjected to the terrifying ordeal of having Richardson throw knives from a canteen of cutlery at him, while shouting, 'I'm the boss and if I tell you what to do, you'll do it!'

'What have I done, Charlie?' cried Blore.

Duval, rather wisely, told the court, 'Naturally, I was quiet sitting in my corner', whilst Blore screamed, 'Don't do it to me!'

Eventually, Richardson told two of his henchmen to go to Blore's company in Cannon Street, collect the stock and books and make it appear that there had been a break-in. He also directed that Blore, who was covered in blood and crying, be taken to a chemist and 'fixed up'.

Mr E.J.P. Cussen for the prosecution asked Duval, 'Did you go to the doctor or complain to the police?'

Duval replied, 'No. A few days later, I flew to Brussels and then lived in Israel, Paris, Germany and Switzerland. I was too frightened to return to London. I did not return to this country until November 1965, when I was arrested in Leeds for passport offences.'

Cross-examined by Geoffrey Crispin QC for Charlie Richardson, Duval denied that he was the 'mastermind' behind the frauds and that he had concocted the story to save his own skin. He did admit that Richardson had paid large sums of money, up to £1,000, to corrupt police officers and that he (Duval) had named half a dozen of them in his statement but denied that he was hoping to get a lot of money by selling his story to the newspapers. 'I am at present a guest of Her Majesty', he protested, 'and cannot indulge in any business activities while I am in prison.'

These were serious allegations, albeit from a man who was not only used to lying habitually to further his illicit, fraudulent trans-actions but was currently serving a prison sentence. But were they true? When Sebag Shaw had concluded his opening statement for the Crown, he told the court that when Eddie Richardson was arrested and charged he had stated, 'You are undermining the whole structure of British justice by bringing these charges against me when you know full well I am innocent.'

Shaw countered this by saying to the jury, 'You will give that speech all the weight you think fit but we all know that British justice is safe in this court. If half the evidence for the prosecution is substantially accurate, you may think that the charges are amply justified and proved.'

Therefore it would be a matter for the jury, who featured in the next of several hiccups which this trial would experience.

★

It was at this time that an attempt was made to discredit the police. Misinformation had been given to the *Daily Mirror* which made front page news. The newspaper reported: 'Last night some detectives slept at the homes of the jurors they guarded, and when that was not convenient, they waited outside their houses in their cars.'

This allegation was introduced to the court proceedings by Mr T. Williams QC on behalf of the bruised and battered James Moody. There was a good reason for it, since it featured in a conspiracy to pervert the course of justice at the commencement of the trial in which Moody featured prominently – but more of that later.

It was a serious attack on the credibility of the prosecution; when Mr Justice Lawton ordered jury protection, he had made it quite clear that there should be no personal contact between police officers and the jurors whom they were guarding. It was important enough for the Director of Public Prosecutions, Sir Norman Skelhorn KBE, QC, to attend court in person, as did Gerald McArthur, who told the judge that he had instructed his officers that in no circumstances were they to enter the jury members' homes, 'not even if some were offered a cup of tea'.

Mr Justice Lawton dealt with the matter in a simple, straightforward manner. Addressing the jury, he asked, 'Did any officer sleep in your homes during the night?' When the jury unanimously chorused, 'No', the judge remarked, 'No more need be said.'

*

The next witness was Bernard Wajcenberg, another fraudster who had had dubious business dealings with Charlie Richardson and Johnnie Longman. He described going to Richardson's office to be paid at the conclusion of a business transaction but said that Richardson had turned on him, saying, 'There is nothing due to you. You owe the firm £5,000', and adding, 'You'll have to pay up or you know what will happen if you don't.'

Telling Wajcenberg that unless he paid he would not get out of the office alive, Richardson grabbed him by the lapels, saying, 'When I go berserk, you know what happens'; he then opened a cupboard which contained knives, choppers and a shotgun. When Wajcenberg tried to protest that he did not owe any money, Richardson retorted, 'You ratted on me and spoke to a police officer and you must pay . . . you have rich friends.'

Wajcenberg did have rich friends and he borrowed £1,500 each from two of them which was handed over, since he had no doubt that he would be beaten up – or worse – if he defaulted. It was not just that he had had the lapels of his jacket seized and been shown a cupboard full of weaponry; he told the court that on a previous occasion he had seen Jack Duval brought in to Richardson's office: 'He was bleeding from the nose, his eyes had been blackened and his shirt was bloodstained. It moved me. I did not know what this sort of thing was. Business is business but violence is something different. I was paralysed; I could not speak any more.'

But even more chilling was Wajcenberg's description of how Richardson spoke to Duval, in the manner of an exasperated parent to a recalcitrant child: 'Why can't you be a good boy? Why do you misbehave? Must you put people behind prison bars?'

In the meantime, John Simmonds had been promoted and was back on the Flying Squad. He had not been required to give evidence in chief since his statement of arrest had been accepted. But he was twice called to the Old Bailey to clear up matters that had arisen and he described what happened:

> Firstly, when I was protecting Ben [Wajcenberg] we were driving to Fashion Street one morning when he suddenly said, 'Oh my God, I forgot to tell McArthur about a specific criminal activity!' At the time, the DPP had given immunity to witnesses on the basis that they were completely honest and admitted all criminal matters they had committed. Ben went on to tell me of a matter that escaped his mind. I realized the importance of what he was saying so I stopped the car, cautioned him and recorded the details in my pocket book and got him to sign it. Once we arrived at Fashion Street I telephoned Mr Mac and gave him the details and subsequently made a full statement.
>
> Later, I was out in a Squad car when I had a radio message to go to the Old Bailey. On arrival I was met in the foyer and ushered straight into the witness box where I was questioned about this matter. Ben had been in the witness box and had been challenged over this one matter, which they said he had not admitted. He protested that he had and that I had even cautioned him. Clearly I confirmed this and deflated the defence's case. It was later ascertained that my statement had been in one of the bundles and that the defence barrister had missed it.

Next was the turn of Derek John Lucien Harris, who told the court of an encounter with Charlie Richardson when he had gone to collect money owing to him. But Richardson now wanted to trace Jack Duval and told Harris that he had been seen in Duval's company the previous evening. This is what Harris told the jury:

> I told him I did not know and Mr Richardson said, 'I believe you do.' He went on, 'I like you, Lucien, and I don't want to hurt you.' A man named Lawrence Bradbury then punched me five or six times in the stomach, and Charles Richardson threatened me with a knife and kicked me in the wrist, smashing my watch. Roy Hall then brought a portable, hand-operated electric generator into the room, similar to the type used to test sparking plugs. Someone came in with a parcel of scampi and everyone began eating. After he had finished, Mr Charles Richardson screwed his thumbs into my eyes. It was very painful and I could

not see for some moments. On Mr Richardson's instructions, my shoes were removed and my toes were wired up to the generator. Mr Hall turned the handle and the shock caused me to jump out of my chair and I fell to the floor. After that, I was stripped except for my shirt and the shock treatment was repeated. As I rolled on the floor, Mr Richardson said the generator wasn't working very well and orange squash was poured over my feet. Then I was bound and gagged and given further electric shocks to various parts of my body. Finally, Mr Richardson said I was to be taken to the marshes where I gathered I would be killed and dumped, under a pile of refuse. While I was dressing, Mr Richardson pinned my left foot to the floor with a knife. Then his attitude changed and he became very friendly. He apologised and said evidently he had made a mistake and I did not know where Jack Duval was. He then gave me £150. Altogether, I was detained for six hours.

Asked why this matter was not reported to the police, Harris replied, 'I had reason to believe that certain police officers were connected with Charles Richardson.'

The other victims gave their evidence and then, on 25 April 1967, after legal submissions had been made, Jean Goodman was acquitted on the directions of the judge on charges of grievous bodily harm or actual bodily harm in respect of Cyril George Green. She was released on bail, pending her trial on a separate indictment in respect of charges of conspiracy to cheat and defraud.

One week later, the judge directed the jury to acquit Charlie and Eddie Richardson of causing grievous bodily harm with intent to Jack Duval between 1 and 31 December 1962 and between 1 September and 31 October 1963 and also, in respect of Charlie Richardson only, inflicting grievous bodily harm on Alfred Blore.

Now it was the turn of the defence, and when Charlie Richardson gave evidence, any allegation of violence, he said – save for one occasion when he had punched Jack Duval on the nose, in retaliation for being hit with a cup – was a lie, a conspiracy by 'a lot of clever fraudsmen putting these allegations and getting out of their own frauds by blaming me for these incidents'.

In fact, he said, both Duval and Wajcenberg had stolen £32,000 out of Common Market Merchants Ltd., a company in which he had invested £5,000.

The knife-throwing incident with Blore? 'It's lies. It sounds like something out of a James Bond book . . . I don't know about any injury to Blore and I've never struck him.'

And Wajcenberg's ill-treatment? 'All lies'.

The blood on the floor of the office? 'It must have got there when an employee went to get the first-aid box.'

As for Harris's graphic account of his ill-treatment, well, 'I went to the office in the evening, I could see Harris's tie was askew and I could see he had had a fight with Bradbury' (who of course was in prison in South Africa and would not be returning for the trial). 'I thought Harris knew where Duval was. There was an atmosphere and I managed to smooth it over.'

Describing 90 per cent of Harris' testimony as 'perjured evidence', Richardson went on to say, 'As far as I'm concerned, no attack did take place on Harris'; he went on to say he had never possessed an electric generator and knew no one who had.

Questioned about Bernard Bridges who, it was thought, knew the whereabouts of Jack Duval and who claimed that he was punched, kicked, bound with flex, attached to the generator and given electric shocks which were so severe that, 'it made me leap into the air', Richardson's response was, 'No, I've never had a cross word with him.'

The appalling treatment of Benjamin Coulston was very quickly dealt with. Not only had he not been a party to Coulston's torture, the first time Richardson had seen him was 'when he picked me out as one of the defendants at Bow Street Magistrates' Court. It was the first time I had seen him in my life.'

And now there was the matter of James Taggart, whom Richardson denied ill-treating on 15 July 1965. Taggart, said Richardson, had given perjured evidence. He could not possibly have attacked Taggart at the time suggested, because he had picked up his brother Eddie at London Heathrow Airport at 8.45 pm, precisely the time when Taggart had said he was being beaten. Having left the airport at 9.00 pm, they had arrived in Chislehurst at 10.00 pm. Simple. Except that it wasn't.

'Look at this telegram', said Sebag Shaw. 'It bears the date 14 July from Johannesburg and that is the telegram you got, isn't it?'

The telegram revealed that Eddie Richardson's flight would be landing at Heathrow at 10.20 pm. 'You see the time?' asked Shaw, and Richardson had to agree that it was 10.20.

'Not 8.45?'

'I could have sworn it was 8.45', muttered Richardson.

The master manipulator had been outmanoeuvred by a flimsy piece of paper found by the police during the search of his address.

That was on the Friday. On the following Monday, two surprise witnesses were called in respect of Charlie Richardson. The first of these was Mrs Elaine Frances Halin, who told the court that she had received a subpoena at about 5.00 pm on Friday and had prepared her statement over the weekend. She stated that during the evening of 15 July Charlie Richardson had taken her to London airport to meet his brother and, having done so, they had taken Eddie Richardson to his home in Chislehurst, after which she and Charlie had returned to her house at Effra Parade, Brixton, with Charlie leaving at about 1.45 am.

Cross-examined, Mrs Halin was asked if the person serving the subpoena had told her that Richardson had finished his evidence about the night at London Airport, to which she replied, 'No'. She thought the aircraft had arrived at about 10.30 pm. Had anybody told Mrs Halin that Richardson was charged with 'a very nasty assault that very night in Rotherhithe New Rd? Again, she replied, 'No'.

Had she read anything about the proceedings against Charles Richardson? 'No', replied Mrs Halin, telling the court that she had realized only yesterday that a charge against him referred to 15 July.

'You had not the slightest idea you were being called today to provide an alibi for Charles Richardson?' asked Sebag Shaw, and again the answer was 'no'.

The second witness was a man on remand for a matter unconnected with the case who was allowed to write down his name and address. Referred to only as 'Mr F', he told the court that he had known James Taggart for ten to twelve years and that recently Taggart had telephoned him and told him that he – Mr F – had offered him £20,000 to change his evidence. This he denied, but the name Charles Richardson had been mentioned, and he added that Taggart had told him, 'If you did telephone me and offered me this, and told me from whom it came and you have trouble with any business, you can be helped.'

Pointing out that this matter had not been put to Taggart when he gave evidence, Mr Justice Lawton told the jury that this evidence was not admissible and they should disregard it.

Eddie Richardson stated he was convicted in the Mr Smith's affray case because of the allegations made in the present case.

'Are you saying you were unlucky or not guilty?' asked Sebag Shaw, to which Richardson replied, 'Not guilty'.

'So the verdict of the jury in that case was not to be trusted? asked Shaw cunningly.

Richardson cleverly countered with, 'The jury must have been influenced by the publicity I received in the charges I face now.'

Charlie Richardson's alibi for the night of the attack on Taggart had received a nasty dent, but of course he had denied the assault. Fraser would later say that at the time of Taggart's attack he was in Hove; and the assault would also be denied by Thomas Clark, who despite having numerous convictions for dishonesty 'did not believe in violence'.

So the three alleged perpetrators were denying the offence, it being their word against that of a convicted fraudster. Of course, Taggart had said in evidence that Alfred Berman had tried to intercede on his behalf, but Berman himself was charged right along with the other three, with blackmail and grievous bodily harm, and with actual bodily harm as an alternative. Therefore Berman was hardly likely to back up Taggart's story – except that he did, and this bombshell burst on the defence case on 15 May 1967.

★

Going into the witness box, Berman stated that on the night of the attack Charlie Richardson had asked him to bring some food to his office, which he did. When he arrived, there were Richardson, Fraser and Clark, also a naked man in a chair. He told the court:

> When I first saw him, he looked ghastly. I had another look and then I recognized the man as James Taggart, whom I knew. I had to look twice. His head, ears and eyes were swollen. He had marks all over his body. I nearly fainted. I said to Charles Richardson, 'Good God, what's happened? What's this man done to get like this?'

Examined by his barrister, Basil Wigoder QC, Berman said that there was 'blood in front of him, on the floor and on the wall behind' and that Richardson had told him Taggart was an informer and responsible for taking a man's liberty away.

'Charles Richardson was shouting and screaming, saying, "he has done terrible things",' Berman told the jury, adding, 'I was in a daze; I didn't know what I had walked into.'

Berman was asked, 'Could you leave the room?'

He replied, 'I wanted to but my feet would not let me. Everything was tense. I walked towards the door but Charles Richardson told me to sit down and wait.'

After about twenty minutes, Frank Prater – a prosecution witness – had arrived.

'Prater went up to Taggart', said Berman, 'and shouted at him, "Where's the money, where's the money?"'

Taggart finally agreed to make out cheques totalling £1,200, and Prater and Richardson decided they should be made out to Berman.

Just to make matters crystal clear, Mr Justice Lawton now stepped in: 'Your defence can be summarised in a few words: you say you had this misfortune to stumble across the two crimes being committed. One, knocking Taggart about in an unlawful way and the other demanding money from Taggart?'

'Yes', replied Berman.

Pushing the point home, the judge continued, 'You were not there because you wanted to be there or that you were a willing party, but in a way, by chance and your continued presence was not due to a desire to encourage what was going on but was because you did not know how you could get away?'

And having received such a very helpful lifeline, the only answer Berman could possibly give was, 'Yes'.

Frankie Fraser now limped into the witness box with the aid of a stick – it was not needed, except as a prop to try to extract sympathy from the jury – and told the court that he had alibis in respect of the assaults on Coulston and Taggart; and that with the exception of Charlie and Eddie Richardson he knew none of the other defendants in the case.

Pressing this point, Sebag Shaw asked him, 'You say you do not know Alfred Berman, one of your co-defendants, and never knew anything about him before this case?'

Fraser replied, 'That is so.'

'You have never done him any harm that you know of?'

'No'.

'And yet', persisted Shaw, 'right out of the blue, he says you were one of the men in an office in Rotherhithe at the same time as Mr Taggart, and that you were with Charles Richardson and Charles Clark. Do you say that is all nonsense?'

'I'm afraid it is', replied Fraser, but he did not sound particularly convincing.

The second time that John Simmonds was called to the Old Bailey related to the arrest of Roy Hall. He explained what had happened:

Both the Hertfordshire DC and I had been summoned to the Old Bailey in the middle of the day; the DC got there early afternoon and had gone into the witness box. I forget why now but I was not able to get there until the next day. I was to be first witness on, and on my way my car broke down at Finchley. I rang Vic Evans who was now in charge of the witnesses and said I would be late; he said I could not be late. He asked me my location and I told him I was in a call box in Finchley. He told me not to move, and a few moments later a Traffic Patrol car with headlights and bell going pulled up. 'DS Simmonds?' shouted the passenger. I nodded, he said, 'Get in', and we roared off to the Old Bailey and I had time for coffee!

I was questioned in respect of the arrest. Great emphasis was placed on the fact that we had handcuffed the prisoner and led him out of the house like that, as if it was some heinous crime. I said that the prisoner had been violent and tried to escape and that we had cuffed him for our own safety and I considered it to be justified when we found a loaded hand gun on the premises. To this day I cannot understand why they bothered to call us but I felt they did more harm to their case by doing so.

The last of the defendants to give evidence was Thomas Charles Clark, who described his twelve convictions – including receiving, possessing electric detonators and storebreaking – before denying any involvement with the torture of Taggart, saying, 'The press has brought all this out. All this gang talk is a myth.'

He initially described himself as nothing more than an acquaintance of Charlie Richardson, but cross-examination revealed that whilst he was serving a three-year sentence Richardson had sent money to Clark's wife which resulted in him writing a letter to Richardson from prison ending with the words, 'Your pal, forever'.

'Until Mr Berman gave evidence in this court', asked Sebag Shaw, 'did you regard him as an enemy or a friend?'

'I feel very sorry for Mr Berman', replied Clark, adding, 'He has other charges to face.'

'To put it in everyday language', interjected the judge, 'he shopped you in the witness box?'

'Not only me', replied Clark.

Sebag Shaw now asked, 'He had never done anything to you before which was unkind?'

'No, quite the contrary', replied Clark.

'And he had never done anything which might suggest that he would play a dirty trick on you?'

'No'.

'And yet he shopped you and Charles Richardson, the man you have described as "your pal, forever"?'

To this Clark replied, 'I think he would even shop his own mother if he saw a chance of getting out of the mess he's in.'

'What about Mr Taggart?' asked Shaw. 'You have said although you never knew him and never had any dealings with him, that he has told lies about you. Why should he want to do that?'

It is one thing for a defendant to issue denials and quite another to make the kind of smart remark which Clark now did: 'He has told lies but he had his motives. I think he's a top grass. He's in trouble over his bankruptcy and so he runs off to Welwyn Garden City to see Uncle Mac.'

This was a sneering reference to Gerald McArthur, bracketing him with Derek McCulloch OBE, known as Uncle Mac, the much-loved BBC Radio presenter of *Children's Favourites* and *Children's Hour*. It did not help that McCulloch was in poor health and in fact died within ten days of Clark making his remark, which brought this frosty rebuke from Mr Justice Lawton: 'Everybody throughout this trial has been at pains to address you and your co-defendants correctly. Do you mind doing the same?'

This resulted in a fulsome apology from Clark, but in all honesty the defence case was not progressing very well, especially after Berman's counsel told the court that after his client 'had left the comparative safety of the dock . . . and said that James Taggart was telling the truth . . . he [Berman] will not be able to walk along any street in this country or anywhere in the world without constantly glancing over his shoulder.'

Oh, dear. It was what's known in the trade as a 'cut-throat defence'.

★

The judge took several days to deliver an impeccably fair summing-up, and on 7 June 1967, after a trial which had lasted forty-five days, the jury consisting of eleven men and one woman returned their verdicts after a retirement lasting nine hours and twenty-six minutes.

Moody was acquitted but still had to face charges of assaulting the police. In the case of Berman, the jury were unable to agree.

Charlie Richardson was found guilty of nine of the charges against him: assaulting and robbing Duval with violence, demanding £5,000 with menaces from Wajcenberg, assaulting Blore, causing grievous bodily harm to Harris, Bridges, Coulston and Taggart and demanding £1,200 from Taggart. He told the court, 'I am completely innocent of these charges.'

Eddie Richardson was found guilty of just two of the charges: actual bodily harm on Duval and inflicting grievous bodily harm on Coulston.

Longman was found not guilty of demanding with menaces in respect of Wajcenberg, but the judge directed that he remain in custody 'in respect of other matters'.

Roy Hall was found guilty of inflicting grievous bodily harm on Harris, Bridges and Green and of causing actual bodily harm to Bickers.

Frankie Fraser and Thomas Clark were both found guilty of demanding £1,200 with menaces from Taggart as well as inflicting grievous bodily harm on him. Fraser was also found guilty of inflicting grievous bodily harm on Coulston.

The following day, 8 June, the sentences were passed. Telling Charlie Richardson, 'It must be clear to all those who set themselves up as gang leaders that they will be struck down by the law, as you will be struck down', the judge sentenced him to concurrent terms totalling twenty-five years and ordered him to pay two-thirds of the prosecution costs, not exceeding £20,000; he also ordered an investigation into how, with assets of £250,000 in mining interests in South Africa, it had been possible for Richardson to obtain legal aid.

According to his biographer, Richardson took his sentence 'like a man', half-bowed to the jury and quietly said, 'Thank you very much'.

Not, however, according to the 9 June edition of *The Times*, which reported, 'As Richardson turned to leave the dock, he stopped suddenly, glared at the jury . . . and snarled, "Thank you very much".'

It was a slight, but subtle difference.

Next in the dock was Eddie Richardson, described by McArthur as 'one of his brother's first lieutenants'; he was sentenced to ten years' imprisonment, to run consecutively to the five-year sentence in respect of the Mr Smith's Club charge.

Roy Hall, who the judge said had 'behaved in a callous, sadistic and vicious way, a willing party to the degradation of these men', was also sentenced to ten years.

Thomas Clark, described by the judge as being 'yet another victim of Charles Richardson', was sentenced to eight years' imprisonment. Sentence was deferred on Fraser.

Mr Justice Lawton praised the work of McArthur and his team, telling them:

> I want to thank all of you on behalf of the court – and I think I am speaking on behalf of every law-abiding citizen in this country – for the work you have done in breaking up one of the most dangerous gangs I have ever heard of.

The jury was handsomely thanked by the judge, and upon leaving court one of them told the waiting pressmen, 'No comment and that is the verdict of us all. We have agreed among ourselves not to say anything to the press or anyone.'

This turned out to be the case. John Barnes, who had guarded one of the jurors, told me that afterwards the juror and his wife became lifelong friends of Barnes and his wife. The couple have since died, but Barnes told me, 'It's interesting, over the years that we knew them, the trial never, ever got a mention and neither of us ever raised the issue!'

Meanwhile, the prisoners, under massive security, were shipped off to 'E' wing at the top security Durham Prison; but the proceedings were not yet over, not by any manner of means.

CHAPTER 18

Monkey Business

Frankie Fraser would later say that whilst Taggart was giving evidence 'the trial wasn't going well for us. By the seventeenth day of the trial, I thought Lawton's attitude was vindictive.' He wanted a change of judge and gave fresh instructions to his barrister, Charles Lawson, who told Mr Justice Lawton:

> He [Fraser] tells me that about the end of 1964, the beginning of 1965, he had arrived at Victoria Station for the purpose of catching a train. He was then apparently travelling to Brighton. He saw your Lordship on the railway station, he thinks between platforms 14 and 15, approached your Lordship and asked whether your Lordship was Sir Frederick Lawton. Your Lordship replied, 'Yes'. I gather that he then made derogatory, defamatory remarks about your father and that your Lordship walked away up the platform, I think pursued by my client, who was continuing to make these remarks.

This came right out of the blue, and Mr Justice Lawton was furious, angrily denying it had ever happened.

Fraser bellowed, 'Yes it did!'

And in fact, something of the kind had occurred, because the judge's father, William Lawton, had been a prison governor whom Fraser detested and had attacked more than once. Mr Justice Lawton later returned to the court and when he addressed Fraser's barrister, it is worth recording word for word what he said:

> There is a matter I want on place on record with regard to your application. You did not do me the courtesy of giving me any warning of the application you were going to make, or of the basis upon which you were going to make it, and as a result I had to put my mind directly on to the problem there and then, and I want to say as emphatically as I can that I have no recollection whatsoever of having spoken to your client. During the hour or so which has transpired since you spoke to me I have been running through my mind the occasions in my life when strangers have come and spoken to me, and I can just – but only just – recollect

one occasion on a London station on a winter's evening when somebody spoke to me and was abusive. I have no recollection of any abuse relating to my father. I feel if there had been any abuse relating to my father, I should have remembered it. I have no recollection whatsoever if it was your client, none whatsoever, and I am quite certain if it had been your client I would have remembered . . . in the circumstances it would be no grounds whatsoever for my not going on with this trial.

But Fraser's attempt to change the judge did not occur, as he claimed, on the seventeenth day of the trial, i.e. 26 April, or when Taggart was giving evidence. In fact, it did not happen when anybody was giving evidence because it was on 12 June 1967, five days after Fraser and other defendants had been found guilty. The judge had been expecting to try the case of Fraser, his nephew James and Johnnie Longman for assaulting and demanding £350 with menaces from Christopher Glinski and to sentence Fraser for the other offences of which he had been found guilty. The reason Fraser had tried to disrupt proceedings was that he did not want this judge to sentence him, especially since he had heard that, two days prior to his outburst, the latest conspiracy to nobble the jury in the torture trial had been thwarted. This was his first opportunity since hearing the news to air his spurious grievances in court.

On 15 June James Fraser and Johnnie Longman both pleaded guilty to assaulting Christopher Glinski. Their plea of not guilty to demanding money with menaces was accepted, and because they had spent so long in custody they were given sentences of imprisonment which would permit their immediate release – in Longman's case only as far as that indictment was concerned, since there was more to come.

No evidence was offered against Frankie Fraser on that indictment, and on the charges of which he had been found guilty he was sentenced to ten years' imprisonment, to run consecutively to the five-year sentence which had been imposed for the Mr Smith's Club affray. So what of the frustrated conspiracy? Read on . . .

*

From the time that the jury in the Torture Case had been sworn until 31 May, two men – Albert John Stayton (the brother of the defendant William Stayton, who had been discharged in respect of the attack on Coulston) and Leslie George McCarthy (who had worked at Atlantic Machines) – had conspired with others to pervert the course of justice. They had approached the brother of a jury member and told him that they 'would like to do business'. The juror's brother refused the offer and contacted the police. Fraser stated in his memoirs that he had refused because 'the police slept in his brother's house' – hence the disinformation to the newspaper which was thoroughly aired in court at the time. The men were not caught until much later, and when they appeared at Bow Street Magistrates' Court on 10 June, Detective Inspector John Morrison (later Commander Morrison OBE, QPM) told the court he feared intimidation of witnesses. Although McCarthy had stated that he was of no fixed address, his solicitor, one Norman Beach, heroically stepped in, offering to supply his address in writing and claiming that McCarthy's brother ('a man of substance') would stand surety in the sum of £10,000 – all to no avail.

When the men were committed in custody to stand their trial at the Old Bailey, DI Morrison told the court, 'I have evidence that people are still trying to get at these witnesses. Twice in the past week, attempts have been made to approach witnesses in this case' – this despite the fact that the witnesses had been permitted to write down their names and addresses.

On 25 October 1967 both men were found guilty at the Old Bailey and sentenced to eighteen months' imprisonment; a third man was acquitted. And that was just one of the conspiracies.

★

The first one – at least the first that was known about – had happened between 2 & 5 August 1966; in other words, within three days of Charlie Richardson's arrest. Christopher Glinski was approached on 4 August by two men, Arthur Robert Baron (who had known Charlie Richardson for years and had worked for him part-time in his metal yard) and Alfred Joseph Fraser (who, it will be remembered, had been arrested by Ted Greeno in 1955 and sent down for ten years' for his part in the Martin's Bank raid and who worked at Atlantic Machines); both men were aged fifty. Glinski had been told that with regard to the alleged attack on him by Charlie Richardson and others he would 'get plenty of girls and drink if he went away to the country' for the duration of the forthcoming trial. Moreover, he was told that he would be 'allowed to join the Richardson gang and become one of the boys', that Richardson was sorry about what had happened and that he would be 'recompensed'; and all this would happen if he were to swear an affidavit exonerating Richardson and James Fraser from taking part on the attack on him in Vauxhall Bridge Road Glinski appeared to accept the offer: on the first occasion, he met the men in the Globe public house in Baker Street and accepted £100, promising to swear the affidavit. But in the meantime he had informed the police, and on the following day, 5 August, the handover of the second £100 was witnessed by them. The pub's doors were locked, handcuffs claimed the wrists of the two men and Glinski's hand-written notes were found in Baron's pocket.

At the committal proceedings at Bow Street Magistrates' Court, Baron shouted, 'This man Glinski is telling lies, surely you can see that?'

But the magistrate, Mr Geraint Rees, obviously could not see it, told Baron to 'Keep quiet' and committed them in custody at the Old Bailey.

On 7 December 1966 Judge Graham Rogers told a jury at the Old Bailey that they would be under surveillance by plain clothes police officers to ensure no improper approach was made to them. And so they were: seventy-two officers were split into teams of six, one team for each juror, and two at a time they performed eight hour tours of duty. After a trial lasting seven days both men were found guilty and sentenced to two years' imprisonment; the jury sent the judge a note expressing their appreciation of the tactful and helpful manner in which the police had discharged their duties.

With hindsight, it was all a waste of time; six days later, the charges of causing actual bodily harm and demanding money with menaces from Glinski in respect of Charlie Richardson and Roy Hall were thrown out at their committal proceedings at Bow Street Magistrates' Court; and six months after that, those charges were dropped against Frankie Fraser, whilst Jimmy Fraser and Johnnie Longman pleaded guilty.

★

The next conspiracy was hatched between 1 December 1966 and 11 January 1967. Benjamin Coulston had already given compelling evidence at Clerkenwell Magistrates' Court in September 1966 of the torture meted out to him by Charlie and Eddie Richardson and Frank Fraser. Now, Coulston was approached by Evelyn Brindle, Frank Fraser's sister, who according to Fraser's memoirs had been eager to assist her brother in the past. When he was on trial in 1949, she had sat with his children in an ABC restaurant used by the jury, saying in a loud voice as they entered the restaurant, 'Don't you worry, your Dad'll be home soon, he's innocent' – although he actually got six months. In 1952 she tried the same trick at Bedford

Quarter Sessions, this time with even less success, because on that occasion Fraser went down for three years.

Still, practice makes perfect, and in a pub in Brixton on 17 December Brindle told Coulston that he would receive £500 to swear a false affidavit exonerating her brother, another £500 afterwards and a further £1,000 when the trial was over. To assist her she employed the services of Albert Edward Wood (who had known Fraser for years and had invested in Atlantic Machines) and Charlie Richardson's secretary, Josephine Louise Shaer. A five-page handwritten affidavit was prepared, but although they approached various Commissioners for Oaths on 2 January 1967, they were unable to get it signed. Coulston then notified the police, Evelyn Brindle's address at Denmark Road, Camberwell was searched and Detective Superintendent Vic Evans found, wrapped in brown paper, five pages of hand-written notes completely contradicting Coulston's previous testimony, together with £596. 'Give me that statement!' shouted Brindle. 'You can't take it; it's all I've got to prove my brother is innocent.'

There was a great deal more shouting at Bow Street Magistrates' Court from two girls in the public gallery when the trio were remanded in custody; and at a later hearing, when Superintendent Evans was giving evidence, Evelyn Brindle shouted to her husband, 'You know that is lies, Jim. I hope you'll bring my two daughters to prove it' and to Evans, 'Do you want me to get fifteen months or two years like poor Jimmy Fraser?'[5]

Some of the case was heard in camera before it was committed to the Old Bailey, where once more Judge Rogers had no hesitation in providing police protection for the jury.

Giving evidence, Evelyn Brindle told the jury that she had heard, via Wood, that Coulston was now saying he had made a false identification at Clerkenwell Court when he stated an attempt was made to pull out his teeth with pliers. 'I got in touch with Jose Shaer, who was Charles Richardson's secretary, as I wanted the matter put right', she said. She said that she would prepare a draft of what Coulston had to say, which he would have to sign in front of a solicitor. No one, she assured the jury, had ever suggested that Coulston should receive £2,000, adding that the only reason he had given false evidence in court was because he was afraid that the police

---

[5] This was probably a reference to James Fraser, who had been sentenced to fifteen months' imprisonment after he fell foul of Detective Sergeant Harry Challenor MM. Fraser's conviction was later quashed.

would prefer further charges against him if he did not. She admitted lying to the police when she initially denied being in possession of an unsigned document, because she feared the police might destroy it: 'It was the only evidence I had that he had told lies.'

Not bad, but not good enough. When she and her two co-defendants were found guilty on 21 March 1967, four young women made such a disturbance in the public gallery – they were a bellicose family – that they had to be forcibly ejected.

The following day, Gerald McArthur told the court that there were still a number of 'in-between' persons operating in London who might attempt to interfere with witnesses in the forthcoming Torture Trial (he was right), and Evelyn Brindle and Albert Wood were each sentenced to two years' imprisonment, while Miss Shaer received a six-month sentence.

Three conspiracies to pervert the course of justice, all of which suggested the involvement of Frankie Fraser. They were, of course, fit-ups. Eddie Richardson made that quite clear when he later said, 'Anyone who was around us was fitted up.'

This had been a bad conspiracy, no doubt about that, but the final conspiracy case, which featured Charlie Richardson and Johnnie Longman, put it in the shade.

*

This was in connection with the trial of Eddie Richardson and others in the Mr Smith's Club affray case. One of the witnesses had allegedly already been paid off and sent on a train to Manchester. Another, a doorman at the club, had received threatening telephone calls, as had his wife and children, telling them that their milk delivery would be poisoned; the doorman later suffered a nervous breakdown.

As for the jury, well, that was relatively easy. The names of the jurors were read out in court as they came to the jury box to be sworn. Charlie Richardson was in the public gallery, as was his associate, Johnnie Longman. When the names were read out, so they were jotted down; as the jurors left the court at the end of the day, they were identified to other members of the Richardson gang, who followed them to their home addresses. Several of the jurors were contacted, including one named Charles North, who was confronted on two occasions by two different people; he immediately reported the matter to the judge. It was on the second occasion that North had a milk bottle thrown through the front room window of his home address. Inside was a note, which read:

'Charlie bring them in guilty or else. A lot more where this came from. You're not alone amongst the twelve.'

The bottle-thrower was Charlie Richardson. The anomalous message, according to Richardson's twisted psyche, was aimed at confusing Mr North, in the same way that the victims in the torture sessions were unnerved and confused. Who could be responsible? Certainly not associates of anybody in the dock; they would hardly tell a juror to find them guilty, would they? No, it was almost certainly the police – probably Tommy Butler himself, whom Richardson hated with a passion. Soon he would have every reason to dislike him even more.

It was Tommy Butler who investigated this matter and he had a lot of help from Longman's former paramour, Mrs Daphne Clements. By the time she came to give evidence at the Old Bailey on 12 July 1967, Charlie Richardson was already one month into his twenty-five-year sentence. She told the court that the previous July she had gone with Longman to Richardson's address, where Longman was making telephone calls to jurors whose names had been jotted down on Richardson's list. She added that Richardson had appeared annoyed at the way one of the witnesses had given his evidence and had said, 'He would have to be punished.'

On another occasion, Mrs Clements told the jury, while she waited outside Richardson's address alone, in Longman's car, Richardson and Alf Fraser came out of the house in a great hurry. Longman then emerged briefly from the house telling her that he had to wait, in case there was a phone call; but when he came out again and told her he was going to take her for a drink he warned her, 'If anybody asks you, you've seen nobody leave this house tonight. Don't dare mention my friends' names to anybody or I'll punch you in the mouth, shoot you up the arse and arrange a convenient accident for you.' When they returned to Richardson's house, Richardson also came back and Longman went inside, only to emerge jubilant shortly afterwards. He then told her that they had thrown a bottle through North's window and said, 'I hope the bottle went through the television screen or hit his old woman on the head.'

It was a pity that Longman had mistreated Mrs Clements by knocking her about during their stormy relationship as common-law husband and wife; had he possessed even a modicum of common sense, he would have realized that that sort of behaviour often prompts a battered partner to give evidence against her bullying spouse.

When Richardson's house was searched at the time of his arrest, a sum of money was found, also a cigarette packet with Charles

North's name written on it, as it was on a piece of paper with the word 'wit' (probably an abbreviation for 'witness'). When he was charged, Richardson replied, 'The charges are ridiculous and a frame-up.' Longman, who probably realized he had said too much already, said nothing at all.

But the jury clearly did not believe that the charges were 'ridiculous' and after retiring for just over two hours found both men guilty. On 20 July 1967 Mr Justice O'Connor told Richardson, 'You, Richardson, deliberately set your face against society and as a part of your activities you thought you could bend the administration of justice to fit your own creed'; he then sentenced him to twelve years' imprisonment, to run concurrently with his twenty-five-year sentence. Describing Longman as 'Richardson's lapdog', the judge sentenced him to eight years' imprisonment.

It was all over. On the same day, charges were dropped against Richardson and Jean Goodman for making false statements to obtain passports, and Jean Goodman pleaded guilty to possessing sixteen Preludin tablets, a banned stimulant – she received an absolute discharge.

One month previously, on 20 June 1967, Berman, whose relationship with Charlie Richardson was described by Sebag Shaw as being that of 'the man who rode on the back of a tiger', changed his plea to one of guilty to demanding £1,200 with menaces from Taggart and also to causing actual bodily harm to a Michael O'Connor; since he had spent eleven months in custody awaiting trial, he was sentenced to a term of imprisonment to permit his immediate release. He also pleaded guilty to keeping 300 uncustomed watches and was fined £500; his pleas of not guilty to causing grievous bodily harm to both Taggart and O'Connor were accepted.

The following day, charges of conspiracy to cheat and defraud were dropped against Charlie Richardson, Jean Goodman, Johnnie Longman, Roy Hall, Brian Morse and Derek Brian Mottram.[6] The same applied to charges of larceny and storebreaking in respect of Charlie Richardson, Brian Morse and James Henry Kensett.

In a different court, Judge Graham Rogers sentenced Jimmy Moody to a term of imprisonment to coincide with his immediate release for attacking the three police officers, since he had been in

---

[6] Mottram had been certified too ill to stand trial on any of the charges, the court having been told that 'he could die at any moment'. Nevertheless, he bravely soldiered on until he expired fourteen years later.

custody for fifteen months since the time of his arrest for the affray at Mr Smith's Club.

And on 22 June appeals were lodged in respect of all those sentenced to imprisonment. This was expected of them, but it did them no good at all.

There was one other matter. Eddie Richardson's finger had been firmly placed in a rather lucrative pie in 1964 when he helped cream off illicit takings of £100,000 per year, courtesy of a sophisticated fraud run between 1962 and 1966 at the London Airport car parks. Twelve men were convicted and on 11 December 1967 were sentenced to a total of thirty-two years' imprisonment, with some being ordered to pay costs of £9,860.

However, Eddie Richardson was not among them. Neither was Frankie Fraser. There were two people with that surname who were acquitted, but not from the same family, I'm sure.

CHAPTER 19

Richardsons – the Aftermath

C harlie Richardson settled down to a disruptive life in prison. John McVicar described him as 'unscrupulous, treacherous and ruthless', and when he was unsurprisingly refused parole for the seventh time, having served fourteen years, he decided to escape and in 1980 did so, from an open prison. He was at large for seven months, but was arrested on his forty-seventh birthday in his brother's porn shop.

Layton Williams interviewed him at Coldingley Prison in 1983 regarding the murder of a previously released inmate who had been on the same wing as Richardson. In fact, Williams interviewed the entire wing and found Richardson to be 'polite and co-operative as he surely didn't want to jeopardise his release date . . . the prison warder informed me that Richardson was expecting an officer of at least the rank of detective superintendent, as he considered himself of such important notoriety.'

It must have come as a crushing blow to Richardson's ego to discover that he was being formally interviewed about a murder by an aid to CID.

Finally released in July 1984, Richardson remarried and had another child. He wrote his memoirs, *My Manor*, published in 1991 – his hatred and contempt for just about everyone spewed out of its pages. A heavy smoker all his life, he died of emphysema in September 2012.

★

Eddie Richardson was released in 1976, having served just over ten years. He opened a porn shop and then went back into the metal business.

He later opened a club named J. Arthur's in Catford managed by Roy Hall, who had been released in 1972 and had suffered several heart attacks. There were reports of drug abuse around the premises as well as a series of assaults which culminated in January 1986 when a young man was stabbed to death. Fifteen people were present; all of them claimed to have seen nothing. Chief Superintendent John Taylor successfully applied for the club's licence to be revoked.

Then, as Richardson would later say, 'I made a mistake.' This 'mistake' was being involved in the importation of two tonnes of cannabis, as well as 153 kilos of cocaine worth £43m to feed the habits of the country's 475,000 cocaine users. The quantity recovered amounted to one-third of the United Kingdom's total seizure of cocaine during 1989. At Winchester Crown Court in 1990 Eddie Richardson was sentenced to twenty-five years' imprisonment.

In prison he made friends with Lord Longford and turned out to be an accomplished painter; he was released in 2001.

★

Frank Fraser had been sentenced to fifteen years; following his involvement in a prison riot, he was finally released after serving twenty. Following a hunger strike ('People cheered and shook my hand') he began to commit his usual catalogue of misbehaviour in prison, chucking pots of urine and excrement over prison governors and attacking warders; it seemed illogical that a man who had pulled every possible stroke to get himself acquitted did just about everything he could, once he was convicted, to prolong his stay behind bars. Martin Gosling, the senior probation officer at Norwich Prison when Fraser arrived, told me that he asked Fraser through the Judas flap of his cell door if anyone needed to be notified of his arrival. 'He immediately leapt from his bunk', Gosling recalled, 'shouting, "Fuck off you sodding bastard!"' This outburst was accompanied by inaccurate spitting. 'He came to Norwich again a year or two later and succeeded in evading the clutches of two prison officers while on a reception board; for some reason he attacked the prison padre who was present, ripping from his neck the crucifix that he wore.'

Following his release, Fraser was 'amazed' to be convicted of receiving stolen coins in 1987 and sentenced to three years' imprisonment – later reduced on appeal to two.

In 1991, as he was leaving a club named Turnmills in Clerkenwell, he was shot in the head; naturally, he claimed that undercover police were responsible.

Fraser was a man who had been flogged, moved over a hundred times whilst serving sentences – sometimes spending just two days and nights in any one prison – and had spent forty-two years of his life behind bars; all this he recounted in a couple of dire memoirs. When he was in his eighties and was asked in a television interview if it was true he had killed forty men, he replied, 'Who am I to argue?' He later twice threatened violence to the interviewer and the year before his death was handed an ASBO (Anti-Social

Behaviour Order) for threatening a fellow resident at a care home. He died aged ninety in 2014.

My enduring memory of Frankie Fraser comes from a television documentary in which he leered at the camera and beseeched the viewers to believe that, 'We woz rascals, weren't we?' Well, it's a matter of opinion, isn't it? If you accept that 'rascal' fits the description of an unrepentant, perjuring, violent, torturing thief who was completely out of control, then yes, he probably was.

*

Jimmy Moody was a rudderless ship following his release, with no Charlie Richardson to guide him. Within a year, he and his brother Dickie gate-crashed a party, and when a row developed about the music being turned down, a fight ensued which resulted in twenty-one-year-old William Day being kicked and his skull smashed in with bricks. The brothers were convicted of his manslaughter and each sentenced to six years' imprisonment, with Jim Moody having a year added for attacking paedophile prisoners. He was later arrested for a series of armed robberies; whilst awaiting trial he escaped from Brixton Prison with the assistance of his brother Dickie, who was sentenced to eighteen months' imprisonment. But Jimmy Moody was never recaptured. He was on the run for thirteen years before finally being shot dead in an East End pub in 1993. It was rumoured that during the intervening years he had been a contract hit-man; no one has ever been convicted of his murder.

*

Henry Botton, the possessor of nine convictions, had only just been released from eight years' preventative detention for breaking into a bank before his involvement in the Mr Smith's Club affray; he was said to be a police informer. He was sixty-three years of age when eighteen-year-old Cornelius Burke, dressed as a police officer, tricked him into opening the front door of his house in Shooters Hill Road, Blackheath in July 1983. He then killed Botton with a shotgun helpfully supplied by Burke's associate, William Clarkson; both men were sentenced to life imprisonment the following October.

*

Following her release, Jean Goodman married a painter and decorator. Jean La Grange visited Charlie Richardson, campaigned for his release for a while and later, it is believed, went back to South Africa and her husband.

As for the rest, Bernard Wajcenberg had several more scrapes with the law: in July 1980 the fifty-three-year-old fraudster was sentenced to thirty months' imprisonment for his part in a £100,000 swindle. When he was arrested in Switzerland, his wife contacted John Simmonds to ask if his sentence could be served in England. However, Simmonds – who said to me, 'Benny was best described as a likeable rogue' – regretfully had to explain to Maria Wajcenberg that such an undertaking was beyond his jurisdiction. And Jack Duval? He was convicted of a £300,000 long firm fraud in 1972 and sent down for nine years.

★

So that was the story of the Richardsons and the Torture Trial. Gwyn Waters told me that Charlie Richardson had far more brains than the Kray twins but 'whatever enterprise Richardson was concerned with, violence had to be involved'.

CHAPTER 20

The Krays – Revisited

When the Krays received word of the affray at Mr Smith's Club they were delighted. They were not, of course, immediately apprised of the full facts but they were aware that the Richardson gang had been seriously disabled. Frankie Fraser had been shot, as had Ronald Jeffrey (both seriously), as well as Eddie Richardson; William Stayton had vanished – they were unaware that he had fled to Gibraltar but it mattered not, he was out of the way; Charlie Richardson had not been involved since he had been in South Africa; but for many of the gang, injured or not, with Dickie Hart dead there were charges pending.

Eddie Richardson and Fraser had had the fruit machines in the West End; they were now out of the running, so who was to stop the Krays making substantial inroads into the West End themselves? Albert Dimes? 'Albert can't fight for fuck', the twins dismissively remarked, and in fairness, Dimes, now in his fifties, would have found the combination of Reg and Ron difficult to contend with. And the word was that the US mafia wanted the twins to arrange gambling junkets for them. So all this could have led to a very smooth, trouble-free takeover.

At least it would have done, until two nights after the Smith's Club affray, when Ronnie Kray shot dead George Cornell at the Blind Beggar public house.

*

There had been bad blood between Ron and Cornell for some time. As a member of the Watney Streeters, Cornell – known then as George Myers – had fought with Ron and, unusually, Ron had come off worse. That was one, not unimportant matter; another was that there had been a confrontation between the two just prior to Christmas 1965, when Cornell had publicly referred to Ron as 'a fat poof'. In addition, Cornell had told the brother of a nineteen-year-old boy that the reason Ron was taking the attractive young man to Newcastle was not, as he claimed, to further the lad's boxing career, but for more salacious purposes. And lastly, and probably least importantly, Cornell ran porn shops in the West End which the twins wanted.

On the evening of 9 March 1966 John Dickson drove John Alexander 'Scotch Ian' Barrie and Ronnie Kray to the Blind

Beggar pub in the Mile End Road, Stepney after one of Ronnie's 'boys' had excitedly informed him, 'Cornell's in the Beggars'. Visiting the pub was, of course, a deliberately provocative act on Cornell's part, because it was in the heart of Kray territory; but not only was Cornell unafraid of Ron, he was openly contemptuous of him. Macabrely, the jukebox was playing a popular song of the day, the Walker Brothers' *The Sun Ain't Gonna Shine Any More*, and for George Cornell, who was sitting at the bar, it didn't. He had just time to sneer, 'Well, look who's here?' as the two men entered the pub, before Barrie let off two shots to scatter and disorientate the customers, whereupon Ronnie Kray fired his Luger, hitting Cornell in the forehead. Cornell's two companions – Albie Wood and Johnny Dale – fled, the barmaid ran into the cellar, other customers, including Michael Flannery, made themselves scarce; and as Cornell lay dying on the floor, Ron and Barrie nonchalantly strolled out of the pub, got into their waiting car and drove off.

The post-mortem was carried out at Westminster mortuary by Professor Cedric Keith Simpson CBE, FRCP, FRCPath; removing a single bullet from Cornell's head, he deduced that due to the absence of powder marks, the shot had been fired from a few feet away.

Although Ron needed no justification to commit a murder he would later say that it was in revenge for the killing of Dickie Hart who, he claimed, was a cousin; and since it appeared that Hart had been dispatched by a rival firm of which Cornell was a member even though he had not been present at the murder, that was reason enough.

By the following morning every man and his dog in the East End knew about Cornell's killing and, more importantly, who was responsible. Tommy Butler was detached from his duties as head of the Flying Squad to investigate what was, on the face of it, a straightforward murder carried out in full view of any number of witnesses and to solve it in no time at all.

But he didn't. No one was talking. No one had seen anything. And when Ronnie Kray was put up for identification, no one picked him out. No one, apparently, knew anything – with the possible exception of Gerald McArthur. John Simmonds told me:

> On the night of the Blind Beggar shooting, Mr Mac had info that something big was coming down with the Krays and the Richardsons. He deployed DS Don Jones and myself to keep obs on the Britannia public house which was in the back streets of Whitechapel. We had a 5 RCS radio so we couldn't listen in or speak to the Met.

We heard a lot of police and ambulance activity but the Britannia was dead quiet. Only when we heard the news on the BBC did we realize we had been at the wrong location – perhaps fortunately!

The fact that no one had spoken was beyond the twins' wildest dreams. They left the country – nobody tried to stop them – and flew to Morocco, where they met up with Billy Hill (who by now was privately describing the twins as, 'brainless cunts'). Reg was followed by Christine, a hostess from London, whilst Ron sought the attentions of any available 'brown boy' in Tangiers.

Then they returned home – and still nobody was saying anything.

Perhaps someone was doing something, however. Apparently, two days after the murder, two unknown men called at the flat of Cornell's elder brother James at Welstead House, Cannon Street Road, Stepney and handed him a parcel containing a revolver and twelve rounds of ammunition, telling him, 'You might need this'. At least, that was the story about its possession given to the bench at Thames Magistrates' Court on 6 August 1966. It appeared that Cornell did not need it and he was fined £50.

*

The twins had always treated the police with contempt ('Coppers is dirt') but nevertheless, they did on occasion try to ingratiate themselves with the force. Mike Warburton recounted the story of how the detective chief inspector from Limehouse and his men were having a drink in The Blue Posts in West India Dock Road when the Krays and some of their followers entered the pub. One of the camp followers sidled over and said, 'Mr Kray sends his compliments and asks if you'd care to have a drink with him?'

To this, the DCI – a rather tough character – replied, 'Please tell Mr Kray, thank you. On this one occasion, I'll have a whisky and soda with him . . . but please also tell him that if he ever sets foot on my manor again, it'll be the worse for him.'

In those days, CID officers were just as territorially inclined as the brothers Kray!

Nevertheless, they still used corrupt members of the Force for their own ends. One such was a bent detective sergeant who, it was said, demanded a sum of money from Ronnie – £20 per week, £50 per week or a flat, one-off payment of £50, it matters not – for unrestricted use of an East End pub. Unable to resist scoring off the hated police, Ron recorded an incriminating conversation with the cop on a concealed tape recorder and then handed it into the Yard. It appeared, however, that Ronnie had not grasped that in doing so he would be required to give evidence at the cop's forthcoming trial; when a witness summons was issued, he promptly went into hiding, and after a retrial in Ron's absence the cop was acquitted.

By December 1966 nobody appeared to be busying themselves about Cornell's murder and the heat was lifting off Ronnie regarding his non-appearance at the bent cop's trial. It was therefore time for the twins' next piece of unparalleled stupidity – engineering Frank Mitchell's escape from Dartmoor.

★

Frank Samuel Mitchell was born in 1929 with learning difficulties; many regarded him as a gentle soul, and so he could be when he was mending watches or making model cars. But he was also dangerously psychotic and could turn from gentle giant to raving lunatic in a split second. He was first arrested at the age of nine, and a string of offences led him on three occasions into Borstal, where he was the ringleader in a riot. Imprisonments followed: for receiving a stolen revolver, then storebreaking and housebreaking. Given a three-year sentence for burglary in 1954, within two days of entering prison he had attacked a warder, for which he received fifteen strokes of the cat. He was transferred to Rampton Psychiatric Hospital the following year and in 1957 he escaped, broke into a house, threatened to kill the married couple who lived there and attacked the husband with an iron bar. When arrested he was found to be in possession of hatchets as well as the iron bar. Sentenced to nine years' imprisonment for larceny and wounding with intent to murder, he was certified as insane and transferred to Broadmoor Psychiatric Hospital.

In July 1958 he escaped once more. When sixty-four-year-old Mr Edward Charles Peggs heard someone, attempting to push his car out of the garage of his remote house near Wokingham in the middle of the night, he called out to the intruder. This resulted in Mitchell, armed with an axe, leaping over a hedge and in through the window.

'Yeah', Kray supporters and Mitchell apologists sagely remark, 'but 'e jus' frettened 'im – 'e didn't 'urt 'im.'

Didn't he? This is what Mr Peggs had to tell the court at Mitchell's committal:

> I looked for something and all I could find was my walking stick. I met him half-way up the stairs. He started to aim blows at me with the axe. I warded off as many as I

could from my head with my stick but he got several blows about my shoulders and arms. Luckily, before he got to the top of the landing, the axe-head came off the handle. He got me in a sort of commando grip which nearly broke my back and gripped me by the throat until I fell unconscious. When I came to, he had my wife on the floor and he had her by the throat. He then ordered me to get up. I couldn't.

Mitchell produced a large billhook, threatened the couple, stole clothes and money and tied up fifty-nine-year-old Mrs Eva Ellen Peggs, whom he had dragged out from underneath the bed where she was hiding, before escaping in Mr Peggs' Ford Prefect. Their whole ordeal had lasted from 3.45 to 5.15 am.

'Jus' frettened'? When the couple were examined by Dr John Ambleton, both were in a state of nervous collapse. Mrs Peggs was weeping (she later said, 'I still shake when I think about that night') and Mr Peggs had bruising on his arms and shoulders.

Later the same morning, Mitchell was caught on a bus. He smilingly surrendered to the police, but when he appeared in court he was transformed into a raving lunatic. At Berkshire Assizes on 2 October 1958 he pleaded guilty to two charges of robbery, asked the court to take two other charges of larceny into consideration and, after Mr Justice Byrne described him with reasonable accuracy as 'a danger to the community', was sentenced to concurrent terms of ten years and life imprisonment.

It appears that the penal authorities took his statement in court ('I want to prove I am sane and know what I'm doing') at face value; he was sent to Hull prison, where in April 1962, during an attempted mass break-out, he attacked a prison warder, permanently maiming his right hand. One month later, he slashed another warder in the face with a knife who required seventy-five stitches; for this he received fifteen strokes of the birch. But within four months he was transferred to Dartmoor, where he was given a great deal of freedom. There were two reasons for this: first, the prison had developed a rather more liberal regime, and secondly, the warders were terrified of him. At six feet one, with a fifty-four inch chest and arms like legs, Mitchell was a physical fitness fanatic, spending endless hours in the gym lifting heavier and heavier weights or in his cell performing hundreds of press-ups and sit-ups. When he wasn't breeding budgerigars and slashing warders, he would demonstrate his enormous physical strength by grabbing two warders by their belts and lifting them, one in each hand, above his head. They probably thought that a little humiliation of this kind was preferable to having their faces slashed open.

So what had this to do with the twins? Simply this: Mitchell wanted a release date and by springing him from prison – not a difficult task, because he was out of doors, practically unsupervised with an 'Honour Party' – they could hide him, send letters to the people who mattered and when the Home Secretary kindly provided a release date, Mitchell could peacefully surrender to the authorities, return to prison and mend a few more watches, gleefully awaiting his release. Of course, the twins could not publicly benefit from this act of humanity in the same way that they could be acclaimed for their 'charitable' events, but the word of their benevolence would flash through the East End like a bushfire.

This imbecile line of reasoning, plus a complete inability to foresee the disastrous consequences of their own actions, suggests that the twins were even more educationally challenged than Mitchell.

★

On 12 December 1966 Mitchell emerged from the Devon moorland and on to Princetown Road, where a grey Humber hired by Billy Exley was waiting. Two members of the Firm, Albert Donoghue and 'Mad Teddy' Smith, provided a change of clothing and persuaded Mitchell to relinquish the knife which accompanied him; and by the time it was realized that he was missing, Mitchell was safely ensconced at 206a Barking Road, East Ham. This was a flat usually inhabited by Lennie 'Books' Dunn, so called because he sold magazines and books from a Whitechapel stall. He had previously been a Kray hanger-on; now he really believed that his status had been elevated to full membership of the Firm.

It started off well. Lisa Prescott, an attractive nightclub hostess, was given £100 and provided as company for Mitchell. Next, letters were laboriously written, verified with Mitchell's thumbprint, to newspapers and the Home Secretary. But although he was occupied and becoming besotted with Miss Prescott, in between obsessively cleaning his teeth and performing press-ups Mitchell was becoming restless. Reg had been to see him just once; Ron, not at all.

And when the Home Secretary declared in Parliament that consideration could only be given to providing him with a date of release once he had returned to prison, this was not something that Mitchell wanted to hear. He grabbed Billy Exley's gun and started making threats against the twins, who quickly got to hear of it.

What could they do? If they anonymously grassed Mitchell's whereabouts to the police, there was a very good chance that he would grass them in return. No, on 23 December there was a council of war at which it was decided that Mitchell had to go – and not back to prison either.

Versions differ as to what happened next. Donoghue would later say that Mitchell was taken just around the corner to Ladysmith Avenue, where four men, including Freddie Foreman, were waiting in a Thames van. He had been told that he was going to be taken through the Blackwall Tunnel, that Lisa would be following in another car and that they would be reunited, with Ronnie Kray present as a bonus, at a farm in Kent. Mitchell believed it, probably because he wanted to believe it, but once he got in the back of the van, with Donoghue in the front, the slamming of the back doors was the signal for the shooting to start. Possibly thirteen shots were fired in all; probably the last two killed him.

Foreman would later say he wasn't even there; the other three men never stood trial; and Mitchell's body has never been found.

Donoghue made what he said was a prearranged telephone call to Reggie Kray saying, 'That dog has won.' This was a coded message, in case Reg's telephone calls were being intercepted, and since Donoghue stated that he had no idea that Mitchell was going to be murdered, he claimed it meant that Mitchell was on his way to Kent. Lisa, however, had a different recollection; she would later state that Donoghue had said, 'The dog is dead' – which did tend to put a different interpretation on the matter. The flat was cleaned to rid it of fingerprints, and Lisa, who had heard the shots, was told to say she hadn't; she was threatened by Reggie Kray to make her keep her mouth shut. She did.

*

Christmas came and went and Ronnie's mind was starting to unravel more and more; he developed a severe identity crisis, never being sure if he was a reincarnation of Al Capone, Lawrence of Arabia or Gordon of Khartoum. He was also convinced that he had lost one of his fingers, although this could be attributed to his lack of numeracy skills rather than his hallucinations. On the plus side, business was still booming, with the sale of stolen bearer bonds from the USA and Canada. Although Reggie was drinking more and more, he tried to revive his unhappy marriage with Frances. Despite her previous suicide attempt they tried a reconciliation; he booked tickets for a holiday in Ibiza, but the following day, 8 June 1967, Frances was found dead following a massive overdose of phenobarbitone.

Reg was beside himself with grief; naturally, he blamed everyone but himself (or Ron) for his unhappy wife's demise – especially her parents, 'who turned her against me'. The funeral at Chingford cemetery was predictable in its bad taste even by East End gangster standards: the ten limousines, the hundreds of flowers and, in the midst of genuine sorrow, the seething hatred between Reg and the Shea family.

Belatedly, the twins took over the running of the fruit machines and pornography shops in the West End which had recently been vacated first by Eddie Richardson and Frank Fraser and then by George Cornell. Reg's drinking was getting worse and so was his violent behaviour – two shootings and a knifing.

Ronnie was becoming more and more suspicious of Leslie Payne, who knew so much about the twins' illicit dealings; he came to believe that if Payne were ever arrested he would give the police chapter and verse about their activities. Therefore he gave Jack 'The Hat' McVitie a gun and a deposit of £100 to shoot Payne, with a balance of £400 to be paid when the job was done. McVitie either bungled the job or, more likely, had no intention of doing it. He made excuses to Ronnie, promised he would do it and then staggered into the Regency Club under the influence of an unwise concoction of drink and barbiturates, waving a sawn-off shotgun and threatening, in the twins' absence, to shoot them. By the following day the Ron and Reg had become aware of this stupid, drunken threat. It would sign McVitie's death warrant.

Three matters were the catalyst for Jack the Hat's demise. The first was that Ronnie – referring to Cornell – would incessantly say to Reg, 'I've done mine, now it's time to do yours.' Secondly, McVitie had had the impudence to dare to threaten the twins. Lastly, Reg was consumed with mawkish sorrow for his dead wife (who, he believed, had been transformed into a little robin) which was combined with his drinking, his rage and his desire to extract a suitable revenge on somebody – in fact, anybody – for Frances' death. It could not be anyone from the Shea family; in his disintegrating state of mind he believed that Frances, looking down from heaven, would know, and never forgive him. Therefore Jack the Hat would be a suitable candidate.

★

The preparations were meticulous. The scene was set when Ron and Reg arrived at a basement flat at 71 Evering Road, Stoke Newington on the evening of 28 October. The occupier was Mrs Carol Ann Skinner, known as 'Blonde Carol', who lived there with her two young children; she had planned a party there which Ronnie had obviously heard about because he asked her, 'Weren't you expecting us?'

She was directed to hold her party elsewhere, which she did; Ronnie Hart – the twins' second cousin and nine years their junior – was told to go to the Regency Club and tell Tony Barry to come and bring a .32 pistol with him. At the same time, the Lambrianou brothers, Chris and Tony, petty criminals who each had convictions for possessing knives and who were friends of Jack the Hat, were to find him and bring him to 'a party' at the address. That was what happened. Barry gave the pistol to Reg and announced the arrival of McVitie and the Lambrianous. A boxing programme was being shown on the television and a record player was ready to be turned on, to drown the noise of the shots.

McVitie, completely unsuspecting, burst into the room, shouting, 'Where's the birds? Where's the booze?' – but Reg was behind the door and pulled the trigger of the pistol, which failed to fire. Reg then grabbed McVitie but he struggled free and tried to dive head-first through a window, whereupon he was dragged back and pulled to his feet.

'Be a man, Jack!' screamed Ronnie and received the reply, 'I'll be a man but I don't want to die like one!'

Ronnie then grabbed McVitie in a bear-hug from behind, trapping his arms, and shouted, 'Kill him, Reg – do him!'

And Reg, ever the subservient one, did – he stabbed McVitie in the face and, as he sank to his knees, stabbed him again and again, in the stomach, chest and throat.

McVitie murmured, 'Oh no . . . oh no', obviously feeling the life draining from his body.

Reg now pulled the knife from McVitie's throat and thrust it in again, using two hands and twisting it. By the time McVitie was carried up to Blonde Carol's bedroom and thrown on to her bed, in the room where her children were asleep, he was quite dead.

*

Covered in McVitie's blood, the twins – Reg with a cut on his hand from the knife he had wielded – were taken by Ronnie Hart to the flat of someone they had known for years, a friend of their parents named Harry Hopwood. Hart took the knife and the gun, which he threw into a canal near Queensbridge Road, and while the twins bathed at Hopwood's address, Hart fetched fresh clothing for them from Vallance Road He cleaned the twins' jewellery, their rings and cufflinks, burnt their paper money, then put their bloodstained clothes in a suitcase that was disposed of by Hopwood's relative, Percy Merricks, who soaked it in paraffin and burnt it. Charlie Kray arrived and was furious when he found out about the murder; later, Ronnie Bender came and told everyone – and this was obviously a reference to McVitie – 'He's in the car'. The twins told Bender to dump the body in the East End; they were angry when he telephoned to say he had driven the car across London Bridge and abandoned it, leaving the body in the back covered with an eiderdown. It was left to Charlie to cover up for his siblings and to contact Freddie Foreman to see about disposing of the body.

Now came the gruesome business of clearing up the scene of the murder; not the twins' job, of course. When Carol Skinner returned to her flat at 4.00 am she was denied access to the basement by Ronnie Bender who, she noticed, had a pair of her little boy's socks on his hands. Understandably annoyed at being told what to do in her own home, she asked why she couldn't come in, to be told that there had been some trouble and 'We're just clearing up'. That was an understatement; Bender was carrying her washing up bowl containing a mixture of blood and water, which he emptied down the lavatory, there was smashed glass everywhere, the floor was wet where it had obviously been washed and the carpet, folded in a heap, was bloodstained.

Later that evening, Albert Donoghue arrived to help clean up. The walls were scrubbed down and re-plastered where necessary, wallpaper was removed and replaced with tar paper stuck down as an aid against damp – unfortunately, when the tar paper was later stripped off by the police, blood-spots matching McVitie's group were found underneath it. Blood had got under the lino, which had to be taken up; felt was put down and a new carpet laid. In the space of twelve hours the basement was completely redecorated, all the old furniture was removed and new furniture was put in place.

Apart from the smell of fresh paint, it was as though nothing had happened at 71 Evering Road. McVitie's common-law wife, Mrs Sylvia Barnard, reported him missing, but the police did not launch a nationwide search; Jack the Hat had wandered off before and he would probably re-appear. And the twins? After leaving Hopwood's address they had gone to Tommy 'The Bear' Brown's flat in Tottenham – it was Brown's brother who supplied the new furniture – before moving on to stay with their friend Geoff Allen, who at that time was living in Lavenham, Suffolk.

After a couple of weeks, they returned to London. The police weren't looking for them because nobody was talking. Once again,

they'd got away with murder. They were apparently invincible.
George Cornell's widow Olive was making a nuisance of herself
– she had smashed every window at Fort Vallance and a sympa-
thetic magistrate had fined her a pound – and it was thought that
Carol Skinner and Ronnie Hart's common-law wife Vicky (who
had also been at Evering Road) might be a problem. But Ronnie
Kray wasn't too concerned. He mentioned that if necessary, he had
a woman lined up to poison the three of them.

CHAPTER 21

Re-enter Nipper Read

Following his success with the Richardson enquiry, Gerald McArthur planned to take on the Krays; in fact, he had already started to collate information, but when this was discovered, the top brass at the Yard were furious and demanded that he hand over every bit of evidence to them. This was because the Assistant Commissioner (Crime), Peter Brodie, had had his nose put firmly out of joint when the complainants in the Richardson case had gone to McArthur in Hertfordshire because they felt the Met could not be trusted. True, McArthur had done a fine job with his mixture of Met, Hertfordshire and No. 5 RCS officers, plus he had been rewarded with an MBE. However, the Commissioner, Sir Joseph Simpson KBE, had died suddenly in office; his deputy, Sir John Waldron KCVO, had stepped into a caretaker role, but Brodie could foresee that he himself stood a very good chance of becoming Commissioner. And this was not vanity on his part; like Simpson, Brodie had been a product of what had been known as Lord Trenchard's (the pre-war Commissioner) 'officer class'. What he needed was the ability to show the powers that be that not all of the Met detectives were bent and that 'his chaps', as he referred to his CID officers, could produce a resounding success. What he needed, in fact, were the Krays, arrested, convicted and in prison.

A month prior to McVitie's murder, Nipper Read had been promoted to the rank of detective superintendent and posted to C1 Department at the Yard – erroneously referred to as the Murder Squad. Within days, he was summoned to Brodie's office to be told that he would be responsible for catching the Krays.

Read was not best pleased; he had received a humiliating setback with the Krays' acquittal in the blackmail case, and any attempt to prosecute them again would be seen in many quarters as victimization. Still, orders were orders, and he commenced work under the direction of Commander John du Rose OBE – with a staff of just two detective sergeants – at Tintagel House.

First, Read assembled a list of names, people who had been associated with the Krays, from his previous investigation; carefully, he worked his way through the list to determine who might help him, cautiously avoiding those who might report back to the twins.

Finally, he hit pay dirt in the shape of Leslie Payne. Read had heard that Payne was on 'Ronnie's hit list' – Payne had not. During the next three weeks Payne, with immunity from prosecution granted by the Director of Public Prosecutions, dictated a 137-page statement which became a catalogue of many of the twins' misdeeds. Names were named, other witnesses came forward and more detectives were added to the team.

Of course, Read knew about the Cornell shooting – everybody did – and he was aware of Frank Mitchell's disappearance. 'Mad Teddy' Smith had also vanished. Billy 'Jack' Frost, Ronnie's driver, had similarly not been seen for some time. About McVitie he knew only that he was missing – until an informant pointed him in the direction of the murder scene, where to his dismay Carol Skinner denied knowing anything about it.

But when Read received information regarding a murder plot set up by Kray associate Alan Bruce Cooper (known as 'ABC') involving explosives, he had a young man named Paul Elvey arrested in Glasgow. All the evidence was there: three dozen sticks of dynamite, a suitcase concealing a hypodermic needle containing cyanide and, for equally silent killing, a crossbow. When the cross-bow was tested, it was found to have a velocity of 130ft per second and to be accurate to a range of at least 50yds. Cooper, too, was arrested; slim, with a stutter and an American accent, he hardly gave the impression of being a contract killer, although the late Detective Sergeant Bill Waite BEM told me, 'He was the coldest man I ever met.'

Read was stunned, then furious, when Cooper told him that he had been working as an informant for John du Rose, who duly confirmed that this was true. Read told me, 'I took him out on the staircase of Tintagel House and let him have it' – meaning, of course, verbal rather than physical abuse. Du Rose tried to calm the situation by telling Read that he had not used Cooper as an informant 'as such' and assured him that if he had received pertinent information he would have immediately passed it on – something that Read had great difficulty accept-ing. However, it could have been true; Du Rose, fine detective though he was, did not have experience of handling informants, allowing the manipulative Mr Cooper to oversee the situation and use it to his best advantage when he was placed in a precar-ious position such as being implicated in a murder plot with the brothers Kray.

Cooper's assassination plans were the subject of scornful com-ment later in court, when he was asked if it was true that because of his 'silly schemes' he was known as 'silly bollocks'?

To this, Cooper replied, 'This is quite news to me. If I was called "silly bollocks", the Krays must have been more stupid than I, to have taken me into their confidence.'

When Joey Kaufman – a member of the US mafia – visited Cooper and told him that the latest batch of stolen bearer bonds were due to be delivered to him, by post, at his London hotel within a few days, Read realized that matters would now have to move very fast. Cooper was not under arrest and it was possible he would get word to the Krays; Read therefore called a pre-arrest meeting at Tintagel House during the early hours of 8 May 1968. His meagre staff was supplemented by officers from the Regional Crime Squads – over a hundred detectives were now assembled to raid twenty-four addresses and arrest twenty-six suspects in an operation synchronized for 6.00 am.

When Nipper Read forced the door of the twins' ninth floor flat at Braithwaite House, Reg, Ron and their minders were all arrested. Reg was in bed with a girl and Ron was on a sofa in a state of tender intimacy with the son of a highly placed member of the Firm; the lad's father was either unaware of the relationship or was exceptionally broad-minded.

On being arrested, Ron replied, 'All I can say is, it's ridiculous. I don't know anything about murder, do I?'

But he did.

Reg replied, 'We've expected another frame-up for a long time. But this time, we've got witnesses. There are plenty of people who will want to help us.'

And there were those who wouldn't.

Others were brought into West End Central police station, their premises having been searched. Charlie Kray had been arrested, as had Tommy Cowley, who exclaimed, 'Murder? Whose murder? What are you talking about? I'm not a gangster or something. I'm not a gangster, Guv'nor.'

Few questions were answered and no admissions made by the prisoners at West End Central; much of the time was spent typing up the carbon copy charge sheets, and not everybody on Read's list had been caught – Ronnie Hart and 'Scotch Ian' Barrie, for example, escaped. But after fifty hours eighteen men were charged with a variety of offences, including conspiracy to murder, demanding money with menaces, inflicting grievous bodily harm and conspiracy to defraud. The last charge included mafioso Joey Kaufman, dragged protesting from his room at a Mayfair hotel; the stolen bearer bonds which were indeed en route to him through the post arrived within a couple of days, valued at $190,000.

On 10 May 1968, amidst a noisy motorcycle and marked police car escort, the men appeared at Bow Street Magistrates' Court. Nine of the prisoners were granted bail by the resident magistrate, Mr Kenneth Barraclough; the Kray brothers were not among them.

After a much-needed sleep in a proper bed, Read marshalled his troops. Protection for the witnesses was paramount – and so was the need to bring in those who had escaped the initial swoop. Three days after the first court appearance, Lennie 'Books' Dunn walked into West Ham police station; in the same way that Payne had drawn up a catalogue of the frauds, Dunn outlined a blueprint for Mitchell's murder. Billy Exley and Alfred Charles 'Limehouse' Willey, both charged with one offence of conspiracy to defraud, had been two of those granted bail at Bow St; now, the day following Dunn's revelations, they contacted Read and added their own input on Mitchell's murder. Lisa Prescott was traced and she, too, made a compelling statement.

Charlie Mitchell had been remanded in custody charged with five offences relating to fraudulent transactions; he asked to see Read and, apart from informing him that he had been told to find the money for a £50,000 contract to murder both him and Leslie Payne, he also made a full confession. When Mitchell appeared in court with the other defendants and the magistrate was informed that no evidence was to be offered against him or Billy Exley and that they were to be used as prosecution witnesses, it was the first indication to the slack-jawed Kray brothers that their defence was not as tight as they might have wished.

Others were arrested. Cornelius Whitehead asked to speak to Read in prison in order to feel things out – a few days later in court, he complained of being threatened, as did Wally Garelick, both of them charged with being concerned in Mitchell's escape and also harbouring him. Tommy Cowley and 'Scotch Jack' Dickson also nervously saw Read; they made no admissions but they, too, were on a fishing expedition.

John 'Scotch Ian' Barrie turned up drunk in the East End and was arrested; he told Detective Chief Inspector Henry Mooney, 'I feel sick. I have been like an animal for some days. I knew you would come for me and such a lovely day, too. I didn't shoot Cornell. I wish I could tell you what happened but I would get shot.'

He was duly picked out by the Blind Beggar barmaid as being the man with Ronnie Kray on the night he had murdered Cornell. And there was more.

Albert Donoghue had also been arrested, and on 31 May Read charged him and Reg Kray with the murder of Frank Mitchell. But when Donoghue – probably the twins' most trusted lieutenant – later met the three brothers in the solicitors' room at Brixton prison he was coolly told that Barrie was going to admit the murder of Cornell, Ronnie Bender would accept responsibility for McVitie's murder and that he, Donoghue, would take the rap for the murder of Mitchell. They, the brothers, would graciously accept responsibility for the frauds and any miscellaneous violence.

The following day, during visiting hours, Donoghue passed a note to his mother asking for Read to come and see him. When he did so, Donoghue made a full statement stressing that he had nothing to do with Mitchell's murder, and Read believed him. His admissions covered forty pages.

Things were now falling into place. Having previously denied any knowledge of the events surrounding McVitie's murder, Carol Skinner was seen again; now she told the full story. Harry Hopwood and Percy Merricks also gave their accounts of what had transpired after McVitie's murder, the misfiring pistol used in his murder was recovered and Ronnie Hart – later used as a prosecution witness – gave himself up over McVitie's murder and was minded by aid to CID Peter Burgess at a safe house in Harwich.

The Lambrianou brothers were arrested for McVitie's murder as was Ronnie Bender; they were all charged as, two weeks later, was Tony Barry. Freddie Foreman, charged with being an accessory after the fact replied, 'It's ridiculous.'

Initially, the Krays asked for reporting restrictions to be lifted, in order to (a) extract the maximum amount of publicity and (b) show the world how cruelly they were being treated. However, when compelling evidence of their duplicity was continually revealed, they tried to put a stop to the newspapers' reporting, going as far as the High Court to do so; they were unsuccessful.

Arthur Porter told me, 'After transporting the Richardson gang to and from Court, by comparison the Krays were perfect gentlemen.'

However, their civilized demeanour in court broke down as the evidence against them began to unfurl. When Ronnie Hart gave evidence of the McVitie murder, there were shouts from the court of 'That's a lie because it never happened', 'You're known as a liar in the East End' and 'You fucking rat'.

Nor was their invective restricted to the witnesses. When Reg Kray complained that detectives had taken away his grandparents' pension books and Geraint Rees, the magistrate, told him that it would be brought to the attention of the authorities for what it was worth, Reg Kray shouted, 'It's worth a lot to us, you old bastard!'

The number of defendants in the dock had slowly been whittled down, the committals for trials had been in stages, but eventually the most important charges, those of the three murders, had been committed to the Old Bailey, and it was on 7 January 1969 that the trial for the murders of George Cornell and Jack McVitie got underway.

*

It is quite likely that the caustic Mr Justice Melford Stevenson was the sternest judge at the Old Bailey since Lord Goddard. He had outraged bookmakers when he collectively described them as 'a bunch of crooks', and the fact that he referred to the 1967 reform of the law on homosexuality as 'a buggers' charter' cannot have endeared him to Ronnie Kray; but it was Melford Stevenson who presided over the first of the Kray Firm's trials.

Kenneth George Illtyd Jones QC (later Sir Kenneth and a High Court Judge) had served during the Second World War as a staff captain with the Royal Artillery and had been Mentioned in Dispatches; war service had interrupted his law degree, but not for long. Florid and overweight, his powerful delivery and skill as a prosecutor had resulted in the Attorney General's selecting him to lead the prosecution of the Krays.

Fifty newspapermen and members of the public were admitted to No. 2 Court by numbered ticket only, issued by Leslie Boyd, the Clerk of the Court. An equal number of police officers were also present. The judge rejected requests for the murders to be tried separately.

The jury were provided with police protection; one of those involved was Robin Jackson, an aid to CID. He had been briefed at the Yard and shown photos of those likely to attempt nobbling of the jury; at the end of each day, he and his partner would shadow their selected juror home. He told me:

> We never spoke to them; we strictly had no communication with them, whatsoever . . . my colleague and I followed our juror home every evening to East Ham. On one occasion, on a crowded Central Line train, we sussed a few unsavoury characters in the same carriage and duly reported it. So the next evening returning home, we recognized at least half a dozen surveillance officers riding that Tube with us and our unaware juror. This was a magnificently run operation; woe betide you if, as the detective superintendent drove around in the middle of the night, with us parked outside our juror's home, you were found asleep in your car. That was you out, and off back to uniform.

Back in court, Ronald Kray and Barrie pleaded not guilty to murdering Cornell; Reg denied harbouring them.

The twins, the Lambrianou brothers, Ronald Bender and Anthony Barry all pleaded not guilty to murdering McVitie. Charlie Kray, Cornelius Whitehead and Freddie Foreman all pleaded not guilty to being accessories after the fact. Albert Donoghue, however, pleaded guilty.

Probably recalling his time as a Judge-Advocate during war crimes trials in 1945 – and perhaps unwisely – Melford Stevenson ordered that the defendants wear numbered cards around their necks in the dock. The prisoners were furious, with Ronnie Kray exclaiming, 'This is not a cattle market!' and they tore off and ripped up the cards. It could be they had a point. An agreement was finally reached by which numbers were placed in front of them, on the outside of the dock. And after that bit of courtroom drama, there was more as Kenneth Jones described to the jury 'the horrifying, deadly effrontery' of the murder of Cornell and that of McVitie as, 'terrified, bathed in sweat, like a caged animal, he tried to escape by throwing himself through a window.'

The barmaid from the Blind Beggar took centre stage at the Old Bailey when, asked if she recognized the man who shot Cornell, she pointed dramatically at the dock and replied, 'It was Number One over there – Ronald Kray.'

Asked if she could identify the man with him, again there was no hesitation when she pointed to Barrie in the line-up and correctly identified him as being 'Number Two in the dock'.

Any doubts regarding Ronnie Kray? 'Oh no, that was him.'

Or Barrie? 'None whatsoever'.

Asked why she told lies at the inquest, she replied, 'I was terrified I would get shot like George Cornell if I told the truth. I was scared stiff.'

Reg Kray would say, much later, that following the murder he had 'had a word' with the barmaid and had 'given her a few quid to keep her happy' – it's likely this was sheer invention.

The Krays had presented a good front for the jury: smart suits, crisp linen, sober ties – and no shouting at a woman witness. This did not apply when John Dickson gave evidence that he had driven Ronnie Kray and Barrie to the Blind Beggar and that afterwards Ron had told Reg that he had shot Cornell. 'If what he says is true, why isn't he here on a murder charge?' shouted Reg Kray.

Dickson, who had previously served a prison sentence for safebreaking and was currently serving a nine months' sentence having pleaded guilty to harbouring Mitchell, shouted back, 'It's because of you that I'm here!'

Probably the most telling moment in Dickson's testimony was when he was asked why he had changed his account of what had happened. His reply was both simple and dramatic: 'Because the murders had to stop'.

Another witness told the court that Reg Kray had told him, 'Ronnie has just shot Cornell. He's a funny fellow, Ronnie; he never lets on what he's going to do.'

Billy Exley told the court that he was present at a flat in Stoke Newington when Reg Kray, Barrie and Ron Kray were discussing the murder of Cornell, with Ron saying, 'I'm glad he's dead.'

Matters between Exley and Ronnie's counsel, Mr John Faithful Fortescue Platts-Mills MP, QC, became rather heated when Exley asked, 'Would you like to know why Ronald Kray killed him? Would you like to know why Ronald Kray told me he killed him?'

Platts-Mills replied, 'I am not willing to make myself a party to further abuse and invention.'

This resulted in the judge rebuking him: 'That was a wholly improper thing to say.'

Ronald Hart gave a graphic, eye-witness account of the murder of Jack McVitie; his chilling testimony was interrupted by Reg Kray shouting, 'If any stabbing was done, it must have been done by you – that's why you're telling lies in the case. You're a bully and a coward.'

But Hart, who had convictions for assault and fraud, was not easily put off; he told the court what had happened after the murder and admitted, under cross-examination being instructed to shoot a man: 'When Ronald Kray tells you to do something, you do it, because if you don't, you get shot yourself.'

Looking straight at the dock, Hart exclaimed, 'Reggie Kray murdered McVitie and Ronald helped him and everyone sitting there with him knows it – and everyone in the East End knows it.'

This provoked a shouting match from the dock, with the judge warning, 'If this goes on, all the defendants will go back to the cells.'

Just as controversial was the moment when McVitie's widow Sylvia pointed at the dock and screamed, 'It's them! They killed him! It took ten of them – ten of them, it took to kill him, because he was a man and he wouldn't bow down to you!'

Harry Hopwood – friend of the twins' parents and fellow Army deserter with Charles Kray Sr. – told the court how, following McVitie's murder, the brothers turned up at his flat 'smothered in blood'.

John Dickson, who had given evidence in the Cornell case, returned to say that following the McVitie murder he had met

Charlie Kray outside a Bethnal Green café who told him that, 'McVitie had been "done" by the twins at a party'; when Dickson asked Ron how badly he was done, Ronald Kray had replied, 'He was done proper'.

Nipper Read gave evidence that Chrissie Lambrianou denied ever being at the party at Evering Road and that when he suggested to Ronnie Bender that he had been concerned in the killing, he replied, 'It's a joke to me.'

When Read charged the twins with McVitie's murder, Reg had replied, 'Not guilty', whilst Ron's response was, 'Your sarcastic insinuations are far too obnoxious to be appreciated' – make of that what you will!

Ronnie Kray went into the witness box to deny murdering Cornell, going to the Blind Beggar or going anywhere else with Barrie that night – and when he heard of the murder, he had got drunk in case the police blamed him, 'because they blamed me for other things I hadn't done'. Suggestions that he had changed his clothes were 'lies and rubbish', and he had not been identified on a parade that autumn which was run by Tommy Butler who, he claimed, had told a national newspaper that he was convinced that Mr Kray had nothing to do with the crime. Right.

A witness was called to say that another man had killed Cornell and that Ron was 'a good bloke'. The witness's name? Francis Davidson Fraser, aka 'Mad Frankie', currently serving his fifteen-year sentence from the Torture Trial. Since he and Cornell had been fellow torturers, it was just a wonderful excuse for a day out and another chance to snub the authorities; as he left the witness box, calling out, 'Good luck, Ron', nobody was in any doubt about Ronnie's sanity in calling him in the first place. John Platts-Mills must, by now, have favoured slitting his wrists.

From the dock, Ian Barry denied both Cornell's murder and the incriminating statement which he had made to Harry Mooney.

Nipper Read had previously produced a statement made to him by Cornelius Whitehead – who had three previous convictions, including one for assaulting the police – in which he said that the twins explained to him why they had killed McVitie and that Reg had told him that if the police ever asked about the party, he was to say he had never been there.

It was alleged by the prosecution that Mrs Whitehead and her son were afraid of Reg and that this was a matter which had to be addressed. Reggie Kray did not give evidence but, as he was allowed to, he made a speech from the dock. Telling the court that the evidence against him was 'a pack of lies', he was permitted to read aloud a poem which he had dedicated to Whitehead's son, also named Connie. It is only right that this twenty-seven line poem in its full horror should be revealed here. Speaking softly and seriously, Reg Kray recited:

> Little Connie
> Is bright and bonnie,
> With mischief in his eyes.
> A saucy smile,
> He stood
> And pondered for a while.
> 'I mustn't tell lies, yet I must go out to play',
> Thought little Connie.
> 'Wonder what I can say?'
> He knew it was getting dark
> But he did fancy having a lark.
> 'Mum, can I go out on my bike?
> I'll only be a little while'.
> 'No', said Mum,
> 'You've got to get your sleep'.
> Connie made out to weep
> And said the other kids did as they liked.
> 'Still, you have got to go to bed.'
> Connie did as Mum said,
> And a Beano comic he read.
> A twinkle in his eyes,
> The comic made him smile.
> He felt, after a while
> Like going to sleep,
> Remembering tomorrow, he could play all day
> And that night, for Mum and Dad he could pray.
> Then little Connie was sound asleep.

As he sat down, the other defendants writhed in embarrassment and gazed at their shoes. Eye contact was impossible. A detective who was present stated that in order to prevent himself laughing out loud he had bitten his lip so hard it almost bled.

Things were going downhill. Chrissie Lambrianou denied that Mrs Skinner had seen him carrying a bucket of blood and water ('She's been watching too many Dracula films . . . it's a wonder she didn't say I drank it as well.') His brother Tony declared, 'I'm being framed' and said that he did not believe for one minute that McVitie was dead, while Ronnie Bender – a man with four previous convictions, which included a three-month sentence for possessing a firearm – denied disposing of McVitie's body ('I'm no magician'). He added that Ronnie Kray was 'a benevolent man; I think the word is philanthropist.'

But the following day, Reg Kray was on top form. When Kenneth Jones was cross-examining a witness, Reg leapt to his feet shouting, 'You fat slob! What's it got to do with this case?' Next in line for Reg's disapprobation was Detective Sergeant Trevor Lloyd-Hughes. Referring to Frances' funeral, he shouted, 'I'll tell you something. He followed me to the funeral . . . he followed me to the mortuary – didn't you? You pigs, fat slobs, bastards!' Pointing at Lloyd-Hughes he screamed, 'You dirty pig! I've got witnesses, you stinking pig!'

Mr Justice Melford Stevenson, who must have possessed the patience of Job, had just about had enough and now he snapped: 'Take him down.'

As he was dragged off to the cells, Reg Kray shouted at the judge, 'You're biased; I've had enough of your comments!' And when this had little or no effect, he screamed at Kenneth Jones, 'You fat slob – sit down and don't laugh at me!'

The façade of calm, respectable businessmen facing trumped-up charges had not just crumpled, it had disintegrated. Ronnie Kray, in particular, when asked by Kenneth Jones about his nickname ('The Colonel'), shouted, 'Your name is Taffy Jones to all the prison officers. So you have a nickname as well. We both have nicknames and mine is better than yours!' Ron's repartee had sunk to the level of name-calling in the school playground.

Tony Barry, one of those on trial for McVitie's murder, told the jury that he had taken the gun to the party because 'if I hadn't gone round with the gun, they would definitely have come back . . . and I would have ended up getting hurt as well as McVitie.'

The gun which he had thrown into a canal had been retrieved by the Yard's Underwater Search Unit, exactly at the spot where Barry had said he had discarded it. Examination revealed that the mechanism was defective and would have caused the weapon to misfire, just as it had when Reg Kray had tried to shoot McVitie.

Barry also mentioned that he had seen Reg slash an ex-boxer named Henry 'Buller' Ward in the face with a knife; when this was corroborated by Dennis Clarke, a doorman at the Regency Club, Reg Kray leapt to his feet shouting, 'Can we have Buller Ward in court?' Dock officers tried to restrain him, while Reg shouted that this was not a fair trial and demanded, 'Get him here and ask him – this is a trial within a trial!' It was just as well for Reg that Ward was not called; examination of his face would have revealed that the knife wound had required thirty stitches.

Tony Barry's brother John, a co-manager of the Regency Club, told of one of the doormen being badly assaulted by the Firm, after which he paid £50 per week to Ronnie Kray.

Freddie Foreman believed the twins to be 'very nice people', and Barrie denied any involvement with the shooting of Cornell. At the time, he had been drinking elsewhere with several people, including Charles Kray Sr. Believing that the police would blame the Krays for the murder, he thought it best to leave the district and adopt a false name, because although he had nothing to hide, everyone connected with the Krays was being 'scooped up and put in prison'.

Mr Platts-Mills' final speech for Ronnie Kray lasted twelve hours and five minutes; William Howard QC for Barrie suggested that the barmaid at the Blind Beggar was 'not absolutely sure' when she identified his client; and Paul Wrightson QC for Reg Kray asked the jury, perhaps rather helplessly, 'Is it not unfortunate to be a Kray twin?'

James Ross QC, counsel for Tony Lambrianou, described Ronald Hart's testimony as 'unspeakable', while Tony Barry's barrister, Mr W.M.F. Hudson, did very well in rowing his client to the shore, saying, 'Barry is here today because he carried that gun and for nothing else. What a diabolical way to get a man bound to silence.' Charlie Kray did not give evidence, but his counsel, Desmond Vowden, said there was no reliable evidence against his client; and Tom Williams QC for Foreman urged the jury to consider only the evidence and not its implications.

During his summing-up, Mr Justice Melford Stevenson commented that Ronnie Kray's defence to both charges was, in effect, 'I wasn't there'. But if he had gone to 'Blonde Carol's' flat, why deny it? And with regard to Tony Barry, was he under duress when he took the gun to Evering Rd?

The all-male jury's retirement lasted six hours and fifty-five minutes before unanimously reaching their verdicts. They did believe that Tony Barry had been placed under duress since they acquitted him of McVitie's murder; and as a woman in the public gallery cried out, 'Thank God!', he was discharged. Ron Kray and Barrie were found guilty of Cornell's murder. Both twins, the Lambrianou brothers and Ronald Bender were found guilty of McVitie's murder. Charlie Kray, Freddie Foreman and Cornelius Whitehead were found guilty of being accessories to McVitie's murder.

Sentences were passed the following day, 5 March 1969. Albert Donoghue had changed his pleas to guilty in respect of a conspiracy to effect Frank Mitchell's escape from prison and harbouring

Mitchell. He had already pleaded guilty to being an accessory following McVitie's murder, and for these three offences he was sentenced to, respectively, two periods of eighteen months and one of two years' imprisonment, all to run concurrently. He adhered to his not guilty plea to murdering Mitchell, and Kenneth Jones offered no evidence on that charge, saying it was proposed to call Donoghue at a later stage for the prosecution.

'I'm not going to waste words on you', the judge told Ronald Kray. 'The sentence is that of life imprisonment. In my view, society has earned a rest from your activities.' In sentencing Reggie Kray, the judge said, 'For the same reasons I have already indicated when dealing with your brother Ronald, you will go to prison for life and I recommend that you also be detained for thirty years.'

Charlie Kray was sentenced to ten years, the judge telling him, 'I am satisfied that you were an active helper in the dreadful enterprise of concealing the traces of the murder.' The same sentence was imposed on Freddie Foreman, the judge saying that he had played an essential part in disposing of traces of the murder. Connie Whitehead received a seven-year sentence; this was consecutive to a two-year sentence for possessing forged American dollars.

John 'Scotch Ian' Barrie received the mandatory term for Cornell's murder, with a recommendation that he serve twenty years; Ronald Bender got the same sentence for McVitie's murder; and the Lambrianou brothers received fifteen-year recommendations.

The judge praised the jury and also Nipper Read, of whom he said, 'I cannot part with this case without saying that the debt owed to Detective Superintendent Read and the officers who served under him cannot be overstated and can never be discharged.'

It was all over. The trial had lasted thirty-nine days, one of the longest criminal trials in British legal history. Twenty-eight self-confessed criminals had volunteered their services to the prosecution. Twenty-three barristers had been employed, including nine Queen's Counsel (five of whom were Recorders), two MPs and one former MP, an Attorney-General of the County Palatine of Durham and an Old Bailey Commissioner. The legal costs were in excess of £75,000, to which the Krays contributed nothing.

They had been granted legal aid.

CHAPTER 22

The Mitchell Murder Trial

The next trial at the Old Bailey, with Mr Justice Lawton presiding, commenced on 15 April 1969. The three Kray brothers pleaded not guilty to the murder of Frank Mitchell, as did Freddie Foreman. Also named was a Ronald Olliffe, who had failed to appear; a warrant was issued for his arrest. Connie Whitehead pleaded not guilty to harbouring the defendants knowing they had murdered Mitchell.

The three Krays, Whitehead, Patrick 'Big Pat' Connelly (currently serving a two-year sentence for possessing a gun) and Wally Garelick all pleaded not guilty to conspiring to effect the escape of Mitchell from Dartmoor; and although Charlie and Ron Kray denied harbouring Mitchell after his escape, this was admitted by Reg Kray, Tommy Cowley and Connie Whitehead.

After Kenneth Jones for the prosecution had stated that Cowley and Whitehead were 'minor characters' in the case, the judge jailed each of them for nine months, in Whitehead's case this being consecutive to his previous sentence. Perhaps surprisingly, Garelick and Cowley were both granted bail, with substantial sureties. This was especially surprising in Garelick's case because his former girlfriend, who was receiving continuous police protection, was due to give evidence.

Jurors were challenged, at the request of John Platts-Mills on behalf of Ronnie Kray, to determine whether or not they were partial, given the enormous amount of publicity generated by the previous trial. Perhaps this was superfluous, because Mr Justice Lawton told them they would be receiving police protection.

Before the trial got underway, Garelick changed his plea to guilty and the Crown offered no evidence against Whitehead for harbouring Mitchell's alleged murderers.

The court heard evidence of Mitchell's lifestyle at Dartmoor: of his almost unrestricted freedom, his womanizing in a nearby town and his ability to purchase large amounts of spirits and cider. In fact, a former prisoner told the jury that there was an unwritten law at the prison that Mitchell could do what he wanted. Possibly recalling his father's draconian regime as a prison governor, the judge remarked, 'This just sounds like cloud-cuckoo land, does it not?'

Over the next few days, evidence was heard of Mitchell's escape and of his behaviour becoming more and more disruptive at the Barking Road flat, but the prosecution now rested on the testimony of Albert Donoghue. He stated that he had visited the flat several times while Mitchell was there and that following a meeting with four men he was told to be outside the flat, with Mitchell, at 8.00 pm on 23 December. One of the men, whom he referred to as 'Jerry', was standing by a van door and signalled him to bring Mitchell out. Donoghue told the court:

> I brought Frank out and he got rather excited when we passed a policeman on patrol. I took him to the van and Jerry told him to get in. The other three men were in the van. Frederick Foreman and a man called Gerrard were sitting on the left. Ronald Olliffe was driving. Foreman told me to go to the front of the van and tell the driver the route. As I walked up and got in, both doors closed and two guns started firing as the van drove off. I spun round and saw Mitchell on his knees, clutching his chest. The guns were just blasting away at him. One was a small revolver, which Gerrard had. The other was a black automatic with a silencer. It was Foreman's. Mitchell fell back on his shoulders, his knees were up. Mitchell started making noises from his throat. Foreman held the gun about a foot away from Mitchell's chest and fired three shots. The material of Mitchell's coat was jumping up and down. Mitchell made some more noise and Gerrard said, 'The bastard's still alive. Give him another one, Fred; I'm empty.'

Donoghue later told of seeing Foreman at his pub and handing him an envelope from Reg Kray containing £1,075; he said that Foreman had described disposing of Mitchell's body, courtesy of an unknown man in the country whom Foreman described as 'a funny old fella'. Donoghue believed the body had been dismembered because Foreman had described Mitchell's heart as being 'ripped and burst' and, cupping his hands to indicate size, had said it was 'surprising how small his brain was, for a big man like that'. There was, said Donoghue, a reference to putting Mitchell's body 'into the pot', which he took to be an incinerator.

If Donoghue's testimony was to be believed it was pretty impressive, and damning too. As to other alleged murderers, Ronnie Olliffe had disappeared, as had Jeremiah Callaghan and Alfie Gerrard, wanted by the police for car thefts and assaults.

Freddie Foreman's barrister, Tom Williams, tore into Donoghue, accusing him of being the murderer and suggesting that the whole story had been manufactured between him and Billy Exley – something which was just as resolutely denied.

On 24 April, after legal submissions had been made, the judge directed the jury to acquit Charlie and Ronnie Kray on the murder charge. However, the case was rather weakened after Nipper Read gave evidence that police had received thirty-five sightings of Mitchell, with twelve people saying they had seen him on various occasions.

Reggie Kray now took the stand to say that on 23 December he had been at Pat Connelly's birthday party and had given John Dickson £200: £100 each for Lisa Prescott and Mitchell who, he understood, was going to be spirited out of the country by boat.

Lisa Prescott had previously told the court that Reg Kray had told her that if she ever mentioned anything about Mitchell, no matter when or where, he would always find her. She said, 'He was not rude at all, very quiet spoken. He meant he would kill me.'

Asked by his barrister, Paul Wrightson, if he had told Miss Prescott not to tell anyone, Reg blandly replied, 'I didn't think there was any reason to.'

In fact, he stated that Donoghue had told him there had been an argument about Mitchell wanting to leave with Miss Prescott, whereupon Mitchell had grabbed him by the throat and Donoghue had panicked and shot him.

'You also say Donoghue has given false evidence about you?' asked Wrightson.

Reg replied, 'I shouldn't think there's any doubt about it.'

High time for a few more outbursts. Charlie Kray was cross-examined by Kenneth Jones, who asked him if his family was a close one – a good enough reason for Ronnie Kray to shout out, 'Families usually are, aren't they, you big slob?'

Charlie Kray broke down after stating that three witnesses had given false evidence, saying, 'My name is Kray, remember. I'm doing ten years for nothing, for all their lies.'

Cue Reg Kray, who still had it in for Trevor Lloyd-Hughes. Jumping to his feet, he told the judge, 'Could I say something? I have a lot of respect for you and the way you've run this trial – the other was like a circus – and for Mr Wrightson. I don't like being provoked by these officers in front. Mr Hughes provoked me and if he continues I can't be responsible for my actions. If he likes to come round the back with me or down the cells . . .'

At this point, Ron chimed in with 'He keeps sneering.'

This was typical gangster manipulation: offer false praise on one hand and damning condemnation with the other.

Pat Connelly stated that he did nothing to help Mitchell escape, and Freddie Foreman said that he had never met Donoghue until after Mitchell's disappearance, when he saw him with two other men at his pub demanding protection money from him – which he gave them.

He remembered the night of 23 December because he had been visiting his wife in a Harley Street nursing home; Nipper Read told the court that this was being 'thoroughly investigated'. Terry Spinks MBE, the 1956 Olympic flyweight boxing champion (and friend of the Krays, having attended Reg's wedding), gave evidence that on the night of the murder he had been drinking with Ronald and Danny Olliffe at the notorious Log Cabin Club in Wardour Street and had been in their company for over four hours until 9.30 pm. Danny Olliffe confirmed this and added that on another occasion he had been attacked by Donoghue, who threatened to burn Foreman's pub down. Why, asked the judge, had he not reported this alibi to the police? There was no point, replied Olliffe. He knew his brother could not possibly have been involved in the murder of Mitchell, because at the material time he had been with him – and with Terry Spinks, of course. Far better to inform Freddie's solicitors.

Summing up for the Crown, Kenneth Jones stated that seventeen witnesses had been called by Foreman's defence to establish bias against Donoghue, as well as four alibi witnesses. But Foreman's alibi that he had been visiting his wife at the nursing home was 'dishonest and false' – the nursing home's staff party had been held on 22 December but for the purposes of the alibi it had been transferred to the night of the murder.

In summing up the evidence for the murder charge, Mr Justice Lawton told the jury:

> This is a case of murder or nothing. I am not going to ask you to consider manslaughter. If Donoghue is telling the truth, then it is as simple as that and they are guilty. If not, they should be acquitted. I am going to put it as bluntly as that . . . It has been put to you that Donoghue was the murderer of Mitchell. You have to ask yourselves if that is so. If it is, you cannot believe a word he says and he is the biggest rogue ever to pass through this witness box. Do not take an over-simplified view of this point. There is a lot more in confessions than meets the eye. If he is telling the truth, he may have come to the state where he felt he must tell someone about it.

After twenty-three days of listening to evidence the jury retired; but after six hours of deliberations on 16 May 1969 they returned to tell the judge that they were unable to agree on the murder charge. This prompted Freddie Foreman to leap to his feet and bellow, 'I'm innocent! I never murdered anyone in my life – I'm a publican, not a murderer!' He was told to 'sit down and stay sitting down'.

Another hour and forty minutes went by. Eventually, everybody was acquitted of all the charges, with the exception of Reggie Kray. He was found guilty of conspiring to effect the escape of Mitchell and was sentenced to five years' imprisonment; for the same offence Wally Garelick received eighteen months' imprisonment. For harbouring Mitchell, to which he had pleaded guilty, Reg received nine months, concurrent. Since these terms were also concurrent to his life sentence, it meant that he would serve not one extra day.

★

Three days later, the Krays were back in court to face further charges: that they conspired to possess stolen bonds, that they and eight other men conspired on four separate charges to cheat and defraud and that they had demanded money with menaces. The twins were charged that they and others had conspired to murder, and Ronnie Kray was charged with inflicting grievous bodily harm. All of those charges were effectively dropped, not because of a lack of evidence, of which there was a sufficiency, but because of the cost of the trials and the certainty that in the event of a conviction nothing would be added to their existing sentences.

This was not to the liking of Alfred Charles Willey, one of six men remanded on bail in respect of one of the conspiracy charges on which the Krays had been acquitted. He was led from the dock shouting, 'You pigs! I'll go to the ends of the earth to see you dead – you can shoot me in the back of the head, as well!' He received a judicial bollocking for this intemperate outburst.

Naturally, everybody who received lengthy prison sentences appealed, but at the High Court on 22 July 1969, dismissing the appeals, Lord Justice Widgery said:

> When such cases are brought to justice, it is not sufficient to pass exemplary sentences on the leaders alone. It is equally necessary for the court to show that a grave view will be taken of the activities of the lesser fry. The more

responsible the part played by the accessory, the heavier the sentence which he can expect.

Perhaps the last word should go to Mr Justice Melford Stevenson – a strong advocate of the death penalty – who retired to his house ('Truncheons' in Surrey) ten years after the Kray trial. He remarked that the twins only told the truth twice during their trial: first when one brother referred to the prosecution counsel as 'a fat slob' and secondly when the other stated that the judge was biased!

CHAPTER 23

Time to Leave the Stage

It had been strongly hinted that Nipper Read's enormous contribution to the dismantling of the East End's most destructive crime family would be recognized in the Honours List, possibly even with a knighthood, and that he would certainly be the next Met Commander. But when two far less qualified officers were promoted ahead of him, a disgruntled Read applied for the job of Assistant Chief Constable of Nottinghamshire and got it; he later served for five years as the National Co-ordinator of the Regional Crime Squads and was awarded the Queen's Police Medal for distinguished service when he retired in 1976.

Why was he overlooked? The Kray enquiry had bestowed a great deal of favourable publicity on Nipper Read – quite rightly, too. But public approbation had missed Brodie, and jealousy set in. In addition, Robert Mark (later Sir Robert Mark GBE, QPM) was now deputy commissioner; what was more, he had the backing of the Home Secretary. He had made it quite clear that he wished to break the power of the CID and to introduce interchange between the departments (that included assistant commissioners), all of which was in total opposition to Brodie's views on the management of 'his chaps'.

It was clear that Brodie would never become Commissioner; Mark did, and the day before his appointment, Brodie resigned. His place was taken by an officer who had spent most of his career in the Traffic Department.

When coupled with the Police and Criminal Act 1984 and the introduction of the Crown Prosecution Service, this sounded the death knell for the Criminal Investigation Department.

*

The Krays passed into East End folklore; they became far more famous after they were incarcerated than they ever were when at large. In the same way that after the Second World War a number of shifty French citizens untruthfully claimed that they had been members of the Resistance, huge numbers of Bethnal Green residents professed close kinship with the Krays. Books were and still are being written about their exploits by the unlikeliest of people, and practically every person who was convicted with the Krays had their own story to tell. Some sought the assistance of professional writers in an effort to provide some semblance of plausibility; others did not, with predictably hilarious results.

Not only did the twins now admit the murders which they had previously strenuously denied, they positively gloated about them in print; it appeared they had more interest in their royalties than a favourable hearing from the parole board.

Freddie Foreman went one step further; in his book *The Godfather of British Crime* he admitted Mitchell's murder, as he did when he was interviewed by Carlton Television. In fact, in the same book he admitted involvement with Alf Gerrard in the murder of 'Ginger' Marks, whose body, like those of Mitchell and McVitie, has never been found. He and Gerrard were charged with Marks' murder; they were acquitted. Then he was interviewed by police, since when he has not only given no further details about the murders but has refused to talk about them at all.

By 1971, Charlie Mitchell, who had provided evidence against the Firm, no longer had the protection of Detective Constable Hugh Parker, who was armed when he minded him at his house in Fulham ('The six month period was an education you could not buy', Parker told me), so he was lucky to evade a blast from a sawn-off shotgun fired from a passing car outside his address in Ellerby Street His luck finally ran out when he was murdered in Spain a few years later.

★

Violet Kray died in 1982; the Twins attended her funeral under tight security. Also present was Detective Constable Alick Morrison, who was an authorized shot. He told me:

> At the church I spent twenty minutes in the vestry with Reggie as we waited for the arrival of Ronnie. Reggie was very chatty and we temporarily swapped watches. He jokingly offered to sell me his but commented that it would cost me at least a year's wages. When Ronnie eventually arrived, it was fascinating to see them greet each other and listen to the conversation. People say to me that it's a pity I didn't have the forethought to record or video the events. For a start, we didn't have today's modern gadgets but more importantly, I had a job to do and after all, it was a funeral, not a circus. Pity the press and the public didn't feel the same.

These were sentiments shared by Charlie Kray. When their father died, seven months later, Charlie mentioned that he had wanted his funeral to be a quiet affair, unlike his late wife's; but in any event, the twins did not attend.

Ronnie Kray never was released; certified insane in 1979, he was transferred to Broadmoor and after a couple of rather odd marriages died of a heart attack at the age of sixty-one in 1995.

Reg followed him to the grave five years later; he was released from prison on compassionate grounds, suffering from inoperable bladder cancer. He had remarried in 1997 and after leaving hospital on 22 September 2000 he had just eight days of freedom before he died in his sleep.

Charlie was released in 1975; I was immediately on his tail with a team from the Serious Crime Squad to see if he would resurrect the Kray empire; but he didn't. He led us to a Kray associate who was far more interesting and who was jailed for seven years for conspiracy to cheat and defraud.

Richard 'Dickie' Bird was a former police constable employed as Charlie's chauffeur following his release. He told me, 'Everyone he met was in awe of him', and added that an element of philosophy had crept into his persona: 'Although Charlie felt wrongly convicted with the murder trials, he also felt the ten years he received were due to him, for the things he got away with.'

They finally caught up with Charlie in 1997, when he was convicted of conspiracy to import cocaine with a street value of £39m plus supplying two kilos of the drug, valued at £63,500, to undercover officers. Not even an eloquent character reference from Frankie Fraser could save him from being sent down for twelve years, claiming, naturally, that the police had set him up; he died of natural causes aged seventy-three, six months before Reg.

And that was the shabby story of the Kray Firm. There are still ill-advised people who will claim that they were 'the salt of the earth', 'staunch' but above all, 'diamond geezers'. Were they really?

Epilogue

Throughout these pages, you have read of some of the worst examples of bloody gang warfare, which spilled over to affect the lives of decent men and women who, through no fault of their own, were swept up, as witnesses and jurors, into this maelstrom of carnage.

And yet, these gangsters created their own images for public consumption, as though they were role models for succeeding generations. In some cases, their ill deeds were minimized – a favourite criminal trait – so when, for example, a victim had his face slashed open, this would be dismissively referred to as 'I give 'im a couple of slaps'. Others were more forthcoming, gloating and glorying in the violence that they inflicted but always being careful to provide some justification, no matter how fatuous, for their actions.

Because justification is a necessity to a gangster – even if it is difficult to rationalize something like the case of Jack Spot and his wife, when anything up to a dozen of them attacked the defenceless couple like a pack of wild animals, kicking, slashing and beating, armed with lethal weapons, before scuttling away into the darkness.

And is it possible to defend the actions of those who participated in the Richardson Torture Trials, where the terrified victims, surrounded by a bunch of jeering henchmen, were stripped, beaten, electrocuted and degraded and where, in the midst of these depredations, one of the onlookers described the look on Charlie Richardson's face as being like 'someone having sex'?

The Kray Twins are invariably described as being 'proper gents'; as one person (who had never even met the brothers) wrote, with almost supernatural imbecility, 'I loved the Krays'. We're talking about the same Kray brothers who would walk into a pub and smash the living daylights out of somebody completely unknown to them, for no other reason than that he happened to have the impertinence to be in the same bar as them.

Let me leave you with one particular matter which sticks in my memory.

It's an account of a conversation – which as far as I'm aware has never been denied – between Roy Hall and John McVicar whilst they were serving their respective sentences. Hall – who had operated the electric generator on some of the Richardson victims – apparently stated that people had to tell the truth when they were undergoing torture; then, chillingly, he said this:

> When you put people under the electrodes, they go. They tell you everything . . . They turn into little kids and ask for their mummy. It's something that you have to see to know.

Proper gents? Diamond geezers?
   You decide.

Bibliography

Browne, Douglas G. and Tullett, E.V., *Bernard Spilsbury – His Life & Cases*, George. G. Harrap & Co, 1951.

Clarkson, Wensley, *Moody*, Mainstream, 2003.

Cook, Andrew, *The Great Train Robbery*, History Press, 2013.

Cooper, Henry, *Henry Cooper – an Autobiography*, Cassell, 1972.

Davidson, Earl, *Joey Pyle*, Virgin Books, 2003.

Donoghue, Albert and Short, Martin, *The Krays' Lieutenant*, Smith Gryphon, 1995.

Du Rose, John, *Murder was my Business*, W. H. Allen, 1971.

Fawcett, Micky, *Krayzy Days*, Pen Press, 2013.

Fido, Martin, *The Krays – Unfinished Business*, Carlton Books, 1999.

Foreman, Freddie, *The Godfather of British Crime*, John Blake, 2008.

Fraser, Frankie, as told to James Morton, *Mad Frank: Memoirs of a Life of Crime*, Warner Books, 1994.

Hill, Billy, *Boss of Britain's Underworld*, Naldrett Press Ltd, 1955.

Hill, Justin, with John Hunt, *Billy Hill, Gyp & Me*, Billy Hill Family, 2012.

Kelland, Gilbert, *Crime in London*, Harper Collins, 1993

Kennison P. and Swinden, D., *Behind the Blue Lamp*, Coppermill Press, 2005.

Kirby, Dick, *Rough Justice – Memoirs of a Flying Squad Detective*, Merlin Unwin, 2001.

Kirby, Dick, *The Real Sweeney*, Robinson, 2005.

Kirby, Dick, *You're Nicked!*, Robinson, 2007.

Kirby, Dick, *Villains*, Robinson, 2008.

Kirby, Dick, *The Guv'nors*, Pen & Sword, 2010.

Kirby, Dick, *The Sweeney*, Wharncliffe, 2011.

Kirby, Dick, *Scotland Yard's Ghost Squad*, Wharncliffe, 2011.

Kray, Reg, *Born Fighter*, Century, 1990.

Kray, Reg, *Villains we Have Known*, Arrow Books, 1996.

Lisners, John, *The Rise and Fall of the Murdoch Empire*, John Blake, 2012.

Lucas, Norman, *Britain's Gangland*, Pan Books Ltd, 1969.

Mark, Sir Robert, *In the Office of Constable*, Collins, 1978.

McDonald, Brian, *Gangs of London*, Milo Books, 2010.

McVicar, John, *McVicar – by Himself*, Artnik Publishing, 2004.

Morton, James, *East End Gangland*, Warner Books, 2001.

Morton, James, *Gangland*, Vols 1 & 2, Time Warner, 2003.

Morton, James, *Gangland: The Lawyers*, Virgin Books, 2003.

Morton, James and Parker, Gerry, *Gangland Bosses*, Time Warner, 2005.

Morton, James, *Gangland Soho*, Piatkus, 2008.

Murphy, Robert, *Smash and Grab*, Faber & Faber, 1993.
Narborough, Fred, *Murder on my Mind*, Allan Wingate Ltd, 1959.
Parker, Robert, *Rough Justice*, Fontana, 1981.
Pearson, John, *The Profession of Violence*, Panther Books, 1973.
Progl, Zoe, *Woman of the Underworld*, Arthur Barker, 1964.
Read, Leonard and Morton, James, *Nipper*, Macdonald & Co, 1999 .
Richardson, Charlie *My Manor*, Pan, 1992.
Richardson, Eddie, *The Last Word – My Life as a Gangland Boss*,
    Headline, 2005.
Simpson, Keith, *Forty Years of Murder*, Harrap & Co, 1978.
Stoodley, Roger, *My Incompetent Best*, privately published, 2012.
Teale, Bobby, *Bringing down the Krays*, Ebury Press, 2012.
Thomas, Donald, *Villains' Paradise*, John Murray, 2005.
Thorp, Arthur, *Calling Scotland Yard*, Allan Wingate, 1954.
Tibbs, Jimmy, *Sparring with Life*, Sport Media, 2014.
Wickstead, Bert, *Gangbuster*, Futura Publications, 1985.
Wilkinson, Laurence, *Behind the Face of Crime*, Frederick Muller, 1957.

Index